This is the rare book that delivers more than it promises. Pick it up to learn about the true joy of sex: you will, and you'll also learn about the joy of God.

—MARVIN OLASKY, editor-in-chief, *World* magazine

This book is a glorious start to forming a Christian mind that expresses delight in God's gift of marital intimacy—a Christian mind that so desires to delight in that which God delights in, that it revels in rejecting the cheap substitutes pawned off on this passing age as true pleasure, and instead only finds satisfaction in what is purest and highest and noblest and best. The book considers the subject of human sexuality biblically, theocentrically, Christologically, and thus helps form a well-rounded Christian outlook on sex.

—J. LIGON DUNCAN III, Senior Minister,
First Presbyterian Church, Jackson, MS, Moderator,
General Assembly of the Presbyterian Church in America

In a culture that's desperately asking sex to be the alpha and omega, this book shows how sex is better when Christ is the Alpha and Omega.

—ANDRÉE SEU, Senior Writer, *World* magazine

I cannot think of any gift of God that has been more abused and misused than that of sex. What was intended to be a stunning, pure, earthly picture of amazing heavenly, eternal realities, has been perverted into an alluring but false god that is in fact a grotesque caricature of the true God. The contributors to this volume have provided a refreshing, insightful, and much-needed treatment of this sacred subject, calling us to bring our thoughts and lives into captivity to the supremacy of Christ and to reflect our ravishment with our heavenly Bridegroom in our sexuality. I pray that this resource will make a profound difference in how God's people think and live.

—NANCY LEIGH DEMOSS, author, host of
"Revive Our Hearts" radio program

Sex is a wonderful gift from God; but it makes a terrible idol, brutal and unyielding in the misery it inflicts. These authors are a breath of fresh air, because unlike our culture's self-proclaimed "sexperts," they respect biblical authority and warmly embrace the Lordship of Christ. Hence, they can lift up the torch of divine truth and expose the enemy's lies about sex that have penetrated not only the darkest corners of our culture, but of our churches. I pray that *Sex and the Supremacy of Christ* will demonstrate to readers that Christ being Lord of all means that he must be Lord of all we think, say, and do about sex—and that in his lordship we will find deliverance and joy.

—RANDY ALCORN, author, *The Purity Principle*

Another Christian book on sex? This is so much more. We don't need another book on how not to look at the girl in the miniskirt. We've read that. We don't need another bedroom guide with chapter titles containing the word "hot." Basically, we don't need another book on sex that's all about us. We need to have our gaze lifted. We need to consider the God who made us sexual creatures for his glory. This book will help you form a Christ-centered, Bible-shaped understanding of sex. This is something we all need.

—JOSHUA HARRIS, author, *Sex Is Not the Problem (Lust Is)*

# Sex and the Supremacy of Christ

John Piper | Justin Taylor

EDITORS

CROSSWAY BOOKS

A PUBLISHING MINISTRY OF
GOOD NEWS PUBLISHERS
WHEATON, ILLINOIS

Cover design: Jon McGrath

Cover photo: Getty Images

First printing 2005

Printed in the United States of America

**Library of Congress Cataloging-in-Publication Data**
Sex and the supremacy of Christ / edited by John Piper and Justin Taylor.
    p. cm.
    Includes bibliographical references and index.
    ISBN 13: 978-1-58134-697-8
    ISBN 10: 1-58134-697-2 (tpb)
    1. Sex—Religious aspects—Christianity. I. Piper, John, 1946-    .
II. Taylor, Justin, 1976-    .
BT708.S474    2005
261.8'357—dc22                    2005002312

| ML | | 15 | 14 | 13 | 12 | 11 | 10 | 09 | 08 | 07 | 06 |
|----|----|----|----|----|----|----|----|----|----|----|----|
| 15 | 14 | 13 | 12 | 11 | 10 | 9 | 8 | 7 | 6 | 5 | 4 | 3 |

*To all single Christians
who keep themselves pure for Christ's sake
and all married Christians who keep their promises
till death do them part*

# Contents

## Part 5: History and Sex

# Contributors

**Scott Croft.** Elder, Capitol Hill Baptist Church (Washington, D.C.).

**Mark Dever.** Senior Pastor, Capitol Hill Baptist Church.

**Michael Lawrence.** Associate Pastor, Capitol Hill Baptist Church.

**C. J. Mahaney.** President of Sovereign Grace Ministries (Gaithersburg, Maryland).

**Carolyn Mahaney.** Wife, mother, and leader of the Titus 2 Ministry, Covenant Life Church (Gaithersburg, Maryland).

**Carolyn McCulley.** Media Specialist, Sovereign Grace Ministries.

**R. Albert Mohler, Jr.** President, The Southern Baptist Theological Seminary (Louisville).

**Ben Patterson.** Campus Pastor, Westmont College (Santa Barbara).

**John Piper.** Preaching Pastor, Bethlehem Baptist Church (Minneapolis).

**David Powlison.** Counselor and teacher, Christian Counseling and Educational Foundation; Lecturer in Practical Theology, Westminster Theological Seminary (Philadelphia).

**Matt Schmucker.** Director of 9Marks Ministries (Washington, D.C.).

**Justin Taylor.** Director of Theology, Executive Editor, Desiring God (Minneapolis).

## Contributor Websites

IX Marks Ministries—9marks.org

Albert Mohler—albertmohler.com

Carolyn McCulley—carolynmcculley.com

Council of Christian Education Foundation—ccef.org

Desiring God—desiringGod.org

Sovereign Grace Ministries—sovereigngraceministries.com

# INTRODUCTION

JUSTIN TAYLOR

These are among the Bible verses most often quoted by evangelicals. But *quoting* Scripture texts is different than *shaping a worldview around them*. If the church today truly took seriously the significance of the term "all things," wouldn't we witness a steady stream of provocative sermons and books on the theme of "How to Have Sex to the Glory of God"? Instead, the mere suggestion of preaching such a sermon would probably elicit little more than a nervous chuckle or red-faced embarrassment.

The genesis of this volume and its attempt to answer that question was the Desiring God National Conference (2004), entitled "Sex and the Supremacy of Christ." We wanted to approach the topic with frankness and reverence, with the supremacy of Christ as both our foundation and our aim. What do sex and the supremacy of Christ have to do with each other, and what implications should this have for our everyday lives?

## What the Bible Says About Sex

Suppose you wanted to know what the Bible teaches about sex. How would you go about finding out? A word search on variants of the word *sex* in an English Bible shows that it almost always occurs in the context of *sexual immorality* (Greek, *porneia*—from which we derive the word "pornography"). So you might conclude that the Bible does not have much to teach us about sex, and that when it does address sexuality, it does so only in a negative, prohibitory, prudish fashion.

But this would be a rather shallow conclusion. *Scripture has a lot to say about sex, because Scripture has a lot to say about everything.* So rather than searching the Bible only for the word *sex*, a more productive strategy would be to search the Bible for the term *all things*, since *sex* is obviously a subset of *all things*. Here is a sampling of what this kind of search would reveal in God's authoritative Word:

- Sex is created by God ("by him *all* things were created"—Col. 1:16).
- Sex continues to exist by the will of Christ ("in him *all* things hold together"—Col. 1:17).
- Sex is caused by God (he "works *all* things according to the counsel of his will"—Eph. 1:11).
- Sex is subject to Christ ("he put *all* things under his feet"—Eph. 1:22).
- Christ is making sex new ("Behold, I am making all things new"—Rev. 21:5).
- Sex is good (*"everything* created by God is good"—1 Tim. 4:4).
- Sex is lawful in the context of marriage (*"all* things are lawful"—1 Cor. 10:23).
- When we have sex, we are to do it for the glory of God (*"whatever* you do, do *all* to the glory of God"—1 Cor. 10:31).
- Sex works together for the good of God's children ("for those who love God *all* things work together for good, for those who are called according to his purpose"—Rom. 8:28).
- We are to thank God for sex (*"nothing* is to be rejected if it is received with thanksgiving"—1 Tim. 4:4).
- Sex is to be sanctified by the Word of God and prayer (*"everything . . .* is made holy by the word of God and prayer"—1 Tim. 4:4-5).
- We must be on guard not to be enslaved by sex ("I will not be enslaved by *anything*"—1 Cor. 6:12).

- We are not to grumble about sex ("do *all* things without grumbling"—Phil. 2:14).
- We are to rejoice in the Lord during sex ("rejoice in the Lord *always*"—Phil. 4:4).
- We are to be content in sex ("having all contentment in *all* things at *all* times"—2 Cor. 9:8 mg.).
- We are to practice and pursue sexual relations in holiness and honor ("each one of you [is to] know how to control his own body [KJV: "possess his vessel"; RSV: "take a wife for himself"] in holiness and honor"—1 Thess. 4:4).
- Spouses are not to "deprive one another [sexually], except perhaps by agreement for a limited time," that they might devote themselves to prayer (1 Cor. 7:5).
- But then they are commanded to "come together again [sexually], so that Satan may not tempt [them] because of [their] lack of self-control" (1 Cor. 7:5).
- In this fallen age, sex is both pure and impure—"To the pure, *all* things are pure, but to the defiled and unbelieving, *nothing* is pure; but both their minds and their consciences are defiled" (Titus 1:15).

What a sermon series this would be! A careful study of these verses, in the context of the whole counsel of God, would show that sex cannot be understood rightly or practiced properly without seeing how sex relates to God. It is our hope and prayer that the chapters collected in this volume will help you orient your entire life and worldview—including your sex life and views on sexuality—around the glory of God in Christ.

### Shame in the Church

One of the hindrances to a frank and edifying discussion of sexuality is the issue of shame. Shame can be healthy, and shame can be sinful. By and large, our culture is hell-bent on shedding any vestiges of propriety and shame in all things sexual. As an overreaction, the church is often too timid to even broach the topic, for fear of violating Paul's command that "it is shameful even to speak of the things that they do in secret" (Eph. 5:12). But this proper shame can easily morph into improper embarrassment and an unhealthy reticence to apply the whole counsel of God to an issue of paramount significance. Such is not an option, however, for the body of Christ, as Al Mohler so helpfully reminds us:

> Christians have no right to be embarrassed when it comes to talking about sex and sexuality. An unhealthy reticence or embarrassment in dealing with these issues is a form of disrespect to God's creation. Whatever God made is good, and every good thing God made has an intended purpose that ultimately reveals His own glory. When conservative Christians respond to sex with ambivalence or embarrassment, we slander the goodness of God and hide God's glory which is intended to be revealed in the right use of creation's gifts.[1]

## Sex in the World

In the 1950s, there was broad assent to an external moral order outside of ourselves, governing and framing our discourse and our ethics. That shared understanding collapsed in the 1960s with the advent of the sexual revolution. In its place a new ethic arose. Some suggest that what we have instead is rampant relativism and narcissistic nihilism. But such an analysis tends to miss the mark. The new ethic—sometimes called an "ethic of authenticity"[2]—"insists that the inner voice is morally authoritative and should be followed without question."[3] Dinesh D'Souza refers to this as the "imperial self."[4] To worshipers and obeyers of the Imperial Self, a bare appeal to "objective morality" is not likely to make significant inroads. Frederica Mathewes-Green writes:

> These students have an objective morality. It's just different from ours. They believe that it's objectively wrong to dump someone in a callous way. It's wrong to have sex with someone who isn't willing. It's wrong to transgress any one of a hundred subtle etiquette cues about who may sleep with whom under what circumstances. There is plenty of objective morality on their side, and they think it's better than ours. As far

[1] R. Albert Mohler, Jr., "The Seduction of Pornography and the Integrity of Christian Marriage," an address delivered to the men of Boyce College (March 13, 2004), available online at www.sbts.edu/docs/Mohler/EyeCovenant.pdf (accessed 1-14-05). This address is an absolute must-read for all men.
[2] See Charles Taylor, *The Ethics of Authenticity* (Cambridge, Mass.: Harvard University Press, 1991).
[3] Dinesh D'Souza, "The Imperial Self," available online at http://www.tothesource.org/12_1_2004/12_1_2004.htm (accessed 1-26-05). I am dependent on D'Souza's analysis here for this section.
[4] Ibid.

as they can see, theirs is working and ours looks pointlessly difficult. Why should they switch? This argument sounds like nothing more than "because I said so."[5]

"Because I said so" is not very persuasive to five-year-old children throwing a temper tantrum, and "because I said so" is not very effective with twenty-five-year-old college students in bed with one another. What is needed in its place is a worldview built around the proposition that *God said so*. Our calling is not merely to parrot those words, but to set forth a biblical theology that takes seriously the gracious prescriptions and the gracious prohibitions of our holy, loving Creator.[6] As we challenge the church and the culture, we must strive to live out Paul's description of the Christian life as "sorrowful, yet always rejoicing" (2 Cor. 6:10). We must learn to speak both frankly and yet with discretion; prophetically and yet with nuance; with boldness and yet with a brokenhearted spirit. In short, we must learn to become who we are: the redeemed body of Christ—sinners being sanctified who reflect both the tough and the tender mercies of our Lord and Savior.

### Sex Is a Pointer to, Not a Substitute for, God

Bruce Marshall, in his novel *The World, the Flesh, and Father Smith,* wrote a very provocative sentence: "The young man who rings the bell at the brothel is unconsciously looking for God."[7] What Marshall saw—and what few are saying—is that there is a deep connection between God and sex. Peter Kreeft sees it. After arguing that "sex is the effective religion of our culture," he explains:

> Sex is like religion not only because it is objectively holy in itself but also because it gives us subjectively a foretaste of heaven, of the self-forgetting, self-transcending self-giving that is what our deepest hearts are designed for, long for and will not be satisfied until they have,

---

[5] Frederica Mathewes-Green, "What to Say at a Naked Party," *Christianity Today,* February 2005, available online at http://www.christianitytoday.com/ct/2005/002/14.48.html (accessed 1-21-05).

[6] Those looking for resources to aid in this task need look no further than the following two outstanding books recently published by Crossway Books: Daniel R. Heimbach, *True Sexual Morality: Recovering Biblical Standards for a Culture in Crisis* (Wheaton, Ill.: Crossway, 2004); and Andreas J. Köstenberger with David W. Jones, *God, Marriage, and Family: Rebuilding the Biblical Foundation* (Wheaton, Ill.: Crossway, 2004). For a study largely confined to the foundational teaching of Genesis, see O. Palmer Robertson, *The Genesis of Sex: Sexual Relationships in the First Book of the Bible* (Phillipsburg, N.J.: Presbyterian & Reformed, 2002).

[7] Bruce Marshall, *The World, the Flesh, and Father Smith* (Boston: Houghton Mifflin, 1945), 108.

because we are made in God's own image and this self-giving constitutes the inner life of the Trinity.[8]

Sex is designed to be a pointer to, not a substitute for, God. The human
heart, as Pascal observed, is a God-shaped vacuum that can be filled only
by God himself:

> There once was in man a true happiness of which now remain to him
> only the mark and empty trace, which he in vain tries to fill from all
> his surroundings, seeking from things absent the help he does not
> obtain in things present. But these are all inadequate, because the infi-
> nite abyss can only be filled by an infinite and immutable object, that
> is to say, only by God Himself.[9]

It is with these considerations in mind that we can consider the connection between sex and the supremacy of Christ.

## An Overview of *Sex and the Supremacy of Christ*

In the opening two chapters, *John Piper* explores this relationship of
God and sex by suggesting two simple but weighty points. Positively, he
argues that sexuality is designed by God as a way to know God in Christ
more fully; and that knowing God in Christ more fully is designed as a
way of guarding and guiding our sexuality. Or to put it negatively: all
misuses of our sexuality distort the true knowledge of Christ; and all
misuses of our sexuality derive from not having the true knowledge of
Christ. In chapter 2—the second part of Piper's message—he expands
upon this second point, helping us to see and savor the supremacy of
Christ in and over all things. The main obstacle to knowing the
supremacy of Christ is the just and holy wrath of God against us, his
sinful, rebellious subjects. And the solution is the righteousness of Christ
in absorbing that wrath and opening for us the door to eternal life. Piper
concludes, then, by asking and answering the question of how the
knowledge of the supremacy of Christ—opened to us by the gospel—
can guide and guard and govern our sexual lives, making our sexuality
sacred, satisfying, and Christ-exalting.

---

[8] Peter Kreeft, *How to Win the Culture War: A Christian Battle Plan for a Society in Crisis* (Downers
Grove, Ill.: InterVarsity Press, 2002), 95.

[9] Blaise Pascal, *Pascal's Pensées*, trans. W. F. Trotter (New York: E. P. Dutton, 1958), 113.

In his chapter "The Goodness of Sex and the Glory of God," *Ben Patterson* suggests that C. S. Lewis's description of worldly pleasure in *The Screwtape Letters*—"an ever-increasing craving for an ever-diminishing pleasure"—is exactly what's going on in our culture. But God's agenda for sex and pleasure, Patterson argues, is different. Sex is good because the God who created sex is good. And God is glorified greatly when we receive his gift with thanksgiving and enjoy it the way he meant for it to be enjoyed. To show that this is true, Patterson takes us on a tour of the Bible, showing the importance of marriage—in the beginning, at the end, and throughout. In particular, he marvels at the imagery from the Song of Solomon, and its vision of wholesome, richly erotic sex done in the way and within the context God intends, in contrast to the cheaply toxic sex done in the way the world recommends. In the second half of his chapter, Patterson examines the theological foundations for the celebration of sex within the covenant of marriage. God not only created all things good, out of nothing, but he sent his only Son in human flesh, showing that the physical is a fit vehicle for communion with God. And God demonstrated this goodness by creating us male and female, as sexual creatures who were made to be together and to find ourselves as we give ourselves away. Patterson closes his chapter by offering a poignant example from his own life where he experienced afresh the gratitude and joy of being given his wife by a good and gracious God.

In Part Two we turn to issues surrounding sexual sin and brokenness. *David Powlison* argues that we are all engaged in a battle, and it is longer, wider, deeper, and subtler than people realize. We must lengthen our view of the battle, seeing it as a lifelong battle. We must widen our view of the battle, not focusing only upon the high-profile sins and thereby missing the big picture. We must deepen our view of the battle, recognizing that sexual sin is but one expression of a deeper war for the heart's loyalty and primary love. We must also recognize that the battle is subtler than we often think as we begin to see the complex layers of sin in our hearts—some obvious, some subtle; some externally manifested, some only internal; some involving our sin against others; some involving others sinning against us. The goal of the battle is not "just say no" and not just the "means of grace," but rather the goal is to see Jesus Christ himself. For Christ's love is itself longer and deeper and wider than we can imagine. Powlison ends his essay by giving us some practical counsel on getting down to business in today's skirmish of the Great War.

One "marquee sin" in our culture is homosexuality. So much of the discussion in the church and in the culture has been framed in terms of "us" versus "them." But *Albert Mohler* explains why he views "Homosexual Marriage as a Challenge to the Church." The challenge has to do first and foremost with the kind of people that we—the body of Christ—will be. Mohler convincingly argues that "we must be the people who cannot talk about homosexual marriage simply by talking about homosexual marriage"—that is, we must start with the larger issues at stake. "We must be the people who cannot talk about sex without talking about marriage, and the people who can't talk about anything of substance or significance without dependence on the Bible. We must be the people who have a theology adequate to explain the deadly deception of sin, as well as a theology adequate to explain Christ's victory over sin. We must be honest about sin as the denial of God's glory, even as we point to redemption as the glory of God restored. We must be the people who love homosexuals more than homosexuals love homosexuality, and we must be the people who tell the truth about homosexual marriage and refuse to accept even its conceptual possibility, because we know what is at stake."

Part Three of this volume focuses specifically on sex and men. *Mark Dever* opens the chapter on "Sex and the Single Man" by observing the unique challenges faced today by single men, due in part to young men waiting longer to get married and the culture's devaluation of marriage. Dever argues that there is a biblical alternative to this pattern of extended adolescence and passivity toward marriage. In the next section of this chapter, *Michael Lawrence* sets the theological foundation for sex. Far more than a list of do's and don'ts, Lawrence shows us the meaning of sex as God designed it and the implications this has for sexual intimacy and for masturbation. *Matt Schmucker* focuses on the physical intimacy issue, demonstrating that most of us have a double standard when it comes to how married men are to interact with women who are not their wives, and how single men are to interact with women who are not their wives. Schmucker then offers four reasons as to why physical intimacy with a woman who is not your wife should be prohibited. So what *should* a biblical relationship look like? After defining courtship and dating, *Scott Croft* explains their different motives, mindsets, and methods. Working with the biblical principle that commitment precedes intimacy, Croft makes a case that the courtship model is the one most consistent with the biblical rules for a relationship with someone of the opposite sex.

C. J. *Mahaney*, in his chapter for married men, takes us back to the Song of Solomon for instruction on godly sexuality. Along with most contemporary evangelical scholars, he respectfully rejects an allegorical or typological interpretation of the book, arguing instead that the book involves the modeling of a godly, passionate sexual relationship in the covenantal context of marriage. Mahaney argues that one of the main lessons we can draw from this book is that in order for romance to increase in our marriages, we must learn to touch our wife's heart and mind before we touch her body. This involves carefully composed words and the cultivation of romance through intentional planning. He offers practical suggestions for how to touch her mind and heart. In the final section of the chapter, he provides wise and biblical counsel on sex itself and the gift of marital intimacy.

We turn to the subject of "Women and Sex" in Part Four. *Carolyn McCulley* begins by making some observations about sex and the single woman in twenty-first-century American culture. But how, she wonders, can committed Christian single women who are by God's grace avoiding sexual immorality address our culture on this topic? She insists that in order to do so, this counterrevolutionary message must be centered upon the gospel and the sin-bearing, life-changing power of Jesus Christ. She then turns to examine what the Bible teaches about the gift of singleness and the gifts of the Proverbs 31 woman. Along the way she deals with issues like avoiding sexual temptation at work and how singles should function in the church as indispensable members of Christ's body. A single woman's ultimate hope cannot be for marriage, but for the presence of Christ. God's seeming silence is not an indication of rejection, but a preparation of revelation, as single women commit to living their lives for the supremacy of Christ.

*Carolyn Mahaney*, in turn, speaks to the married women about sex. She is not oblivious to the pain and confusion that many women have experienced through past sexual encounters, but she argues that no situation is beyond the reach of God's grace and the power of Christ's cross. She insists that by God's grace all married women can enjoy the sexual relationship with their husbands, and she proposes to examine what such a passionate relationship would look like from a wife's perspective. Recognizing that the Bible does not provide explicit instructions on marital sex, Mrs. Mahaney does see several biblical principles that can cultivate what she calls "Grade A sexual intimacy." Wives, she argues, are to be attractive, available, anticipatory, aggressive, and adventurous. She closes with words of gentle encouragement and wise counsel to those women who are in danger of despairing and losing hope about their sexual relationships with their husbands.

In the final part of the book, "History and Sex," we turn to a historical couple and a historical movement to give us some perspective. In my chapter on "Martin Luther's Reform of Marriage," I look at the life of Martin Luther, the great German Reformer. As Luther set about the task of reforming marriage through his teaching, preaching, and writing, he was convinced that he himself had been called to singleness and would never marry. After all, he thought that he would probably die a martyr's death in just a few short years! But God had different plans, and a crucial component of Luther's rehabilitation and reformation of the marital institution was his brief courtship and long marriage to Katherine von Bora, a young nun whom he had helped escape from a convent. Their life together—along with Luther's teachings on sex, marriage, love, and children—had a revolutionary impact upon Reformation Germany and continues to influence the evangelical church today.

In the final chapter, *Mark Dever* examines the role of the Puritans and sex. The Puritans and sex? Did they ever enjoy such a thing? Isn't "Puritanism" the "haunting fear that someone, somewhere may be happy"?[10] Dever refutes these historically ignorant suggestions and, in quotation after quotation, allows the Puritans to speak for themselves. After surveying the historical background of the Roman Catholic tradition and the Lutheran revolution, Dever details the Puritan view on marriage, sex, romance, sexual sin, and pleasure. Dever shows that the Puritans were not opposed to pleasure per se; they were opposed to plea-

---

[10] H. L. Mencken, *A Mencken Chrestomathy* (New York: Vintage, 1982), 624.

sure insofar as it was insubordinate to pleasure in God. Dever closes by drawing together eight lessons we can learn from the Puritans regarding a biblical view of sexuality. Also attached to his essay is an appendix that surveys the study of the Puritans within the academic world.

May Christ bless you as you read this book. Our prayer is that it would draw you closer to him, as you see his supremacy in all things—including sex.

## Acknowledgments

The process of editing and writing a book never occurs in a vacuum. Our wives, Noël and Lea, graciously and joyfully support us in this ministry, and they deserve special thanks for their help and for their patience. We stand in debt to many friends, without whom this project would not exist. Jon Bloom, the executive director at Desiring God, keeps the wheels turning in this ministry. Scott Anderson, the conference coordinator at Desiring God, labored many long hours to pull the "Sex and the Supremacy of Christ" conference together. Vicki Anderson, our administrative assistant, frees us up to work on projects like this. We would also like to express our appreciation to Carol Steinbach and Robert Williams, who graciously and quickly pulled together the Scripture and Person indexes for us. We express our deep thanks to the contributors to this book, who agreed not only to present their talks in Minneapolis, but also to turn them into written chapters in the midst of hectic ministry schedules.

Most importantly, we acknowledge our debt to Jesus Christ. Our lives once revolved entirely around anything and everything but you. But by your grace, you have placed yourself at the center of our solar system. We pray that this book would honor you and the supremacy of your name.

# Part 1: God and Sex

# CHAPTER 1

# Sex and the Supremacy of Christ: Part One

JOHN PIPER

There is a connection between the beheadings of Jack Hensley and Eugene Armstrong and Nick Berg and Paul Johnson and Kenneth Bigley in Iraq, and this book on *Sex and the Supremacy of Christ*.

I look at them and I see their hands and their eyes. And I think of my hands and my eyes and my death and my faith. And then I hear the words of Jesus put it all in perspective, and in relation to sex.

> You have heard that it was said, "You shall not commit adultery." But I say to you that everyone who looks at a woman with lustful intent has already committed adultery with her in his heart. If your right eye causes you to sin, tear it out and throw it away. For it is better that you lose one of your members than that your whole body be thrown into hell. And if your right hand causes you to sin, cut it off and throw it away. For it is better that you lose one of your members than that your whole body go into hell. (Matt. 5:27-30)

In other words, there is something far more important than to keep your eye or your hand—or your head—namely, to receive eternal life and not to perish in hell. And Jesus links it with the war that we are waging not in Iraq but in our hearts. And the issue is sexual desire and what we do with it.

Everywhere you look in the world, it seems, there are reminders that life is war. We are not playing games. Heaven and hell, Jesus says, are in the balance.

## Two Simple, Weighty Points

I have two simple and weighty points to make. I think everything in this book will be the explanation and application of these two points. The first is that *sexuality is designed by God as a way to know God in Christ more fully*. And the second is that *knowing God in Christ more fully is designed as a way of guarding and guiding our sexuality*. I use the phrase "God in Christ" to signal at the outset that I am going to move back and forth between God and Christ because the biblical assumption of this book is that Christ is God.

Now to state the two points again, this time negatively, in the first place *all misuses of our sexuality distort the true knowledge of Christ*. And, in the second place, *all misuses of our sexuality derive from not having the true knowledge of Christ*.

Or to put it one more way: *all sexual corruption serves to conceal the true knowledge of Christ*, but *the true knowledge of Christ serves to prevent sexual corruption*.

### 1. Sexuality Is Designed by God as a Way to Know God More Fully

God created human beings in his image—"male and female he created them" (Gen. 1:27)—with capacities for intense sexual pleasure and with a calling to commitment in marriage and continence in singleness.[1] And his goal in creating human beings with personhood and passion was to make sure that there would be sexual language and sexual images that would point to the promises and the pleasures of God's relationship to his people and our relationship to him. In other words, the *ultimate* reason (not the only one) why we are sexual is to make God more deeply knowable. The language and imagery of sexuality are the most graphic and most powerful that the Bible uses to describe the relationship between God and his people—both positively (when we are faithful) and negatively (when we are not).

Listen, for example, if you can without embarrassment, to both the

---

[1] I would argue that when God wills singleness for any person he designs it as a way of knowing him more fully. There are unique ways of knowing God through sexual continence in singleness and unique ways of knowing God through sexual intimacy in marriage.

positive and the negative in God's words spoken through the prophet Ezekiel. Keep in mind that God has chosen Israel from all the peoples on the earth to experience his special covenant love, until the day when the Jewish Messiah, Jesus Christ, would come and live and die in the place of sinners, so that the gospel of Christ would overflow the banks of Israel and flood the nations of the world. So what we hear God say about his love for his people Israel in the Old Testament is all the more true of his relationship to those who believe in his Son, the Messiah, Jesus Christ. Here is how God describes that relationship with Israel according to the prophet Ezekiel, chapter 16. He speaks to Jerusalem as the embodiment of his people and rehearses over a thousand years of history. Starting at verse 4:

> "On the day you were born your cord was not cut, nor were you washed with water to cleanse you, nor rubbed with salt, nor wrapped in swaddling cloths. No eye pitied you, to do any of these things to you out of compassion for you, but you were cast out on the open field, for you were abhorred, on the day that you were born.
>
> "And when I passed by you and saw you wallowing in your blood, I said to you in your blood, 'Live!' I said to you in your blood, 'Live!' I made you flourish like a plant of the field. And you grew up and became tall and arrived at full adornment. Your breasts were formed, and your hair had grown; yet you were naked and bare.
>
> "When I passed by you again and saw you, behold, you were at the age for love, and I spread the corner of my garment over you and covered your nakedness; I made my vow to you and entered into a covenant with you, declares the Lord GOD, and you became mine. Then I bathed you with water and washed off your blood from you and anointed you with oil. I clothed you also with embroidered cloth and shod you with fine leather. . . ." (Ezek. 16:4-10a)

That's a picture of God's utterly free and undeserved mercy. That is how Israel was chosen. That's how you were brought from death to life and from darkness to light and from unbelief to faith, if you are a believer. "I said to you, 'Live!' and made you flourish. I married you. You are mine." That's how Israel began. That's how the Christian life begins. The mighty mercy of God. Then he goes on with the image:

"Thus you were adorned with gold and silver, and your clothing was of fine linen and silk and embroidered cloth. You ate fine flour and honey and oil. You grew exceedingly beautiful and advanced to royalty. And your renown went forth among the nations because of your beauty, for it was perfect through the splendor that I had bestowed on you, declares the Lord GOD.

"But you trusted in your beauty and played the whore because of your renown and lavished your whorings on any passerby; your beauty became his. You took some of your garments and made for yourself colorful shrines, and on them played the whore. The like has never been, nor ever shall be. . . .

"Adulterous wife, who receives strangers instead of her husband! Men give gifts to all prostitutes, but you gave your gifts to all your lovers, bribing them to come to you from every side with your whorings." (Ezek. 16:13-16, 32-33)

There's the picture of the faithless Israel. Her idolatry—her turning from the Lord God to foreign gods—is pictured as the work of a whore. And I say again what I said earlier: *God created us with sexual passion so that there would be language to describe what it means to cleave to him in love and what it means to turn away from him to others.* Now comes the word of judgment:

"Therefore, O prostitute, hear the word of the LORD: Thus says the Lord GOD, Because your lust was poured out and your nakedness uncovered in your whorings with your lovers, and with all your abominable idols, and because of the blood of your children that you gave to them, therefore, behold, I will gather all your lovers with whom you took pleasure, all those you loved and all those you hated. I will gather them against you from every side and will uncover your nakedness to them, that they may see all your nakedness." (Ezek. 16:35-37)

It may look as though God was finally finished with Israel. Judgment had fallen. The wife was put away. But that is not the last word. God hates divorce. Therefore, though he judge and separate, he will not finally forsake his covenant people—his wife. He will make with her a new covenant and bring her back to himself at the cost of his Son and by the power of his Spirit:

"For thus says the Lord GOD: I will deal with you as you have done, you who have despised the oath in breaking the covenant, yet I will remember my covenant with you in the days of your youth, and I will establish for you an everlasting covenant. . . . I will establish my covenant with you, and you shall know that I am the LORD, that you may remember and be confounded, and never open your mouth again because of your shame, when I atone for you for all that you have done, declares the Lord GOD." (Ezek. 16:59-60, 62-63)

The end of the story is that God, after giving up his faithless wife into the hands of her brutal lovers, will not only take her back, and not only make with her a new and everlasting covenant, but will himself pay for all her sins. Are there debts this prostitute owes? This husband will pay them. "When I atone for . . . all that you have done, declares the Lord." Indeed he will pay with the life of his own Son.

And so in the New Testament, after Jesus Christ has died and risen and is gathering a people for himself and his heavenly Father, the apostle Paul calls all husbands to live with their wives like this. Model your love on this kind of love:

Husbands, love your wives, as Christ loved the church and gave himself up for her, that he might sanctify her, having cleansed her by the washing of water with the word, so that he might present the church to himself in splendor, without spot or wrinkle or any such thing, that she might be holy and without blemish. (Eph. 5:25-27)

This is the fulfillment of Ezekiel's vision: "I will remember my covenant with you . . . and I will establish for you an everlasting covenant. . . . and you shall know that I am the LORD . . . when I atone . . . for all that you have done" (Ezek. 16:60-63). Jesus Christ creates and confirms and purchases with his blood the new covenant and the everlasting joy of our relationship with God. The Bible calls this relationship marriage, and pictures the great day of our final union as "the marriage supper of the Lamb" (Rev. 19:9).

Therefore, I say again: *God created us in his image, male and female, with personhood and sexual passions, so that when he comes to us in this world there would be these powerful words and images to*

*describe the promises and the pleasures of our covenant relationship
with him through Christ.*

God made us powerfully sexual so that he would be more deeply
knowable. We were given the power to know each other sexually so that
we might have some hint of what it will be like to know Christ
supremely.

Therefore, all misuses of our sexuality (adultery, fornication, illicit
fantasies, masturbation, pornography, homosexual behavior, rape, sexual child abuse, bestiality, exhibitionism, and so on) distort the true
knowledge of God. God means for human sexual life to be a pointer and
foretaste of our relationship with him. That's the first of my two points.

### 2. Knowing God Is Designed by God as a Way of Guarding and Guiding Our Sexuality

My second point is this: not only do all the misuses of our sexuality serve
to conceal or distort the true knowledge of God in Christ, but it also
works powerfully the other way around: the true knowledge of God in
Christ serves to prevent the misuses of our sexuality. So, on the one
hand, sexuality is designed by God as a way to know Christ more fully.
And, on the other hand, knowing Christ more fully is designed as a way
of guarding and guiding our sexuality.

Now on the face of it this will seem to many as patently false—that
knowing Christ will guard and guide our sexuality. Because many will
list off the pastors, priests, and theologians who have committed adultery or who have been found addicted to pornography or who have sexually used little boys or girls. Surely, then, if pastors, who hold the sacred
office of tenderly shepherding Christ's flock, can be so sexually corrupt,
there can be no correlation between knowing God and being sexually
upright, can there?

I think this question should be answered from Scripture, not from
experience, because if the Scripture teaches that truly knowing God
guards and guides and governs our sexuality in purity and love, then we
may be sure that a pastor, or priest, or theologian, or anyone else whose
sexuality is not governed and guarded and guided in Christ-exalting
purity and love does not know God—at least not as he ought. So what

does the Bible teach concerning the knowledge of God and the guarding of our sexuality?

In answering this question let's remember that knowing someone in the fullest biblical sense is defined by sexual imagery. Genesis 4:1, "Now Adam *knew* Eve his wife, and she conceived and bore Cain." *Knowing* here refers to sexual intercourse. Or again in Matthew 1:24-25 we read, "When Joseph woke from sleep, he did as the angel of the Lord commanded him: he took his wife, but *knew* her not until she had given birth to a son. And he called his name Jesus." He "knew her not" means he did not have sexual relations with her.

Now I don't mean that every time the word *know* is used in the Bible there are sexual connotations. That's not true. But what I do mean is that sexual language in the Bible for our covenant relationship to God does lead us to think of knowing God on the analogy of sexual intimacy and ecstasy. I don't mean that we somehow have sexual relations with God or he with man. That's a pagan thought. It's not Christian. But I do mean that the intimacy and ecstasy of sexual relations points to what knowing God is meant to be.

One of the books of the Bible that makes this clear is the book of Hosea. Listen to the way God speaks through Hosea to describe the restoration of his marriage with faithless Israel:

"Behold, I will allure her, and bring her into the wilderness,
    and speak tenderly to her.
And there I will give her her vineyards
    and make the Valley of Achor a door of hope.
And there she shall answer as in the days of her youth,
    as at the time when she came out of the land of Egypt.

"And in that day, declares the LORD, you will call me 'My Husband,' and no longer will you call me 'My Baal.' For I will remove the names of the Baals from her mouth, and they shall be remembered by name no more. . . . And I will betroth you to me forever. I will betroth you to me in righteousness and in justice, in steadfast love and in mercy. I will betroth you to me in faithfulness. *And you shall know the* LORD." (Hos. 2:14-16, 19-20)

I think it is virtually impossible to read this and then honestly say that *knowing God*, as God intends to be known by his people in the new covenant, simply means mental awareness or understanding or acquaintance with God. Not in a million years is that what "knowing God" means here. This is the knowing of a lover, not a scholar. A scholar can be a lover. But a scholar—or a pastor—doesn't know God until he is a lover. You can know *about* God by research; but until the researcher is ravished by what he sees, he doesn't know God for who he really is. And that is one great reason why many pastors can become so impure. They don't know God—the true, massive, glorious, gracious, biblical God. The humble intimacy and brokenhearted ecstasy—giving fire to the facts—is not there.

But I am getting ahead of myself. I haven't shown this from Scripture yet. I only said, *If* the Scripture teaches that truly knowing God—truly knowing Christ—guards and guides and governs our sexuality in purity and love, then we may be sure that a pastor, or anyone else, whose sexuality is not governed and guarded and guided in purity and love does not know God—at least not as he ought.

So is this what the Bible teaches: that knowing God—knowing Christ—is the path to purity? Is it indeed the case that the true knowledge of God promised in Hosea (and Jer. 31:34) brings the powerful passions of the body under the sway of truth and purity and love?

This entire book will be an answer to that question. But let me simply point you to some of the texts that provide the answer.[2] Each of these texts teaches that knowing God as revealed in Jesus Christ guards our sexuality from misuse, and that not knowing God leaves us prey to our passions:

> Since they did not see fit to have God in [their] knowledge God gave
> them up to a debased mind to do what ought not to be done. (Rom.
> 1:28, literal translation)

Suppressing the knowledge of God will make you a casualty of corruption. It is part of God's judgment. If you trade the treasure of God's glory

---

[2] See these other texts not referred to in this chapter: 2 Timothy 2:24-26; Romans 12:2; Philippians 1:9; Romans 10:3; Hosea 4:1, 6; 5:4; 6:3.

for anything, you will pay the price for that idolatry in the disordering of your sexual life. That is what Romans 1:23-24 teaches:

> [They] exchanged the glory of the immortal God for images resembling mortal man and birds and animals and reptiles. Therefore God gave them up in the lusts of their hearts to impurity, to the dishonoring of their bodies among themselves.

This is the old way. When we come to Christ, we take off the old way like a worn-out garment. Ignorance of God's wrath and glory does not fit us anymore. The new way is sexual holiness, and Paul contrasts it with not knowing God:

> This is the will of God, your sanctification: that you abstain from sexual immorality; that each one of you know how to control his own body in holiness and honor, not in the passion of lust like the Gentiles *who do not know God.* (1 Thess. 4:3-5)

Not knowing God puts you at the mercy of your passions—and they have no mercy without God. Here's the way Peter says it in 1 Peter 1:14-15:

> As obedient children, do not be conformed to the passions of *your former ignorance,* but as he who called you is holy, you also be holy in all your conduct.

The desires that governed you in those days got their power from deceit, not knowledge:

> Put off your old self, which belongs to your former manner of life and is corrupt *through deceitful* desires. (Eph. 4:22)

The desires of the body lie to us. They make deceitful promises—promises that are half true, as in the Garden of Eden. And we are powerless to expose and overcome those half-truths unless we know God—really know God, his ways and works and words embraced with growing intimacy and ecstasy.

When Paul describes the new person in Christ, who is putting off the old practices and the old slaveries, he says in Colossians 3:10 that "the new self . . . is being *renewed in knowledge* after the image of its creator." In other words, "I will betroth you to me forever, and you will know me." And in this knowledge you will be renewed—including your sexuality.

Peter's second letter has one of the clearest passages in the Bible on the relationship between knowing God and being liberated from corruption. In 2 Peter 1:3-4 he says:

> His divine power has granted to us all things that pertain to life and godliness, *through the knowledge of him who called us* to his own glory and excellence, by which he has granted to us his precious and very great promises, *so that through them* you may become partakers of the divine nature, having escaped from the corruption that is in the world because of sinful desire.

The divine power that leads to godliness comes "through the knowledge of him who called us to his own glory and excellence." And we become partakers of his divine nature—that is, we share in his righteous character—through his precious and very great promises. In other words, knowing the glorious treasure that God promises to be for us frees us from the corruption of lust and shapes us after the image of God.

Or as Jesus said, most simply in John 8:31-32: "If you abide in my word, you are truly my disciples, and *you will know the truth, and the truth* will set you free." Not *all* truth. The truth that you find in his Word. The truth that you find in relation to Christ as his disciple. And what is that truth? "I am the way, and *the truth*, and the life. No one comes to the Father except through me" (John 14:6). "No one knows the Father except the Son and anyone to whom the Son chooses to reveal him" (Matt. 11:27).

The Son knows the Father with infinite truth and intimacy and ecstasy. The joy that the Son has in the Father is unparalleled. His gladness in God the Father exceeds all gladness (Heb. 1:8-9). And this he shares with us who trust him as Savior and Lord and Treasure of our lives. "These things I have spoken to you, that my joy may be in you, and that your joy may be full" (John 15:11). "No one knows the Father except the Son and anyone to whom the Son chooses to reveal him"

(Matt. 11:27). And if he chooses, we will know the Father. And if we know the Father the way Christ knows the Father, we will be free.

## Conclusion

Let me therefore state again the two points that fly as a double banner over this book: 1) *sexuality is designed by Christ as a way to know God more fully;* and 2) *knowing Christ more fully in all his infinite supremacy is designed as a way of guarding and guiding our sexuality.* All sexual corruption serves to conceal the true knowledge of Christ, and the true knowledge of Christ serves to prevent sexual corruption.

I will come back to this in the next chapter, and all the other contributors to this book will unfold it. And as they do, let the double banner over this book fly with the words of Hosea to the wayward wife of God, and to you: *"Let us know; let us press on to know the LORD;* his going out is sure as the dawn; he will come to us as the showers, as the spring rains that water the earth" (Hos. 6:3).

Amen.

CHAPTER 2

# Sex and the Supremacy
## of Christ: Part Two

JOHN PIPER

In the previous chapter I waved a banner over this book with two convictions written on it: The first was that *sexuality is designed by God
as a way to know Christ more fully.* And the second was that *knowing
Christ more fully is designed by God as a way of guarding and guiding
our sexuality.* And when I speak of knowing Christ, I mean it in the
fullest biblical sense of grasping the truth about Christ, and growing in
fellowship with Christ, and being satisfied with the supremacy of Christ.

What I would like to do in this chapter, by God's grace, is to help
you experience that second conviction. I would like to help you know
the supremacy of Christ more fully and show you a couple of ways this
will affect your sexuality.

My conviction is that the better you know the supremacy of Christ,
the more sacred and satisfying and Christ-exalting your sexuality will
be. I have a picture in my mind of the majesty of Christ like the sun at
the center of the solar system of your life. The massive sun, 333,000
times the mass of the earth, holds all the planets in orbit, even little Pluto,
3.6 billion miles away. So it is with the supremacy of Christ in your life.
All the planets of your life—your sexuality and desires, your commitments and beliefs, your aspirations and dreams, your attitudes and convictions, your habits and disciplines, your solitude and relationships,
your labor and leisure, your thinking and feeling—all the planets of your
life are held in orbit by the greatness and gravity and blazing brightness

of the supremacy of Jesus Christ at the center of your life. If he ceases to be the bright, blazing, satisfying beauty at the center of your life, the planets will fly into confusion, a hundred things will be out of control, and sooner or later they will crash into destruction.

We were made to know Christ as he really is (which is why biblical doctrine is so important). We were created to comprehend—as much as a creature can—the supremacy of Christ. And the knowing we were made to experience is not the knowing of disinterested awareness—like knowing that Caesar crossed the Rubicon, or that ancient Gaul was divided into three parts—but the knowing of admiration and wonder and awe and intimacy and ecstasy and embrace. Not the knowing of a hurricane by watching TV but by flying into the eye of the storm.

We were made to see and savor with everlasting satisfaction the supremacy of Christ. Our sexuality points to this, and our sexuality is purified by this. We are sexual beings so that we may know something more of the supremacy of Christ. And we must know the supremacy of Christ—we must know *him* in his supremacy—in order to experience our sexuality as sacred and sweet and Christ-exalting and secondary— quietly, powerfully secondary.

My prayer for this book, and for all of you one by one, is that you will see and savor the supremacy of Christ—married or single, male or female, old or young, devastated by disordered desires or walking in a measure of holiness—that all of you will behold and embrace the supremacy of Christ as the blazing sun at the center of your life, and that the planet of your sexuality, with all its little moons of pleasure, will orbit in its proper place.

There are many practical strategies for being sexually pure in mind and body. I don't demean them. I use them! But with all my heart I know, and with the authority of Scripture I know, that the tiny spaceships of our moral strategies will be useless in nudging the planet of sexuality into orbit, unless the sun of our solar system is the supremacy of Christ.

Oh, that the risen, living Christ, therefore, would come to us (even now) by his Spirit and through his Word and reveal to us

- the supremacy of his *deity*, equal with God the Father in all his attributes—the radiance of his glory and the exact imprint of his nature, infinite, boundless in all his excellencies;

- the supremacy of his *eternality* that makes the mind of man explode with the unsearchable thought that Christ never had a beginning, but simply always was; sheer, absolute reality while all the universe is fragile, contingent, like a shadow by comparison to his all-defining, ever-existing substance;
- the supremacy of his never-changing *constancy* in all his virtues and all his character and all his commitments—the same yesterday, today, and forever;
- the supremacy of his *knowledge* that makes the Library of Congress look like a matchbox, and all the information on the Internet look like a little 1940s farmers' almanac, and quantum physics—and everything Stephen Hawking ever dreamed—seem like a first-grade reader;
- the supremacy of his *wisdom* that has never been perplexed by any complication and can never be counseled by the wisest of men;
- the supremacy of his *authority* over heaven and earth and hell—without whose permission no man and no demon can move one inch; who changes times and seasons, removes kings and sets up kings; who does according to his will among the host of heaven and among the inhabitants of the earth, so that none can stay his hand or say to him, "What have you done?" (see Dan. 4:35);
- the supremacy of his *providence* without which not a single bird falls to the ground in the furthest reaches of the Amazon forest, or a single hair of any head turns black or white;
- the supremacy of his *word* that moment by moment upholds the universe and holds in being all the molecules and atoms and subatomic world we have never yet dreamed of;
- the supremacy of his *power* to walk on water, cleanse lepers and heal the lame, open the eyes of the blind, cause the deaf to hear and storms to cease and the dead to rise, with a single word, or even a thought;
- the supremacy of his *purity* never to sin or to have one millisecond of a bad attitude or an evil, lustful thought;
- the supremacy of his *trustworthiness* never to break his word or let one promise fall to the ground;

- the supremacy of his *justice* to render in due time all moral accounts in the universe settled either on the cross or in hell;
- the supremacy of his *patience* to endure our dullness for decade after decade and to hold back his final judgment on this land and on the world, that many might repent;
- the supremacy of his sovereign, servant *obedience* to keep his Father's commandments perfectly and then embrace the excruciating pain of the cross willingly;
- the supremacy of his *meekness* and lowliness and tenderness that will not break a bruised reed or quench a smoldering wick;
- the supremacy of his *wrath* that will one day explode against this world with such fierceness that people will call out for the rocks and the mountains to crush them rather than face the wrath of the Lamb;
- the supremacy of his *grace* that gives life to spiritually dead rebels and wakens faith in hell-bound haters of God, and justifies the ungodly with his own righteousness;
- the supremacy of his *love* that willingly dies for us even while we were sinners and frees us for the ever-increasing joy in making much of him forever;
- the supremacy of his own inexhaustible *gladness* in the fellowship of the Trinity, the infinite power and energy that gave rise to all the universe and will one day be the inheritance of every struggling saint.

And if he would grant us to know him like this, it would be but the outskirts of his supremacy. Time would fail to speak of the supremacy of his severity, and invincibility, and dignity, and simplicity, and complexity, and resoluteness, and calmness, and depth, and courage. If there is anything admirable, if there is anything worthy of praise anywhere in the universe, it is summed up supremely in Jesus Christ.

He is supreme in every admirable way over everything:

- over galaxies and endless reaches of space;
- over the earth from the top of Mount Everest 29,000 feet up, to the bottom of the Pacific Ocean 36,000 feet down into the Mariana Trench.

- He is supreme over all plants and animals, from the peaceful Blue Whale to the microscopic killer viruses;
- over all weather and movements of the earth: hurricanes, tornadoes, monsoons, earthquakes, avalanches, floods, snow, rain;
- over all chemical processes that heal and destroy: cancer, AIDS, malaria, flu, and all the workings of antibiotics and a thousand healing medicines.
- He is supreme over all countries and all governments and all armies;
- over Al Qaeda and all terrorists and kidnappings and suicide bombings and beheadings;
- over bin Laden and al-Zarqawi;
- over all nuclear threats from Iran or Russia or North Korea.
- He is supreme over all politics and elections;
- over all media and news and entertainment and sports and leisure;
- over all education and universities and scholarship and science and research;
- over all business and finance and industry and manufacturing and transportation;
- and over all the Internet and information systems.

As Abraham Kuyper used to say, "There is not a square inch in the whole domain of our human existence over which Christ, who is Sovereign over all, does not cry, 'Mine!'"[1] And rule with absolute supremacy. And though it may not seem so now, it is only a matter of time until he is revealed from heaven in flaming fire to give relief to those who trust him and to inflict righteous vengeance on those who don't.

Oh, that the almighty God would help us see and savor the supremacy of his Son. Give yourself to this. Study this. Cultivate this passion. Eat and drink and sleep this quest to know the supremacy of Christ. Pray for God to show you these things in his Word. Swim in the Bible every day. Use the means of grace. Like God-centered, Christ-

---

[1] Abraham Kuyper, *Abraham Kuyper: A Centennial Reader*, ed. James D. Bratt (Grand Rapids, Mich.: Eerdmans, 1998), 488.

exalting books. Get John Owen on the glories of Christ[2] and the mortification of sin.[3] Get C. J. Mahaney on the cross[4] and the glory of God in marriage.[5] Get David Powlison[6] and Ben Patterson[7] and Jonathan Edwards.[8] And with all your getting—whatever it takes—get the all-satisfying supremacy of Christ at the center of your life.

This is the *blazing sun* at the center of your solar system, holding the planet of sexuality in sacred orbit. This is the *ballast* at the bottom of your little boat keeping it from being capsized by the waves of sexual temptation. This is the *foundation* that holds up the building of your life so that you can build with strategies of sexual purity. Without this—without knowing and embracing the supremacy of Christ in all things—the planets fly apart, the waves overwhelm, and the building will one day fall.

### The Main Obstacle to Knowing the Supremacy of Christ

So here we are as sinners. All of us. "None is righteous, no, not one" (Rom. 3:10). We have all sinned and fallen short of the glory of God (Rom. 3:23). We don't know him, we don't trust him and treasure him the way he deserves. So what stands in the way? What is our main obstacle to knowing the supremacy of Christ, with a deeply satisfying and sexuality-transforming knowledge?

The biblical answer to that question is: the absolutely just and holy wrath of God. We cannot know God in our sin because, in our sin, the wrath of God rests upon us. What we deserve in our sin is not the knowledge of God but the judgment of God. And since we are cut off from the knowledge of God by the wrath of God, we are cut off from sexual purity and holiness. God doesn't owe us purity, he owes us punishment. Therefore we are hopelessly depraved and hopelessly condemned.

[2] John Owen, *The Glory of Christ,* in *The Works of John Owen,* vol. 1, ed. W. H. Goold, 24 vols. (1850–1853; reprint Edinburgh: Banner of Truth, 1965).

[3] John Owen, *The Mortification of Sin,* in *The Works of John Owen,* vol. 6.

[4] C. J. Mahaney, *The Cross Centered Life* (Sisters, Ore.: Multnomah, 2003); C. J. Mahaney, *Christ Our Mediator* (Sisters, Ore.: Multnomah, 2004).

[5] C. J. Mahaney, *Sex, Romance, and the Glory of God* (Wheaton, Ill.: Crossway, 2004).

[6] David Powlison, *Seeing with New Eyes: Counseling and the Human Condition Through the Lens of Scripture* (Phillipsburg, N.J.: Presbyterian & Reformed, 2003).

[7] Ben Patterson, *Deepening Your Conversation With God: Learning to Love to Pray* (Minneapolis: Bethany, 2001); Ben Patterson, *Waiting: Finding Hope When God Seems Silent* (Downers Grove, Ill.: InterVarsity Press, 1991).

[8] See the recommended resources in John Piper and Justin Taylor, eds., *A God-Entranced Vision of All Things: The Legacy of Jonathan Edwards* (Wheaton, Ill.: Crossway, 2004), 269-272.

Except for one thing: the good news that Christ has become for us the curse to bear God's wrath and the righteousness to meet God's demand. This is the heart of the gospel. And without it, there is no hope to escape God's wrath, no hope to know Christ's supremacy, and no hope for sexual purity. But here it is for everyone who believes: Galatians 3:13, "Christ redeemed us from the curse of the law by becoming a curse for us—for it is written, 'Cursed is everyone who is hanged on a tree.'" We were under the curse of God's wrath. But Christ became a curse for us. And here it is again: Philippians 3:9, Paul's testimony that he is "found in [Christ], not having a righteousness of my own that comes from the law, but that which comes through faith in Christ, the righteousness from God that depends on faith." God's demand was that we be perfect. We cannot, in our sin, fulfill this demand. But Christ has. And by faith in him, that perfect righteousness is imputed to us.

Therefore, since it is true that Christ has absorbed all the wrath of God that was aimed at me, and since it is true that Christ has performed the perfect righteousness that God demands of me, there is now for me no condemnation. Instead, every thought of God and every act of God toward me in Christ Jesus is mercy. The way is open to know him and all the beautiful supremacy of his Son. The cross of Christ has made the supremacy of Christ knowable.

The best gift of the gospel is not the forgiveness of sins. The best gift of the gospel is not the imputed righteousness of Christ. The best gift of the gospel is not eternal life. The best gift of the gospel is seeing and savoring the supremacy of Christ himself. The greatest reward of the cross is knowing the supremacy of Christ.

### How Then Does the Knowledge of the Supremacy of Christ (Opened to Us by the Gospel) Guide and Guard and Govern Our Sexual Lives?

How does it make our sexuality sacred, satisfying, and Christ-exalting? Of all the ways this works, I will mention only two.

*First, knowing the supremacy of Christ enlarges the soul so that sex and its little thrills become as small as they really are.* Little souls make little lusts have great power. The soul, as it were, expands to encompass the magnitude of its treasure. The human soul was made to see and

savor the supremacy of Christ. Nothing else is big enough to enlarge the
soul as God intended and make little lusts lose their power.

Vast starry skies seen from a mountain in Utah, and four layers of
moving clouds on a seemingly endless plain in Montana, and standing
on the edge of a mile-deep drop in the Grand Canyon can all have a
wonderfully supplementary role in enlarging the soul with beauty. But
nothing can take the place of the supremacy of Christ. As Jonathan
Edwards said, if you embrace all creation with goodwill, but do not
embrace Christ, you are infinitely narrow.[9] Our hearts were made to be
enlarged by Christ, and all creation cannot replace his supremacy.

My conviction is that one of the main reasons the world and the
church are awash in lust and pornography (by both men and women—
30 percent of Internet pornography is now viewed by women[10]) is that
our lives are intellectually and emotionally disconnected from the infinite, soul-staggering grandeur for which we were made. Inside and outside the church Western culture is drowning in a sea of triviality,
pettiness, banality, and silliness. Television is trivial. Radio is trivial.
Conversation is trivial. Education is trivial. Christian books are trivial.
Worship styles are trivial. It is inevitable that the human heart, which
was made to be staggered with the supremacy of Christ, but instead is
drowning in a sea of banal entertainment, will reach for the best natural buzz that life can give: sex.

Therefore, the deepest cure to our pitiful addictions is not any mental strategies—though I believe in them and have my own (called
ANTHEM[11]). The deepest cure is to be intellectually and emotionally staggered by the infinite, everlasting, unchanging supremacy of Christ in all
things. This is what it means to *know* him. Christ has purchased this gift
for us at the cost of his life. Therefore, I say again with Hosea, "Let us
know; let us press on to know the LORD" (Hos. 6:3).

*Second, knowing the supremacy of Christ saves our sexuality from
sin by empowering us to suffer.* Knowing all that God promises to be
for us in Christ both now and for endless ages to come, with ever-

[9] Jonathan Edwards, *The Nature of True Virtue* (reprint, Ann Arbor: University of Michigan Press, 1960), 77.
[10] See, for example, the statistics cited by the *Internet Filter Review,* http://www.internetfilterreview.com/internet-pornography-statistics.html (accessed 1-7-05). "1 of 3 visitors to all adult web sites are women."
[11] See John Piper, *Pierced by the Word* (Sisters, Ore.: Multnomah, 2003), 107-111. This is also available at www.desiringGod.org.

increasing joy, frees us from the compulsion that we must avoid pain and maximize comfort in this world. We need not, and we dare not. Christ died to make our everlasting future bright with the supremacy of his own glory. And the effect he means for it to have now is glad-hearted suffering in the path of love.

Matthew 5:11-12: "Blessed are you when others revile you and persecute you and utter all kinds of evil against you falsely on my account. Rejoice and be glad, *for your reward is great in heaven.*" Yes, namely, seeing and savoring the supremacy of Christ himself. That's the reward, and that's the power to suffer.

Luke 14:13-14: "When you give a feast, invite the poor, the crippled, the lame, the blind, and you will be blessed, because they cannot repay you. *You will be repaid at the resurrection of the just.*" Yes, namely, seeing and savoring the supremacy of Christ himself. That will be your repayment, and that is the power to do the hard thing and serve the poor.

Hebrews 10:34: ". . . you joyfully accepted the plundering of your property, since you knew that you yourselves had a better possession and an abiding one." Yes, namely, seeing and savoring the supremacy of Christ himself. That is the better and abiding possession, and the power to be plundered with joy in the path of love.

Hebrews 13:13-14: "Therefore let us go to him outside the camp and bear the reproach he endured. For here we have no lasting city, but we seek the city that is to come." Yes, the city where the "glory of God gives it light, and its lamp is the Lamb" (Rev. 21:23), and where we will live in the light of his supremacy forever. That is the better city, and that is the power to go outside the camp and bear reproach.

Our knowing all that God promises to be for us in Christ gives us the power to suffer with joy. And here's the link: we must suffer in order to be sexually pure.

Jesus says, " . . . everyone who looks at a woman with lustful intent has already committed adultery with her in his heart. If your right eye causes you to sin, tear it out and throw it away. For it is better that you lose one of your members than that your whole body be thrown into hell" (Matt. 5:28-29). In essence he is saying, suffer whatever you must in order to win the war with lust.

Knowing the supremacy of Christ—being satisfied with all that God is for us in Jesus—gives us the power to suffer for the sake of loving people and being pure.

Therefore, in conclusion, I say again with Hosea: "Let us know; let us press on to know the LORD." It will not be easy. It may cost you your life. But if you keep the supremacy of Christ before your eyes as an infinite prize, you will find the strength to suffer and press on to love and purity, with joy.

## CHAPTER 3

# The Goodness of Sex
# and the Glory of God

BEN PATTERSON

It's risky to talk about the goodness of sex these days, because ours is an age of sexual hyperbole. Never before in history has the goddess of sex offered so much with so little to give. Never before has sexual pleasure been sought with such grim earnestness. Never before has so much merchandise been moved on the implicit promise that it will make you more sexy or get you more sex. If the advertising industry is any indication, the threat of AIDS and STDs, rather than diminishing or disciplining the sexual urge, has simply made it more daring and more exciting. It has raised the stakes and upped the bets, so to speak.

In the 1960s a famous graffiti appeared in Berkeley, California. In a parody of the Nazi slogan, "Arbeit macht frei," or "Work makes free," someone had sprayed on a wall, "Sex makes free." A few years later a friend of mine saw a more erudite version of the same thought scrawled on a rest room wall in the philosophy building of the University of Southern California. It was a parody of philosopher René Descartes' famous formulation, "Cogito, ergo sum," or "I think, therefore I am." It was "*Copulo,* ergo sum," or "I copulate, therefore I am."

With all of this sexual obsession, one is tempted to downplay the pleasures and goodness of sex—to say they are overrated. *But that might do the devil's will as much as the obsession itself.* Pleasure is God's idea, and God is the devil's Enemy. The devil actually hates pleasure, because he hates the God of pleasure.

In C. S. Lewis's *The Screwtape Letters,* the devil Screwtape tries to explain to his nephew Wormwood what he finds most appalling and disingenuous about God: that God is really out to make people happy, and that even the austere parts of his program, the spiritual disciplines, are really ruses, clever deceptions to make them more happy. "He's a hedonist at heart," sniffs Screwtape. "All those fasts and vigils and stakes and crosses are only a facade. Or only like foam on the sea shore. Out at sea, out in His sea, there is pleasure and more pleasure. He makes no secret of it; at His right hand are 'pleasures forevermore'. . . . He's vulgar, Wormwood. He has a bourgeois mind. *He has filled the world full of pleasures.*"[1]

The devil's grand strategy against pleasure is to twist it, to get us to misuse it. "Never forget that when we are dealing with any pleasure in its healthy and normal and satisfying form, we are, in a sense, on the Enemy's [God's] ground. I know we have won many a soul through plea- sure. All the same, it is His invention, not ours. He made the pleasures: all our research so far has not enabled us to produce one. All we can do is to encourage the humans to take the pleasures which our Enemy has produced, at times, or in ways, or in degrees which He has forbidden. Hence we always try to work away from the natural condition of any pleasure to that in which it is least natural, least redolent of its Maker, and least pleasurable. *An ever increasing craving for an ever diminish- ing pleasure is the formula.*"[2]

I think that formula is exactly what is going on in our culture—an ever-increasing craving for an ever-diminishing pleasure. Look at the magazines at the checkout counter of your market. There is a weariness about them, a chatty droning about this technique and that technique, this pleasure point or that pleasure point.

G. K. Chesterton's description of the world's joys applies: these amount to merely "small publicity" when set next to the Christian's "gigantic secret" of joy.[3] The gigantic secret of the joy of sex is this: Sex is good because the God who created sex is good. And God is glorified greatly when we receive his gift with thanksgiving—for the gift points

[1] C. S. Lewis, *The Screwtape Letters* (New York: Macmillan, 1944), 112, emphasis mine.
[2] Ibid., 49, emphasis mine.
[3] G. K. Chesterton, *Orthodoxy* (London: William Cloves & Sons, 1932), 296.

back to the God who gave it—and enjoy it the way he meant for it to be enjoyed.

How do we know this is true? We know it's true because of its place in the Bible. "The Bible is a book about marriage." That's the way David Hubbard put it in his commentary on the Song of Solomon.[4] To say the Bible is a book about marriage is to say that it is also a book about sex and the meaning of sex. For marriage is the only natural condition for the pleasure of sex.

## The Bible Is a Book About Marriage and Sex

There are five ways this is true:

1. *In the very beginning of the Bible there is a marriage.*
Genesis 2:23-25: "The man said, 'This is now bone of my bones and flesh of my flesh; she shall be called "woman," for she was taken out of man.' For this reason a man will leave his father and mother and be united to his wife, and they will become one flesh. The man and his wife were both naked, and they felt no shame" (NIV).

2. *At the very end of the Bible there is a marriage.*
Revelation 19:6-7, 9: "Hallelujah! For our Lord God Almighty reigns. Let us rejoice and be glad and give him glory! For the wedding of the Lamb has come and his bride has made herself ready. . . . Then the angel said to me, 'Write: "Blessed are those who are invited to the wedding supper of the Lamb!"'" (NIV).

Revelation 21:2: "I saw the Holy City, the new Jerusalem, coming down out of heaven from God, prepared as a bride beautifully dressed for her husband" (NIV).

3. *The central themes of the Bible are underlined with marriage metaphors.*
Hosea's bad marriage to a sexually promiscuous wife is a picture of God's marriage to Israel. When the marriage is healed and God and his people are reconciled, the promise is, "No longer will they call you

---

[4] David Hubbard, *Ecclesiastes, Song of Solomon,* The Communicator's Commentary (Waco, Tex.: Word, 1991), 267.

Deserted, or name your land Desolate. But you will be called Hephzibah [my delight is in her], and your land Beulah [married]; for the LORD will take delight in you, and your land will be married. As a young man marries a maiden, so will your sons marry you; as a bridegroom rejoices over his bride, so will your God rejoice over you" (Isa. 62:4-5, NIV).

In the Gospels, Jesus said he is like a bridegroom to his people. Therefore people must be joyful in his presence, for "How can the guest of the bridegroom mourn while he is with them?" (Matt. 9:15, NIV). He said the coming of the kingdom of heaven is like people waiting for a wedding (Matt. 25:1-13). When John the Baptist was asked his opinion of Jesus' rising popularity, he said it was time for him to step aside because his friend the Bridegroom had come. It's now Jesus' party, not his. "He must become greater; I must become less" (John 3:30, NIV).

The apostle Paul saw human marriage as a demonstration of God's marriage to his people. After speaking in some detail about the mutual responsibilities of a husband and a wife in marriage, and of how the two become one flesh (Eph. 5:21-33), Paul says, "This is a profound mystery—but I am talking about Christ and the church" (v. 32, NIV).

4. *The sexual, in the Bible, is a chief arena of the brokenness of sin—and therefore occupies an important place among the things Christ came to redeem.*

Genesis 3:16: the Fall fractures the sexual relationship of the man and the woman. The bearing of children will be painful, and her desire for her husband will be full of anguish and struggle. The marriage bed will become a battleground.

Romans 1:21-24: the heart of our darkness is this: "For although they knew God, they neither glorified him as God nor gave thanks to him, but their thinking became futile and their foolish hearts were darkened." Darkness leads to idolatry. "Although they claimed to be wise, they became fools and exchanged the glory of the immortal God for images . . ." Idolatry shows itself first, and perhaps most tellingly, in our sexuality. "Therefore God gave them over in the sinful desires of their hearts to sexual impurity for the degrading of their bodies with one another (NIV)."

5. *Happily tucked away in the Bible, among the Law and the*

*Prophets, is a little book called Song of Solomon; it is a collection of love and wedding songs.* It offers no liturgy or commandments, no hymns, oracles, or visions—just love songs, the "Song of Songs" (Song 1:1), "the best love song of all."

This is unique in the Old Testament. Because of its concern for the covenant, the Old Testament's interest in sex is mainly with its relation to begetting. There are very few clues as to whether it should be fun. The Song of Solomon fills this gap. It says that along with having children, sex is for pleasure, joy, communion, and celebration. Pregnancy is not even mentioned in the book! It paints a beautiful picture of what redeemed sex looks like. Karl Barth said the tone of the book is *"eros without shame."* He described it as a poetic commentary on Genesis 2:25: "The man and his wife were both naked, and they felt no shame" (NIV). If they didn't feel shame, what did they feel? The Song of Solomon gives the answer. Here are some of the ways they felt:

1:2 (NLT): "Kiss me again and again, for your love is sweeter than wine." This has to be one of the most memorable opening lines in the Bible! Compare it with other famous beginnings: Genesis 1:1, "In the beginning, God . . ."; John 1:1, "In the beginning was the Word . . ." And then we have the Song of Solomon: "Kiss me again and again." The Hebrew is literally something like "Smother me with kisses." The "love" referred to has strong, physically erotic connotations, as in the caresses of lovemaking. And it leaves her feeling more euphoric, headier, more "buzzed" than wine.

1:9 (NIV): "I liken you, my darling, to a mare harnessed to one of the chariots of Pharaoh." When his beloved deprecates her physical beauty, he strongly disagrees and says she is like a mare, a female horse, in Pharaoh's cavalry. But there were no mares in Pharaoh's cavalry, because a mare would excite all the males into a pandemonium of sexual excitement! Precisely. Does she think she is unattractive? He begs to differ. On the contrary, her attractiveness to men is like a mare released in a corral of stallions. She not only looks good to him, she looks good to others, too.

2:3-7 (NIV): "Like an apple tree among the trees of the forest is my lover among the young men. I delight to sit in his shade, and his fruit is sweet to my taste. He has taken me to the banquet hall, and his banner over me is love. Strengthen me with raisins, refresh me with apples, for

I am faint with love. His left arm is under my head, and his right arm embraces me. Daughters of Jerusalem, I charge you by the gazelles and by the does of the field: Do not arouse or awaken love until it so desires."

Apples and raisins and other fruits were all ancient erotic symbols. That's what her lover is like to her. But he is not merely a symbol; he's the real thing. His "shade" is his nearness, and the effect he has on her is like being brought to a banquet hall, literally a house of wine, another symbol of the ecstasy of lovemaking. The "banner" of love seems out of place, the banner being a military metaphor; perhaps it speaks of the ferocity of love. Whatever its meaning, it provides a dramatic picture of a woman swept up under the passion and protection of her man—his left arm under her head, his right arm embracing her.

In her excitement she calls for a vow—a solemn oath—expressing the exquisite passion she feels: "Do not arouse or awaken love until it so desires." Remarkably, she issues a call for restraint in the name of "the gazelles and . . . the does of the field"—further symbols of passion.[5] Her message is that the experience of lovemaking is too powerful, too all-consuming to stir up until the lovers are ready, until they have the commitment proper to sex. She charges restraint in the very name of the things that excite her; for the sake of sex, we must restrain sex until the right time.

The pleasures and goodness of sex are heightened, not lessened by proper restraint, in the same way the Colorado River is made more powerful by the walls of the Grand Canyon. The very narrowness of the river's channel there makes for a greater river. Farther south, as the river flows through the deserts of California and Arizona, it is shallow, wide, and muddy, even stinky in spots. Wider boundaries diminish the river; sharper, stronger, and *narrower* boundaries strengthen it. Less is more. The boundaries and proscriptions of sex in the Bible are for the sake of sex. Again, less is more—at least less as understood by one man and one woman together exclusively till death parts them.

2:16-17 (NLT): "My lover is mine, and I am his. He feeds among the lilies! Before the dawn comes and the shadows flee away, come back to me, my love. Run like a gazelle or a young stag on the rugged mountains."

---

[5] Cf. 4:5 and 7:3, where her lover compares her breasts to fawns, twins of a gazelle; also 2:17 and 8:14, where she invites her lover to her "mountains"—to enjoy her contours.

"My lover is mine, and I am his"—this formula appears at key points in the Song to emphasize the exclusivity of the lovers' commitment to each other. It is also a formula on the human level of what is true of God and his people (Hos. 2:23). In the context of this glorious, amorous, monogamous exclusivity her lover "feeds among the lilies!" The covenant promise has an erotic dimension: they belong to each other to the fullest, and they may and will enjoy each other to the fullest. "Lilies" or "lotuses" describe not only the beauty of the beloved, but are metaphors for a man's lips (5:13), and the part of a woman's body surrounding her breasts (4:5). She enjoys this so thoroughly that she wants it to last all night: "Before the dawn comes and the shadows flee away, come back to me, my love." Specifically, she wants him to "run like a gazelle or a young stag on the rugged mountains." Here she visualizes him enjoying her "mountains," the contours and clefts of her body (cf. 4:6).

He too waxes eloquent with a flurry of metaphors and similes to stimulate the imagination of the most unimaginative reader.

> "How beautiful are your sandaled feet, O queenly maiden. Your rounded thighs are like jewels, the work of a skilled craftsman. Your navel is as delicious as a goblet filled with wine. Your belly is lovely, like a heap of wheat set about with lilies. Your breasts are like twin fawns of a gazelle. Your neck is as stately as an ivory tower. Your eyes are like the sparkling pools in Heshbon by the gate of Bath-rabbim. Your nose is as fine as the tower of Lebanon overlooking Damascus. Your head is as majestic as Mount Carmel, and the sheen of your hair radiates royalty. A king is held captive in your queenly tresses. Oh, how delightful you are, my beloved; how pleasant for utter delight! You are tall and slim like a palm tree, and your breasts are like its clusters of dates. I said, 'I will climb up into the palm tree and take hold of its branches.' Now may your breasts be like grape clusters, and the scent of your breath like apples. May your kisses be as exciting as the best wine, smooth and sweet, flowing gently over lips and teeth" (7:1-9, NLT).

Put simply, he feels about her the way a student expressed to me his love for his fiancée: "I look at her . . . and I can't breathe!" Breasts like grape clusters? A navel like a goblet of wine? Thighs as finely shaped as jewels? Is this really in the Bible, the Word of God? It really is! How wholesome and richly erotic sex can be when enjoyed in the ways and within the context God intended. How much better it is than the cheap, toxic ways the world recommends. Contrast the joy of this text with the confusion and shame a young man experiences as he walks past the lingerie in the window display of a Victoria's Secret store:

Just what kind of secret is
Victoria trying to keep?
What blushing mystery pauses
before the pursed lips of the
mannequin in the window?

Whatever it is,
or whoever plastic *she* is,
I have shuffled to a stop,
hoping no one spies my
lingering.

We've all done it—men, that is.

I'm not the first to be fascinated
by the accoutrements of
feminine mystique,
which are so many things,
but not secretive;

panties, bras, frills, straps, and lace
brandish a secret badly kept,
a message plain as an eye-shadowed wink.

Suddenly, I get the message.

A purr from behind
the window
hooks its finger,
peeling blushes off my skin,
revealing bleeding secrets beneath.[6]

---

[6] This poem is by Andy Patterson, a senior at Westmont College, where I am the pastor. He is also my son, I am proud to say.

Victoria's Secret is Victoria's Lie. God's good idea will always out-pleasure the ersatz pleasures of the world.

What are the theological foundations for this celebration of sex—and what does it have to do with the glory of God? The gigantic secret of the joy of sex is this: *Sex is good because the God who created sex is good. And God is glorified greatly when we receive his gift with thanks-giving and enjoy it the way he meant for it to be enjoyed.* The reason we like sex so much is that it is a little bit like the God who created it. Therefore, the more sex is enjoyed in ways redolent of its Creator, the better sex is for all involved—to God's glory and our sanctification and joy. The church father Irenaeus nearly reduced it to a formula when he said, "The glory of God is man fully alive, and the life of man is the vision of God."[7] The vision of God: that's where the theological foun-dations come in. I think there are five.

### Theological Foundations

1. *The goodness of the creation.* God made it, so it must be good. He said so. He made it good because he made it ex nihilo, out of noth-ing. To say God made it all out of nothing is to say he made it with no outside limitations, because when you make something out of nothing, the only limitations are those in your own mind. No one brought God the raw material of creation, dropped it into his lap, and said, "Now see what you can do with this stuff." He wasn't a sculptor bound by the lim-itations of marble or clay, or a painter restricted by watercolors. What we see in this lovely world is not the best that God could do with some inferior material. It was made from the very best of "materials"—the thoughts and desires of a wise and loving God. His only limitations were in his mind.

Not so in the creation stories of the pagans, ancient or modern. Whatever gods there may be were forced to work with some preexistent material, usually inferior in quality. In the Babylonian creation myth, Marduk, the state god of Babylon, formed the world out of a furious struggle with the great sea serpent Tiamat. According to the myth, the world as we know it was formed in violence and death, out of the great serpent's corpse. The message of the myth is that there is pain and evil

---

[7] Irenaeus, *Adversus haereses* 4.20.7.

and sickness and injustice in the world because the stuff the gods had to work with was flawed from the beginning. As the saying goes, you can't make a silk purse out of a sow's ear.

But according to the Bible, this is not how it is with God or his world or our bodies. He created the heavens and the earth graciously and freely, using the finest of materials—whatever was in his loving, wise, and holy heart. Paul says God is for the body (1 Cor. 6:13). He should be: he made it.

Then he did something astounding with what he made: he put us in charge of it, as stewards. What is a steward? A steward is someone entrusted with the management of someone else's property and charged with managing it in the owner's best interest. God's great interest is his glory.

Marriage and sexuality is a stewardship. I must give my wife back better than I received her. And I must give the world we shared back to God better than we received it. Marriage is yet another arena in which to live out your vocation to serve Christ. Dietrich Bonhoeffer once spoke to a love-struck couple in a marriage homily: "In your love you see only the heaven of your own happiness, but in marriage you are placed at a post of responsibility towards the world and mankind."[8] We do nothing in this life unto ourselves alone. Even a happy marriage (or great sex) is not only for the happiness of the husbands, wives, and children; it is for God's glory.

2. *The reality of the Incarnation.* The God who created human flesh deemed that it was a fit vehicle for the Son of God to "tent" among us in (John 1:14). To remember him and his death we are to eat bread and drink wine. As a sign and symbol of the cleansing of new birth we are to use water. Whatever one's view of communion, it should impress us all that he told us to eat and drink something to remember him, his body and his blood. He told us to wash with water to express forgiveness and new birth. These aren't mere psychological transactions, they are physical acts.

The physical is a fit vehicle for communion with God and for a husband and wife. When Adam knew his wife (Gen. 4:1), what happened?

---

[8] Dietrich Bonhoeffer, *Letters and Papers from Prison* (New York: Macmillan, 1971), 43.

Did he gather information? No. She got pregnant! "This is a piquant irony," writes Thomas Howard. "Here we are, with all our high notions of ourselves as intellectual and spiritual beings and the most profound form of knowledge for us is a plain business of skin on skin. It is humiliating. When two members of this godlike, cerebral species approach the heights of communion between themselves, what do they do? Think? Speculate? Meditate? No, they take off their clothes. Do they want to get their brains together? No. It is the most appalling of ironies: Their search for union takes them quite literally in a direction away from where their brains are."[9]

I'll never forget the pastoral visit I had with a woman whose husband had just died that morning. She had nursed him at home through a protracted and painful bout with cancer. When I walked into her living room, his corpse was still on the hospital bed she had wheeled beside the fireplace. I stood on one side of the bed, and she on the other, as I prayed for her. Before I finished praying I opened my eyes to see her massaging her husband's feet, patting his cheeks, and rubbing his calves and hands as she must have done innumerable times in their marriage. I was deeply moved at what I saw, and as I drove home I thought, *This is what sex is finally all about: one man and one woman to the end, loving and caring for each other's bodies, with their bodies.*

3. *God made us sexual creatures.* "So what else is new?" you say. This does not mean, primarily, that we have sexual drives and urges. I will not be less a male when my hormones give out. My masculinity will not be reaffirmed if I am shot to death by a jealous husband when I'm a hundred years old, as my father once quipped. The hormones are part of it, but they are peripheral to the center, which is that we are differentiated as male and female. Apart from this basic differentiation, we cannot be understood as human beings. The words of Jesus are, "Haven't you read, . . . that at the beginning the Creator 'made them male and female'?" (Matt. 19:4, NIV). This is a radically different view of our sexuality than the Greek myth of the androgyne: in the beginning was a sexless androgyne that was later split into male and female. Sexual differentiation was seen as a kind of "fall," with our attraction to each

---

[9] Thomas Howard, *Hallowed Be This House* (San Francisco: Ignatius, 1979), 115-116.

other a desire to "become one" in the sense of getting back to our origin. The goal was to transcend the sexual differentiation, and ultimately the flesh in which we are imprisoned, and become pure spirit, sexless and body-less.

That is not what the Bible means by our maleness and femaleness. To say we are sexual creatures is to say that we cannot be understood except as male and female, and except as male *or* female. As male *and* female we make up one humanity. As male *or* female we make up the two poles of that humanity, with our bodies as concrete expressions of those poles.

4. *We are made to be together.* God said of us that it is not good to be alone (Gen. 2:18). In putting us together he gave us a God-like power over each other. As Adam's "love poem" to Eve expressed it, she was bone of his bone and flesh of his flesh (2:21-23). It is also true that my wife will, in some sense, become boredom of my boredom, fear of my fear, and love of my love. She has the same impact on me. We become what others are to us; and they become what we are to them. I have often regarded as empirical evidence of this truth the number of elderly couples I have seen who actually look alike.

Becoming "one flesh" is one of the truly unique features of a Christian understanding of marriage. Men and women are so very different from each other. This can be cause for frustration or cause for excitement and growth. It is a lifelong adventure to love and understand this woman I live with—so very different from me and yet one with me. We have such a differing sexuality as male and female, we who are one and yet must become one! We have so much to learn from each other that it will take a lifetime! Always when I meet with a couple for pre-marriage counseling, I will urge them to take their sense of humor along with them on their honeymoon, because blessed and few are the couples whose honeymoon reaches the heights of sexual communion. Most of us have a lot to learn, and that is good—it draws us out of ourselves.

5. *We find ourselves as we give ourselves away.* There is great grace in the gift of Eve to Adam; she is given as he sleeps. But it is costly grace; she is formed from his own body. The great mystery of one becoming

two foreshadows the greater mystery of two becoming one. God's math is that one and one don't equal two, but one (Gen. 2:24). And the one flesh is greater than the two that preceded it. In marriage as with the gospel, we find ourselves as we give ourselves away (Luke 9:23-24).

Therein is the tragedy and oxymoron of modern ideas of "trying out" marriage. One can no more "try out" marriage than try out death or birth. For marriage to be marriage, it must be all or nothing. I sometimes counsel students who are fascinated with this "trying out" nonsense to "try out" marriage this way: Don't start living together after a dinner by candlelight; wait till one of you has the stomach flu—then sleep together. My suggestion is, of course, tongue-in-cheek, and it helps to make the big point about the goodness of sex and marriage: that the quality of life does not consist in the number of experiences one has, but in the depth of commitments. Illicit sex can be fun and exciting, like diving off the high dive. But it's the swimmers who get strong.

We lose ourselves to find ourselves. In the mystery of love, as God planned it, "no one can ever figure out who is doing the giving and who the receiving," writes Thomas Howard. Real lovers "know that giving and receiving are a splendid and hilarious paradox in which, lo, the giving becomes receiving, the receiving giving until any efforts to sort it out collapse in merriment or adoration."[10]

## Thank You

There is one more thing to be said about the goodness of sex and the glory of God: Thank you. Sex is good because the God who created sex is good. And God is glorified greatly when we receive his gift with thanksgiving and enjoy it the way he meant for it to be enjoyed. Gratitude may be the greatest joy of sex, and what brings the greatest glory to God, because joy is what you experience when you are grateful for the grace that has been given you. The Greek language gives us a picture of how this works: grace, gratitude, and joy all have the same root, *char*, which is a word having to do with health or well-being. Grace is *charis*, gratitude is *eucharistia*, and joy is *chara*. The three are organically joined, theologically and spiritually. Karl Barth's insight is vivid:

---

[10] Thomas Howard, "God Before Birth: The Imagery Matters," *Christianity Today*, December 17, 1976, 12-13.

"How can anything more or different be asked of man? The only answer to *charis* is *eucharistia*. . . . Grace and gratitude belong together like heaven and earth. Grace evokes gratitude like the voice an echo. Gratitude follows grace like thunder lightning."[11]

I must give a personal testimony here. A few months before I married the wonderful woman who has been my wife all these years, I experienced a chilling fear of commitment. I reasoned that if I said yes to her, I'd be saying no to millions of other women. I knew I didn't have access to millions, but however many of them there might be, the door would be closed after marriage. Marriage seemed so narrow. But I have discovered that its narrowness is the narrowness of the birth canal. There has been a universe in this one person, this mystery I know as Lauretta.

Now fast-forward several years to a family vacation. The six of us have stopped in Blythe, California, to use the rest room in a McDonald's restaurant. Blythe is a town on the California side of the Colorado River. Picture me standing there holding my daughter, a few feet from the rest room doors, as a gorgeous young woman I have come to call The Babe from Blythe emerges from behind those doors. I'll avoid as many details as I can, but she was sexy, tan, and dressed as, well, young women are wont to dress in warm desert climates. And she was looking right at me, smiling warmly! My fatigued mind was suddenly focused. I straightened up and smiled back, flushed with the adolescent conceit that even though I was much older than she was, I must still remain a very attractive man. Babes still take notice! Our smiles and eyes met for longer than could be merely a random encounter as she walked past me. It was then I noticed my reflection in the mirror along the wall and saw who she was smiling at. It was me, all right, but it wasn't Ben Patterson the Mature Hunk. It was Ben Patterson, Mary's daddy. He was middle-aged, a little lumpy, and he was holding a precious child. That's what delighted The Babe. My first reaction was embarrassment, tinged with a little disappointment. *Silly fool, you aren't what you thought you were!* But as I continued to look in the mirror, I decided I liked what I saw there more than I liked what I first thought The Babe saw. I liked being Mary's

---

[11] Karl Barth, *The Doctrine of Reconciliation*, vol. 4, part 1 of *Church Dogmatics* (Edinburgh: T & T Clark, 1980), 41.

daddy. I like it a lot. Ditto for Dan and Joel and Andy. It's better to be a daddy than a stud. My deflation turned into elation.

Whether or not that is what P. T. Forsyth meant by God being an "infinite opportunist,"[12] that's what I mean. He orchestrated my lust and conceit into a blessed realization of my true glory and happiness. God was smiling at me through the smile of The Babe from Blythe. With one deft stroke, he seized the moment, stripped me bare, and clothed me with mercy.

I want to thank God for the gift of sex. But not sex in general; sex in *particular*. You see, there was a teenaged girl from Minneapolis who gave up everything she had known to come to California and live with me, March 27, 1971. She hardly knew me. And I'll never forget the risk she took when she changed her name to mine. And a pigheaded, frightened, and lonely man has been understanding the gospel better because of her—through the one God made to be bone of my bone and flesh of my flesh. Thank you, Lauretta. And to God alone be the glory.

---

[12] P. T. Forsyth, *The Soul of Prayer* (London: Independent Press, 1949), 84.

# Part 2: Sin and Sex

# CHAPTER 4

# Making All Things New:
# Restoring Pure Joy to the
# Sexually Broken

### DAVID POWLISON

For many years, a quilt has adorned one wall of our living room. The artist took swatches of fabric and cut hundreds of tiny squares and triangles. She created a lattice pattern through which you gaze into a luminous, iridescent garden. I view her quilt as an invitation to pause and catch a glimpse into paradise. The latticework encloses, protects, provides structure, revealing wonders. The garden within creates an impression of color and light, flower and air, life and pleasure.

It gives a small picture of our God's great work, the brightness of all creation, the brightness of our salvation.

As such, it gives us a picture of sexuality—and of every other luminous thing that becomes darkened and can be redeemed. Sex is one good strand of God's good work in creation. Sex is one good strand of his good work in salvation. Imagine your sexuality transformed into a garden of delight protected within the lattice. God began to do good work in you, and he is working to complete this. You will flourish in a garden of safety and joy. Wrongs are made right, "and all shall be well, and all shall be well, and all manner of thing shall be well."[1] The highest pleasure, the joy that remakes all lesser pleasures innocent, is our pleasure in Christ, the inexpressible gift. He is light. He is life-giver. In his light, your sexuality transforms into one blossom among all that is good.

I needed a contrasting object lesson, so I stopped in to talk with my

---
[1] Julian of Norwich, *Revelation of Divine Love*, chapter 31.

auto mechanic. He fished a greasy rag from the trash bin at the back of his garage and handed it to me. Unnameable filth had soaked through that scrap of fabric. Ground-in, oily dirt. If your hands are clean, you don't really feel like touching such a sordid rag. If you must handle such an object, you pick it up by one corner between thumb and forefinger, holding it out away from you at arm's length. The filthy rag gives us a second, all-too-familiar picture of sexuality. Sex soaks up dark, dirty stains. We must deal with such ground-in evils if we are to fix what's wrong with us and with others. We understand why Jude evokes an unpleasant sense of wariness even amid his call to generous-hearted love: "To others show mercy with fear, hating even the garment stained by the flesh" (Jude 23).

You can hardly bear to put a name on what some people do, or on what happens to some people. Is your sexuality misshapen and misdirected? Sexual evils are among the dark things that pour forth from within our hearts. Jesus bluntly indicts a roster of sexual wrongs (Mark 7:21-23)—and offers costly mercy to the repentant. Has your sexuality been harmed by others? Some people experience terrible sufferings at the hands of predators, users, misusers, and abusers. Jesus fiercely curses those who trip up others (Matt. 18:6-7)—and offers safe refuge to sufferers.

On the one hand, sex becomes a complex darkness. On the other hand, sex becomes a garden of simple, pure delights. Which picture represents you?

It's not really a fair question. You probably can't answer either-or, because most likely you're somewhere in the middle. This chapter is about *making* new, about the long *restoring* of joys to the broken and dirtied. In other words, it's about the process of change. It's about moving along a trajectory *away from* the dark and *toward* the light. It's about knowing where you're heading while you're still somewhere in the middle.

Of course, some human beings aren't in the middle, but live utterly mired within sexual darkness. They even call "good" what God calls "evil." But they're not likely to have kept reading this far, because they want to feel justified in wrong, not to be remade right. They want more of what they already have. But if you have read this far, that very persevering has been because light, however far away it seems, is drawing you. There is no darkness so deep that it is immune to light. Perhaps you've been wronged sexually and have lived a nightmare of fear and hurt. But you long for light. Such longing is a blossom of light pulling you in the direction of more light. Or, perhaps you've been wrong sexually and have lived in a fantasyland of lewd, nude, and crude. But you feel sick and tired, dirty and ashamed. Such guilt is a blossom of honesty. It pushes you toward the middle. Your sins delight you less and less; they afflict you more and more. *"Kyrie, eleison;* Lord, have mercy, you whose mercies are new every morning." When you know you need help, then you're already moving into the middle, out of the filth.

Are you tilted more toward light? One man did live utterly as that garden of light shining through the lattice. Jesus did no sin. Yet he chose to enter our deepest darkness. He bore your stains, and did so without becoming stained. He is able to sympathize with your particular weakness and struggles because he has entered your plight, facing the temptations of sin and suffering. He is able to help you in your failure and your vulnerability to future failure because he remains unstained. He does not hold you at arm's length. Jesus is willing to deal gently and truthfully, however ignorant and wayward we are. He is bringing us back to the paradise of light.

Perhaps you have come far along this good path already. You have been given much light sexually. Much of the garden of faithful pleasures already flourishes in you. Much of the latticework of loving restraints is set in place. Oh, hopeful joy, so much has already been purified! *"Gloria in excelsis Deo;* glory to God in the highest." But I know, and you know, that oily stains and cracked slats remain in the fabric of every person's life. We must still run the race of renewal.

A contemporary hymn contains this line: "In all I do, I honor you." When I sing that hymn, I always think, *Well, I want to honor you in all I do, but I don't.* The line is truest as a statement of honest intention, but often false as a statement of achievement. We want the garden, but grime still clings to us and oozes from us. Augustine put his struggle starkly: "As I prayed to you for the gift of chastity I had even pleaded, 'Grant me chastity and self-control, but please not yet.' I was afraid that you might hear me immediately and heal me forthwith of the morbid lust which I was more anxious to satisfy than to snuff out."[2] We want the latticework to protect us, but dark creatures slip into or out of our

---

[2] Augustine, *The Confessions,* trans. Maria Boulding (Hyde Park, N.Y.: New City, 1997), book 8, chapter 17, page 198.

hearts. When talking about something as important and troublesome as sex, it is important to affirm that the desire for light is the beginning of the emergence of light in our lives.

One theme runs through this chapter: ". . . he who began a good work in you will bring it to completion at the day of Jesus Christ" (Phil. 1:6). What does that lifelong process look like? How do you get from here to there? How does dirt transform into beauty? What is the battle like? You're somewhere in the middle, but Christ has begun a good work in you. He has washed away true guilt. He has broken your willing bondage. Jesus knows his business well. He is looking out for you. He is working to clear away sin's rot. Jesus is remaking you into a person who actually loves people and who begins to consider their best interests. Your opinions and impulses no longer reign. What he has begun, he will complete. On the final day, he will entirely remove the instincts and energies of sin from you. How does the war work out? We will look at seven aspects.

### 1. Bring Light to *All* That Darkens Sex

You fight on many fronts. There are many kinds of evil, more than you might imagine. Some are obvious, some not so obvious. So what are you up against?

#### a. Unholy Pleasure

The most obvious forms of sexual darkness involve the sins of overt immorality. There are countless ways that sexuality veers into extramarital eroticism. Sex can become like living in a carnival of intoxicating fires, a dream world of erotic arousal, predatory instinct, manipulative intention, and the pursuit of carnal knowledge. In a nutshell, in each of the many forms of wrong, a person has sexual intercourse with the wrong object of desire. Sexual love flourishes as a loving intimacy between one husband and wife. But desire is easily distorted and action misdirected. Wrongful sexual relations can occur either in reality or in fantasy. These are the typical, red-letter, on-the-marquee sins. So what do the weeds of adultery, fornication, homosexuality, pornography, rape, bestiality, voyeurism, incest, pedophilia, fetishism, sado-masochism, transvestitism, prostitution, and bigamy-polygamy have in common? They involve sexual relations, in person or in your imagination, with the wrong object of desire.[3] Other people become objects of unholy desire. These fantasies and interpersonal transactions are the obvious ways in which human sexuality is misdirected into overt sins.

Historically, the behaviors mentioned have usually been evaluated and stigmatized as socially shameful. They have often been named as criminal acts in legal codes. To the degree that cultural values and laws mirror the call of love for others, rather than endorsing lust, they express the way that God sizes up human sexuality. Of course, when mores and laws change for the worse, such behaviors may even be reinterpreted as good, right, and sweet, rather than evil, wrong, and bitter (Isa. 5:20f.). But God teaches us to see things for what they are.

The bold-print sins point in the direction of the fine-print versions of the same sins. Many varieties of flirtation, self-display, foreplay, and entertainment don't necessarily "go all the way" to orgasm: dressing to attract and tease the lust of others, looking voyeuristically, suggestive remarks, crude humor, erotic kissing, petting, and the like. All these actions suggest an intention toward immoral sexual intercourse, whether the intention is consummated or not. Such behaviors (whether occurring in daily life or portrayed on film or page) cross the line of love. Whether or not our cultural context views such things as acceptable, or even as entertaining, they are evils. Love considers the true welfare of others in "the eyes of Him with whom we have to do" (Heb. 4:13, NASB).

Jesus Christ will come even to those who have pursued unholy pleasures. He who hates the gamut of perversities listed in previous paragraphs is not ashamed to love sinners. He does not weary in the task of rewiring sexuality into a servant of love. He is not only willing to forgive those who turn and repent; he takes the initiative to forgive, and to turn us, and to give us countless reasons to turn. He says, "You need mercy and help in your time of need. Come to me. Turn from evils, and turn to mercies that are new every morning. Flee what is wrong. Seek help. Everyone who seeks finds. Fight with yourself. Don't justify things

---

[3] Marriage per se is neither magic nor magically loving. A few of these perversions of sexual goodness can be performed between married parties: e.g., joint use of pornography, sado-masochism, "homosexual marriage," rape, bigamy. But such practices violate the call to loving intimacy before the eyes of God, who created sex good and who defines good sex. The sexual identity and desires of one or both parties can be warped, whatever the marital status. The last part of this section will discuss sexual sins that more typically occur within marriage.

that God names as evil. Don't despair when you find evils within yourself. The only unforgivable sin is the impenitence that justifies sin and opposes the purifying mercies of God. Come to me, and I will begin to teach you how to love."

Our culture thinks that any consenting object of desire is fair game for sexual intercourse. Individual will is the supreme value. But Christ thinks differently, and he gets the last say. He backs up his point of view with a promise of clear-eyed, unavoidable reckoning: "Let no one deceive you with empty words, for because of these things the wrath of God comes upon the sons of disobedience" (Eph. 5:6). He backs up his point of view with a promise of hard-won mercies and with power to patiently change you so that you learn to love him supremely. Each of the perversities makes sex too important (and makes the Maker, Evaluator, and Redeemer of sex irrelevant). Sex becomes your identity, your right, your fulfillment, your need. That is nonsense. Each ends up degrading sex as a mere urge that must find an outlet. That, too, is nonsense. Whether exalted or degraded, sex ends up disappointing, self-destructive, and mutually destructive.

Jesus brings sanity and good sense. He starts by making sex of secondary importance. Sex is a real but secondary good. God neither overvalues nor degrades the good things he has made. By realigning whom you *most* love (away from yourself and distorted pleasures), he makes all secondary loves, including sexuality, flourish in their proper place. That might mean containing sexual expression during a long season, even a lifetime of purposeful celibacy as a single adult. Jesus himself lived this way. It might mean a season of frequent sexual expression within loving marriage. That's the most common calling. It might mean short or long seasons of again containing sexual expression because of the different kinds of celibacy that arise in the course of marital life: e.g., advanced pregnancy and post-partum; forced separation for business or military reasons; a chosen fast from sexual expression because of more pressing needs; the diminution of sexual arousal with advancing age; consequences of prostate surgery or other illnesses; the loss of your spouse by death. Whether by containment or by expression, our sexuality can be remade into love.

When we think about the forms of "sexual brokenness" that need to be made new, it is natural that we think first of the obvious sins. But other evils also begrime us as sexual beings. These also lie within the scope of redeeming love.

### b. Unholy Pain

Many people experience pain and fear attached to sexual victimization. Have you ever been attacked or betrayed sexually? Sex becomes like life in Auschwitz, like a burn survivor, a waking nightmare of hurt, fear, and helplessness from the hands of tormentors. Jesus' kindness redeems both sinners and sufferers. He rights all wrongs. Jesus is merciful to people who do wrong (forgiving and changing you). He is merciful to people who are wronged (comforting and changing you). When you are used, misused, and abused, sex grows dark. If you are or were a victim of sexual aggression, if you were violated, betrayed, or threatened by the sins of others, then the prospect of sex may often cause ambivalence or fear.

The erotic is meant to be a bright expression of mutual lovingkindness. Sex thrives in a context of commitment, safety, trust, affection, giving, closeness, intimacy, generosity. The erotic flourishes as one normal, everyday expression of genuine love within marriage. A man and woman are "naked and unashamed" with each other and under God (see Gen. 2:25). They give mutual pleasure. Sex with your spouse can be simple self-giving, freely given and freely received. Your sexual interactions can express honesty, laughter, play, prayer, and ecstasy. Sex can be open before the eyes of God, approved in your own conscience, and approved in the eyes of family and friends who care for you.

But sex can become very distasteful. Pawing, seduction, bullying, predation, attack, betrayal, and abandonment are among the many ways that sex becomes stained by sufferings at the hands of others. When you've been treated like an object, the mere thought of the act can produce tense torment. Sexual darkness is not always lust; sometimes it is fear, pain, haunting memories. If immoral fantasies bring one poison into sex, then nightmarish memories infiltrate a different poison. The arena for trusting friendship can become a prison of mistrust. The experience of violation can leave the victim self-labeled as "damaged goods." Sex becomes intrinsically dirty, shameful, dangerous. Even in marriage, it can become an unpleasant duty, a necessary evil, not the delightful convergence of duty and desire.

If such things happened to you, you might well feel hatred, terror, and disgust. You might feel guilt, shame, and self-reproach over what someone else did to you. Your thoughts of sex might be filled with loathing and despair, the furthest thing from lustful desire. This, too, is a rag soaked in the grease of nameless dirt. To those for whom sexual experience has resulted in unholy pain, Christ says, "I understand well your experience. I hear the cry of the needy, afflicted, and broken. Come to me. I am your refuge. I am safe. I will remake what is broken. I will give you reason to trust, and then to love. I will remake your joy." For good reason, two-thirds of the Psalms engage the experience of those who suffer violence, violation, and threat (see, e.g., Psalm 10). These sufferings found their point of reference in the God who hears you now, who is your refuge, your hope, who is willing to hear your anguish and loneliness, who overflows with comforts. The reference point makes all the difference. God cares and will patiently repair what has been torn.

In different ways, both violator and violated are stained with the filth of a fallen world. In different ways, Jesus Christ washes both. And there's still other dirt on the shop floor, and other fresh mercies.

### c. Guilt

The activity of doing sin is different from the repercussion of feeling guilt. Temptation arises as internal desire and external allure culminate into action. Then, if the conscience is not seared, comes the typical aftermath: guilt, shame, regret, remorse, resolves to change, penance, self-reproach, despair, making up, concealment, and so forth. Obsession with erotic pleasure yields to obsession with moral failure. Grace addresses both in different ways, because both are part of the dynamic of sexual evils.

Are you haunted by your sins—in the eyes of God, in the eyes of your conscience, and in the eyes of others who might find out? The sin may have just occurred a few minutes ago; it may be a distant but potent memory. Perhaps you don't actively participate in that sin anymore. You've come far, and you no longer feel any allure to a lifestyle you once avidly pursued. Or perhaps you just did it again. But the memory—whether freshly minted or ancient history—fills you with dismay. Perhaps immediate and long-term consequences of your sin run far beyond the repercussions within your conscience: an abortion, sexually transmitted disease, inability to bear children, ongoing vulnerability to certain kinds of temptations, a bad reputation, ruined relationships, wasted time, failed responsibilities. Nobody did this to you; you did it to yourself and to others. You victimized yourself as well as those you betrayed. You, too, feel like damaged goods. For you, sex is no longer bright, iridescent, cheerful, generous, matter-of-fact. It is not a flat-out good to be enjoyed with your spouse or to be saved should you ever marry. You might live with such guilty feelings in your singleness. You might have brought them into your marriage. Perhaps you are afraid of relationships because you know from bitter experience that you can't be trusted. Perhaps it's hard to shake off the train of bleak associations that attach to sexual feelings and acts.

We often underestimate just how radically biblical faith relies on grace. Grace means that what makes things right comes to you from the outside. It's the sheer gift that someone else gives to you. You don't get it by jumping through certain religious hoops. You are forgiven, accepted, saved from death *outside of yourself* and *because of Another.*

Listen to how a man of faith dealt forthrightly with his former sins. The italics highlight how much your hope amid real guilt lies outside of you:

> *Remember,* O LORD, *Your* compassion and *Your* lovingkindnesses,
> For they have been from of old.
> *Do not remember* the sins of my youth or my transgressions;
> According to *Your* lovingkindness *remember* me,
> For *Your* goodness' sake, O LORD. . . .
> For *Your* name's sake, O LORD,
> *Pardon* my iniquity, for it is great. (Ps. 25:6-7, 11, NASB)

David's sexual sin was high-handed. It tore his conscience (Psalm 51; cf. Psalms 32, 38). It brought immediate and long-lasting consequences (2 Sam. 12:10-12, 14). Yet David was truly forgiven (2 Sam. 12:13). He experienced the joy of repentance and the wisdom, clarity, and purposeful energy that real repentance brings (see those same psalms, and the rest of 2 Samuel 12). Notice: David radically appeals to the quality of *"Your* mercy, O LORD." David's own conscience remembers only too well, but he appeals to what someone else will choose to remember: "When God looks at me, will he remember my sin, or his own mercies?"

Sin turns you in on yourself, blinding you to God. Guilt also tends to turn you in on yourself. Self-laceration exalts your opinion of yourself as supremely important; shame exalts the opinion of other people. But living repentance and living faith turn outward to the one whose opinion matters most. What God chooses to "remember" about you will prove decisive. Your conscience, if well-tuned, is secondary and dependent on the stance he takes. If the Lord is merciful, then mercy has the final say. It is beyond our comprehension that God acts mercifully *for his sake,* because of what *he* is like. Wrap your heart around this, and the aftermath of sin will never be the same. You will stand in joy and gratitude, not grovel in shame. You'll be able to get back to the business of life with fresh resolve, not just with good intentions and some flimsy New Year's resolutions to do better next time. This is our hope. This is our deepest need. This is our Lord's essential, foundational gift. The one with whom we have to do freely offers mercy and grace to help us by the lovingkindness of the Lord Jesus Christ (see Heb. 4:13-16, NASB).

### d. Viewing Sexual Sin as Just a Male Problem

Too often, teaching on sexual sin assumes and targets only the struggles of men. Seductive women may be viewed as sources of temptation to men (provocative clothing; participation in making pornography; the temptress at work; the prostitute). But women often slip under the radar when the issue is the struggle with lust. Unvarnished erotic lust is seen as a typically male problem. As one common saying puts it, "95 percent of men struggle with lust . . . and the other 5 percent are lying." But what about the 100 percent of women sitting in churches, either secretly struggling or secretly smug? There are core similarities between men and women, along with some typical differences.

For starters, *the Bible is candid that there is no temptation that is not common to all* (1 Cor. 10:13). This doesn't mean temptations always take exactly the same form, but there are underlying similarities. By God's creation, men and women are primarily the *same* (human). By his creation and providence, we are secondarily different (male-female differences tied to biology; masculine-feminine differences tied to culture). Add it up, and we struggle with the same kind of thing, but may struggle in different *ways*. That does not mean that females are not perfectly capable of the same unvarnished, immoral eroticism that characterizes some males. It takes two to tango in any act of adultery or fornication. The woman may well be the initiator/aggressor in sending out sexual signals or in arranging a liaison. Women have roving eyes and get hooked on erotic pleasures. Women masturbate. Women pursue homosexuality. A woman can pattern her identity around fulfilling sexual self-interest and having a magnetic effect on male sexual interest. When she finds mercy in Christ and starts her journey toward the garden of light, her struggle may directly parallel the struggle of the man who has similarly patterned his lifestyle around immoralities. Both must learn how to love, rather than how to fulfill and arouse lust.

Second, *it is noticeable that female sexuality in America has taken on cruder forms in recent years* (or, at least, is far more willing to be brazen). Open lewdness and frank immorality have replaced coy, suggestive hints of availability. Male or female, the rule seems to be, if you want it, go for it. For example, female athletes increasingly display the openly obscene behaviors that were once the prerogative of male athletes: gutter humor, mooning, streaking, sexualized hazing and initiation rites, predatory sexual acts, an atmospheric grossness. Using obscene language, attending a strip show, and surfing pornographic websites are not exclusively male sins. Women's magazines (e.g., *Cosmopolitan*) have increasingly become manuals for how to have wildly ecstatic sex with your "partner" of choice. Marital status is an optional, irrelevant category. But Jesus Christ is "no respecter of persons": a coarse female is as ugly as a coarse male. Jesus loathes the degradation of sex (Eph. 5:3-8a). His self-sacrificing mercy works to transform sex into an expression of love, light, and fruitfulness (Eph. 5:1f., 8b-10) for females and males alike.

Third, *there are some typical and noteworthy differences between men and women*. Both strugglers and those who minister to them should be aware of variations on the common themes. At the level of motive, for example, male sexual sin and female sexual sin often operate in somewhat different ways. Men are often more wired to visual cues, to anonymous "body parts" eroticism. Women are often more wired to feelings of personal intimacy and emotional closeness as cues for sexual arousal. These aren't absolute differences (notice the "oftens"). But being aware of the tendencies can be helpful. The motives driving adultery, fornication, and promiscuity may follow somewhat different patterns.

Homosexuality provides a particularly obvious example. Lesbianism typically presents a different picture from male homosexuality. Many lesbians were once actively, unambivalently heterosexual, whether promiscuous or faithfully married. They might have conceived, borne, and raised children without much questioning of their sexual identity. But over time the men in their lives proved disappointing, violent, drunken, uncomprehending, or unfaithful. Perhaps during the unhappiness of a slow marital disintegration, or while picking up the wreckage after a divorce, other women proved to be far more understanding and sympathetic friends. Emotional intimacy and communication opened a new door. Sexual repatterning as a lesbian came later. The life-reshaping "lusts of the flesh" were not initially sexual. Instead, cravings to be treated tenderly and sympathetically—to be known, understood, loved, and accepted—played first violin, and sex per se played viola.

Fourth, *the culture of romance novels, soap operas, and women's magazines does not draw nearly as much attention as male-oriented pornography.* Men do graphic pornography. That's an obvious problem. Women do romance. It's the same kind of problem, though the participants keep their clothes on a while longer, and there's more of a story to tell before they tumble into bed. Romance novels are female pornography. The sin comes wired through intimacy lust first and builds toward erotic lust. The formulaic fantasies offer narrative emotion-candy, not visual eye-candy. Romance tells a story about someone with a name, someone you fall in love with. It builds slowly. It's more than a moment of instant gratification with anonymous, naked, willing bodies. But like male pornography, there is a progression from soft-core (e.g., Harlequin series), to more openly erotic (e.g., Silhouette series), to frankly pornographic writings that target women. The male model Fabio made his career posing for formulaic book cover art. A big, strong guy, stripped to the waist, tenderly cradles a beautiful woman. He's the knight in shining armor, protective, gentle, understanding—*and* the handsome hunk. The romantic novel genre has even made a crossover to evangelical Christian publishing houses. The sex is cleaned up; the knight in shining armor is also a deep spiritual leader who marries you before sleeping with you. But the fantasy appeal to intimacy and romance lusts remains as the inner engine that allures readers.

Female versions of sexual-romantic sin are shop-floor rags as much as male versions. Jesus Christ calls all of us out of fantasy, delusion, and lust, whether the fantasyland is filled with naked bodies or with romantic knights. Jesus Christ is about the reality business. Francis of Assisi got things straight: "Grant that I would not so much seek . . . to be loved as to love." Jesus teaches us how to be committed, patient, kind, protective, able to make peace, keeping no record of wrongs, merciful, forgiving, generous, and all the other hard, wonderful characteristics of grace. He teaches us to consider the true interests of others. He teaches us a positive, loving purity that protects the purity of others. Instead of our instinctual ways—narcissism, fascination with our own desires and opinions, self-indulgence—Jesus Christ takes us by the hand to lead us in ways that make *vive la différence* shine brightly.

### e. Sexual Struggles Within Marriage

We mislead ourselves and others if we say or imply that just getting married solves all the problems of sexual sin, sexual pain, sexual confusion. All sorts of remnant sins can carry on in marriage. All sorts of remnant heartaches and fears can still play out. "Making all things new" continues to remake sex within marriage. Here are some examples.

- One person may need to learn that sex is good, not dirty. You can relax rather than tense up. You can give yourself freely, rather than worry about what will happen to you. Pleasure will not betray you. Your spouse is faithful and can be trusted. Only larger, deeper, fundamental trust in God can free us to grant simple trust and generous love to another human being, who *will* in fact let us down and do us wrong in some ways.
- Another person may need to learn that sexual bliss is not the *summum bonum* of human life. You still need to say no to lust. There are seasons and reasons for self-denial and temporary celibacy. Your spouse may struggle, in sex as in other areas, and you will need to learn that "love is patient" (1 Cor. 13:4) comes first in Paul's list for a reason.

- Some people may need to learn whole new patterns of sexual arousal. Sexual gymnastics may have been a part of the fantasies and fornications of your past. But your spouse, God's gift to you, may enjoy quiet, tender moments being held in your arms. The Richter Scale of raw ecstasies may have spiked higher in your past immoralities than in your marriage. But you need to learn that the scale of solid joys and lasting treasures proves incomparably deeper and more satisfying.
- Still other marriages may need to give up evil relational patterns: game-playing, manipulation, give to get, avoidance, bartering sex for other goodies, sulking. Even high-stakes criminal sins—sadistic sexual aggression, violence, and rape—can occur in marriage.
- Still other people must sever the link that equated sex with "success or failure," with "performance" and "identity." As Christ redefines and recenters your identity, he changes what sex *means*. Sex can become a simple and meaningful way to give. It can become a simple pleasure, as normal as eating breakfast. It can become a safe place where failures and struggles can be talked about and prayed through.
- Some marriages may deal with impotence and frigidity ("erectile dysfunction" and "arousal disorder" in the medicalizing jargon of our times). On the male side, Viagra, Cialis, and Levitra present a purely chemical solution for symptoms. The problem sometimes has a significant biological component unrelated to normal aging. But most often there are significant links to spiritual issues: performance anxiety, an unwillingness to face the diminishments of aging, the separation of sex from love, guilt over premarital sex, or unreal expectations of potency that have been learned from the media, pornography, or fornication.
- Still others may be tempted to compare their spouse with previous partners, or with fantasy partners, or with some idealized fantasy of what marital bliss should be like. Wise sex loves *your* husband or wife.
- Still others will continue to struggle with familiar patterns of lust. They may be tempted to flirt, or to cheat, or to view

pornography, or to masturbate in the shower, or to fantasize about past experiences.

- Finally, every person will struggle with garden variety anger, anxiety, grumbling, selfishness, unbelief, and the weight of life's difficulties. The everyday nonsexual sins and troubles don't disappear! Other sins and hardships can clutter the bedroom with nonsexual troubles that greatly affect sexual intimacy. Christ's ongoing mercies will remake your sexuality in part by remaking the worry and irritability and other problems that arise in response to life's pressures.

You get the picture! "He who began a good work in you will bring it to completion at the day of Jesus Christ" (Phil. 1:6). His redemption will touch *every* form of grease. We can't do justice to "sexual brokenness" unless we get the whole problem on the table. Jesus works with us. And it is our joy that he works with far more than just the Technicolor sexual immoralities.

## 2. It's a *Longer* War

One key to fighting well is to lengthen your view of the battle. If you think that one week of "shock and awe" combat will win this war, you're bound for disappointment. If you're looking for some quick fix, an easy answer, a one-and-done solution, then you'll never really understand the nature of the fight. And if you promise easy, once-for-all victories to others, then you'll never be much help to them.

The day of "completion" will not arrive until the day when Jesus Christ returns (Phil. 1:6). When we see him, then we will be like him perfectly (1 John 3:2). The wiping away of all tears, the taking away of every reason for sorrow, crying, and pain, will not come until God lives visibly in our midst (Rev. 21:3-4). Someday, not today, all things will be made new (Rev. 21:5). Much of the failure to fight well, pastor well, counsel well, arises because we don't really understand and work well with this long truth. Consider two specific implications. First, sanctification is a direction in which you are heading. Second, repentance is a lifestyle you are living.

*a. Sanctification Is a Direction*

Too often our practical view of sanctification, discipleship, and coun-seling is shortsighted. If you memorize and call to mind one special Bible verse, will it clean up all the mess? Will prayer drive all the darkness away? Will remembering that you are a child of God, justified by faith, shield your heart against every evil? Will careful self-discipline and a plan to live constructively eliminate all failure? Is it enough to sit under good preaching and have daily devotions? Is honest accountability to others the decisive key to walking in purity? These are all very good things. But none of them guarantees that three weeks from now, or three years, or thirty years, you will not struggle to learn how to love rather than lust. We must have a vision for a long process (lifelong), with a glo-rious end ("the day of Jesus Christ"), that is actually going somewhere (today). Put those three together in the right way, and you have a prac-tical theology that's good to go and good for the going.

Look at church history. Look at denominations. Look at local churches. Look at people groups. Look at families. Look at individuals. Look at all the people in the Bible. They all have a history and keep mak-ing history. Things are never finished. No one ever says, "I've made it. No more forks in the road. No more places I might stumble and fall flat. No more hard, daily choices to make." Look at yourself. Life *never* operates on cruise control. The living God seems content to work in his church and in people groups on a scale of generations and centuries. The living God seems content to work in individuals (you, me, the person you are trying to help) on a scale of decades, throughout a whole life-time. At every step, there's some crucial watershed issue. What will you choose? Whom will you love and serve? There's always *something* that the Vinedresser is pruning, some difficult lesson that the Father is teach-ing the children he loves (John 15; Hebrews 12). It's no accident that "God is love" and "love is patient" fit together seamlessly. God takes his time with us.

In your sanctification journey and in your ministry to others, you must operate on a scale that can envision a lifetime, even while commu-nicating the urgency of today's significant choice. "Disciple" is the most common New Testament term describing God's people. A disciple is sim-ply a lifelong learner of wisdom, living in relationship to a wise master.

The second most common term, "son/child/daughter," contains the same purpose: by living in lifelong relationship to a loving Father, we learn how to love. When you think in terms of the moral absolutes, it's *either* oily rag *or* garden of delights. But when you think in terms of the change process, it's *from* oily rag *to* garden of delights. We are each and all on a trajectory from what we are to what we will be. The moral absolutes rightly orient us on the road map. But the process heads out on the actual long, long journey in the right direction. The key to getting a long view of sanctification is to understand *direction*. What matters most is not the distance you've covered. It's not the speed you're going. It's not how long you've been a Christian. It's the direction you're heading.

Do you remember any high school math? "A man drives the 300 miles from Boston to Philadelphia. He goes 60 miles per hour for 2 hours, 40 miles per hour for 3 hours, and then sits in traffic for 1 hour, not moving. If traffic lightens up, and he can drive the rest of the way at 30 miles per hour, how many hours will the whole trip take?" If you know the formula, "distance equals rate times time," you can figure it out (8 hours!). Is sanctification like that, a calculation of how far and how fast for how long? Not really. The key question in sanctification is whether you're even heading in the direction of Philadelphia. If you're heading north toward Montreal, you can go 75 miles per hour for as long as you want; you'll never, ever get to Philadelphia. And if you're simply sitting outside Boston, and have no idea which direction you're supposed to go, you'll never get anywhere. But if you're heading in the right direction, you can go 10 miles per hour or 60 miles per hour; you can get stuck in traffic and sit awhile; you can get out and walk; you can crawl on your hands and knees; you can even get temporarily turned around. But at some point you'll get where you need to go.

The rate of sanctification is completely variable. We cannot predict how it will go. Some people, during some seasons of life, leap and bound like gazelles. Let's say you've been living in flagrant sexual sins. You turn from sin to Christ; the open sins disappear. No more fornication, sleeping with your girlfriend or boyfriend. No more exhibitionism, wearing revealing clothes. No more pornography, buying *Penthouse* or the latest salacious romance novel. Ever. It sometimes happens like that. For other people (and the same people, at another season of life) sanctification is a steady, measured walk. You learn truth. You learn to serve others constructively. You build new disciplines. You learn basic life wisdom. You learn who God is, who you are, how life works. You learn to worship, to pray, to give time, money, and caring. And you grow steadily—wonder of wonders! Other people (and the same people, at another season) trudge. It's hard going. You limp. You don't seem to get very far very fast. But if you're trudging in the right direction, someday you will see him face to face, and you will be like him. Some people crawl on their hands and knees. Progress is painful. Praise God for the glory of his grace, you are inching in the right direction. And then there are times you aren't even moving, stuck in gridlock, broken down—but you're still facing in the right direction. That's Psalm 88, the "basement" of the Psalms. This man feels dark despair—but it's despair in the Lord's direction. In other words, it's still faith, even when faith feels so discouraged you can only say, "You are my only hope. Help. Where are you?" That counts—it made it into the Bible! There are times you might fall asleep in the blizzard and lie down comatose and forgetful—but grace wakes you up, reminds you, and gets you moving again. There are times you slowly wander off in the wrong direction, beguiled by some false promise, or disappointed by a true promise that you falsely understood. But he who began a good work in you awakens you from your sleepwalk, sooner or later, and puts you back on the path. And then there are times you revolt, and do a face-plant in the muck, a swan dive into the abyss—but grace picks you up and washes you off again, and turns you back. Slowly you get the point. Perhaps then you leap and bound, or walk steadily, or trudge, or crawl, or face with greater hope in the right direction.

We love gazelles. Graceful leaps make for a great testimony to God's wonder-working power. And we like steady and predictable. It seems to vindicate our efforts at making the Christian life work in a businesslike manner. But, in fact, there's no formula, no secret, no technique, no program, and no truth that guarantees the speed, distance, or time frame. On the day you die, you'll still be somewhere in the middle, but hopefully further along. When we lengthen the battle, we realize that our business is the direction. God manages to work his glory in and through *all* of the above scenarios! God's people need to know that, so someone else's story doesn't set the bar in a place that is not how your story of Christ's grace is working out in real life.

## b. Repentance Is a Lifestyle

What was the first trumpet call of the Reformation?

It was not the authority of Scripture, foundational as that is. Scripture is the very voice, face, and revelation of God. A Person presses through the pages. You learn how he thinks. How he acts. Who he is. What he's up to. But "Scripture alone" did not stand first in line.

It was not justification by faith, crucial as that is. We are oily-rag people. Christ is the garden of light. We are saved by his doing, his dying, his goodness. We are saved from ourselves outside of ourselves. No religious hocus-pocus. No climbing up a ladder of good works, or religious knowledge, or mystical experience. He came down, full of grace and truth, Word made flesh, Lamb of God. We receive. That's crucial. But "faith alone" wasn't actually where it all started.

It was not the priesthood of all believers, revolutionary as that is. Imagine, there aren't two classes of people, the religious people who do holy things by a special call from God, and the masses of laity toiling in the slums of secular reality. The "man of God" is not doing God's show before an audience of bystanders. We all assemble as God's people, doing the work and worshiping together, with differing gifts. The one Lord, our common King and attentive audience, powerfully enables faith and love. Yes and amen, but this radical revision of church didn't come first.

The trumpet call, Thesis Number One of Luther's *Ninety-five Theses,* was this: "When our Lord and Master, Jesus Christ, said 'Repent,' He called for the entire life of believers to be one of repentance." That first of Luther's theses dismantled all the machinery of religiosity and called us back to human reality. Luther glimpsed and aimed to recover the essential inner dynamic of the Christian life. It is an ongoing change process. It involves a continual turning motion, turning toward God, and turning away from the riot of other voices, other desires, other loves. We tend to use the word *repentance* in its more narrow sense, for decisive moments of realization, conviction, confession, turning. But Luther uses the word in its wider, more inclusive sense. If we are living in Christ, we are living *from-to*. John Calvin put it in a similar way: "This restoration does not take place in one moment or one day or one year. . . . In order that believers may reach this goal [the shining image of God], God assigns to them a race of repentance, which they are to run throughout their lives."[4] The entire Christian life (including the more specific moments of repentance) follows a pattern of turning from other things and turning to the Lord.

Luther went on to describe the transformation that occurs as we live *from-to*:

> This life, therefore,
> is not righteousness but growth in righteousness,
> not health but healing,
> not being but becoming,
> not rest but exercise.
> We are not yet what we shall be, but we are growing toward it.
> The process is not yet finished, but it is going on.
> This is not the end but it is the road.
> All does not yet gleam in glory but all is being purified.[5]

Lifelong progressive sanctification was the trumpet call back to biblical faith. It was a call back to *this* life—including sex—in which the living God is on the scene throughout your life. He planned a good work. He began a good work. He continues a good work. He will finish a good work. He has staked his glory on the completion of that work. Lengthening the battle heightens the significance of our Savior for every step along the way. We are not yet what we shall be, but we are growing toward it.

### 3. It's a *Wider* War

Sexual sins grab everyone's attention. They haunt the conscience and excite the gossip. They push other sins into the background. They go up on the marquee in red letters ten feet high.[6] But consider the struggle with sin this way. Imagine a multiplex theater screening many movies simul-

---

[4] John Calvin, *Institutes of the Christian Religion*, 3.3.9.

[5] Martin Luther, "Defense and Explanation of All the Articles," Second Article (1521).

[6] This characterization partly arises from tendencies within American Christian culture. Other Christian cultures may do their calculus of the conscience a bit differently. In Uganda, for example, *anger* is particularly shameful, the bogeyman sin that automatically disqualifies from ministry. But Ugandans view sexual immorality the way that Americans view anger outbursts or gluttony. Such behaviors are sinful, but aren't uniquely shocking and damning. Dante's *Divine Comedy* portrays "normal" sexual sins—sensuality, fornication—as meriting a shallower circle in hell. Like gluttony or sloth, these are distortions of normal desires. But sins of treachery, sexual and otherwise, involve betrayal of trust, and they sit in the deepest pit of hell.

taneously. Sexual sin is the "feature film" advertised on the marquee. But other significant films are playing in other screening rooms. The war with sin happens in many places simultaneously. In ministry to people who struggle with sexual sins, you may get the breakthrough in another screening room, with a sin that you might not have noticed or might not have considered to be related. A breakthrough—with anger, or pride, or anxiety, or laziness—may have ripple effects that eventually help disarm the big bogeyman that has been hogging all the attention and concern. It's very important to widen the battlefront and not to let the high-profile sins blinker us from seeing the whole picture. I will give a case study of how sexual sin can and must be located within wider battles.

Tom is a single man, 35 years old. You might be able to fill in the rest of his story, because his pattern is so typical. He came to Christ, with a sincere profession of faith, when he was 15. At about the same time, his 20-year struggle with sexual lust began. It involves episodic use of pornography and episodic masturbation, about which Tom is deeply discouraged. Over the years he has experienced many ups of "victory" and just as many downs of "defeat."

Tom came for help to me as his elder and small-group leader. He was discouraged by recent failures, by the latest downturn in a seemingly endless cycle. Over the years he had tried "all the right things," the standard answers and techniques. He had tried accountability—sincerely. It helped some, but not decisively. Accountability has a way of starting strong, but slipping to the side. At a certain point, to tell others you failed yet again, and to receive either sympathy or exhortation, stops being helpful. Tom had memorized Scripture and wrestled to apply truth in moments of battle. It often helped, but then in snow-blind moments, when he most needed help, he would forget everything he knew. Sex filled his mind and Scripture vanished from sight. Other times he just overrode the truth in an act of "Who cares?" rebellion. Then he would feel terrible—his conscience would go snow-blind for only half an hour at a time! He prayed. He fasted. He sought to discipline himself. He planned constructive things to do with his time, and to do with and for others. He got involved in ministry to teens. He tried things that aren't in the Bible: vigorous exercise, cold showers, dietary regimes. Briefly, he even tried the advice of a self-help book, trying to think of masturbation as "normal, everybody does it, so give yourself permission." His conscience, wisely, could never get around Jesus' words about lust in the heart (Matt. 5:28).

Tom had tried it all. Most things helped a bit. But in the end, success was always spotty and fragile. Tom had gained no greater insight into his heart and into the inner workings of sin and grace. For twenty years it was, "Sin is bad. Don't do it. Just do _____ to help you not sin." His entire Christian life was conceived and constructed around this struggle with episodic sexual sin.

His pattern was as follows: Seasons of relative purity might last for days, weeks, even for a few months. He measured his success by "How long since I last fell?" The longer he went, the more his hopes would rise: "Maybe now I've finally broken the back of my besetting sin." Then he would fall again. He would stumble through seasons of defeat, wandering back to the same old pigsty. "Am I even a Christian? Why bother? What's the point? Nothing ever works." He was plagued with guilt, discouragement, despair, shame. Sometimes Tom would even turn to pornography to dull the misery of his guilt over using pornography. He would beg God's forgiveness over and over and over, without any relief or any joy. Then, for unaccountable reasons the season would change for the better. He would get sick of sin or get inspired to fight again.

That's when he gave me a call. He really wanted deliverance once and for all.

What should I do in trying to help Tom? I was reticent to simply give Tom more of the same things he'd tried dozens of times and found wanting. I didn't want to just give him a pep talk and a Scripture, urge him to gird up his loins to run the race, and offer accountability phone calls. What is he missing? What's happening in the other theaters of his life? Are there motives and patterns neither of us yet sees? What's going on in the days or hours before he stumbles? What about how he (mis)handles the days and weeks after a fall? Why does his whole approach to life seem like so much complicated machinery for managing moral failure? Why does his approach to the Christian life seem so dehumanized and depersonalized? His Christianity seems like a big production, a lot of earnest effort at self-improvement. Why does his collection of truths and techniques never seem to warm up and invigorate the quality of his relationships with God and people? Is the centerpiece of the Christian life really this endless cycle of "I sin. I don't sin. I sin. I don't sin. I sin"? What are we missing?

I asked Tom to do a simple thing, attempting to gain a better sense of the overall terrain of his life: "Would you keep a log of when you are tempted?" I wanted to know what was going on when he struggled. "When? Where? What just happened? What did you do? What were you feeling? What were you thinking? If you resisted, how did you do it? If you fell, how did you react afterwards? Does anything else correlate to your sexual temptations?"

Through all the ups and downs, Tom had maintained a great sense of humor. He laughed at me and said, "I don't need to keep a log. I already know the answer. I only fall on Friday or Saturday nights—usually Friday, since Saturday is right before Sunday." If you have any pastoral counseling genes in you, you light up at an answer like that. Repeated patterns always prove extremely revealing on inspection. I asked, "Why does sexual sin surface on Friday night? What's going on with that?" He said, "I go out and buy *Playboy* magazine as my temper tantrum at God."

Amazing! Look what we've just found out: another movie is playing in a theater next door. Now we're not only dealing with a couple of bad behaviors, buying pornography and masturbating. We're dealing with *anger at God* that drives those behaviors. What's that about? Tom went on to give a fuller picture. "I come home from work on Friday night, back to the apartment. I'm all alone. I imagine that all my single friends are out on dates, and my married friends are spending time with their wives. But I'm all alone in my apartment. I build up a good head of steam of self-pity. Then by nine or ten o'clock, I think, 'You deserve a break today'—I even hear the little McDonald's jingle in my head, and then sexual desires start to look really, really sweet. 'God has cheated me. If only I had a girlfriend or a wife. I can't stand how I feel. Why not feel good for awhile? What does it matter anyway?' Then I hop in the car, head to 7-11, and fall into sin."

Amazing, isn't it? Pornography and masturbation grabbed all the attention, generated all the guilt, defined the moment and act of "falling." Let's call that Screening Room #1. But we've also heard about anger at God that precedes and legitimates sexual sin: Screening Room #2. We've heard about hours of low-grade self-pity, grumbling, and envious fantasies: a matinee performance in Screening Room #3. We've heard Tom name the original desire that leads to self-pity, to anger at God, and finally to sexual lust: "God owes me a wife. I need, want, demand a woman to love me." That's playing in Screening Room #4, an unobtrusive G-rated film, seemingly no problem at all. It's a classic nonsexual lust of the flesh that Tom has never viewed as problematic. In fact, in his mind, it's practically a promise from God: "Psalm 37:4: Delight yourself in the LORD, and he will give you the desires of your heart." "If I do my part, God should do his part and give me a wife."

As Tom and I kept talking, I found out why God owes him a wife: "I've tried to do all the right things. I've served him. I've tried account-ability. I've memorized Scripture. I've tried to be a good Christian. I do ministry. I witness. I tithe . . . but God hasn't come through." In other words, the "right answers" for fighting sin are also the levers to pry goodies out of God. Tom's words sound eerily like the self-righteous whine of the older brother in Jesus' parable of the prodigal son: "I'm good, therefore God owes me the goodies I want." Subsequent anger at God operates like any other sinful anger: "You aren't giving me what I want, expect, need, and demand." This fatally flawed, proud "upside" of the classic legalistic construct has been showing in Screening Room #5. And why does Tom mope in self-lacerating depression for days and weeks after falling, rather than finding God's living mercies new every morning? That's the self-punitive, despairing "downside" of the legalis-tic construct: "I'm bad, therefore God won't give me the goodies." Screening Room #6 is where self-punishment, self-atonement, penance, and self-hatred play out.

It doesn't take much theological insight to see how all these distor-tions of Tom's relationship with God express different forms of basic unbelief. We suppress living knowledge of the true God. We create a uni-verse for ourselves void of the real God's presence, truth, and purposes. Unbelief does not mean a vacuum; rather the universe fills up with seduc-tive, persuasive fictions. Screening Room #7 is showing a blockbuster that Tom had never noticed as trouble. (When Dame Folly keeps her clothes on she sounds like common sense.) In fact, we have found out why Tom is so eager right now to get my counsel and advice. Why does he want to have victory over his lust problem, to try again, to defeat the dragon of lust once and for all? He's recently had his eye on an eligible young lady who started to attend our church. That's reawakened his motivation to fight. If only lust goes, then God owes, and maybe he'll get the wife of his dreams. Even Tom's agenda for counseling plays a bit part in the wider battle: Screening Room #8!

Look how far we've come in half an hour. Tom's "fall" at 9:30 P.M. last Friday was not where he started to fall. It was not even his most devastating fall. For me to assist Tom's discipleship to Jesus is not simply to offer tips and truths that might help him remain "morally pure" on subsequent Fridays. Counseling must be about rewiring Tom's entire life. "Cure of souls" is what ministry does.

You can see why we must widen the battlefront in order to cure souls. Tom concentrates all his attention on one marquee sin that sporadically surfaces, defining and energizing all his guilty feelings. But that narrowing of attention serves to mask far more serious, pervasive sins. As a pastor, friend, or other counselor, you don't want to concentrate all your energies in the same place Tom does. There are other, deeper opportunities for grace and truth to rewrite the script of this man's life. Tom had turned his whole relationship with God into flimsy scaffolding. Self-righteousness ("victory at last") would get him the goodies he really wanted out of life. Though Tom knew and professed sound theology, in daily practice he reduced God to, in Bob Dylan's words, the "errand boy to satisfy [his] wandering desires."[7]

Tom and I put the fire of truth and grace to the scaffolding. Wonderful changes started to run through his life. We didn't ignore temptations to sexual sin, but many other things that he had never before noticed became urgently important. We spent far more time talking about self-pity and grumbling as "early warning sins," about how the desire for a wife becomes a mastering lust, about how the self-righteousness construct falls before the dynamics of grace. Temptations to sexual sin greatly diminished. The topography of the battlefield radically changed. The significance of Jesus Christ's love went off the charts. The lights of more accurate and comprehensive self-knowledge came on. A man going in circles, muddling in the middle, started to leap and bound in the right direction. We experienced the delights of a season of gazelle growth. Ministering to someone who has struggled for

---

[7] "When You Gonna Wake Up," words and music by Bob Dylan, from the album *Slow Train Coming* (1979).

twenty years with the exact same thing is disheartening, and frequently a recipe for futility. Ministering to someone who is starting to battle a half-dozen foes that were previously invisible is extremely heartening! Widening the war served to deepen and heighten the significance of the Savior, who met Tom on every battlefront.

### 4. It's a *Deeper* War

The Bible is always about behavior, but it is never only about behavior. God's indictment of human nature always gets below the surface, into the "heart." His gaze and Word expose the thoughts, intentions, desires, and fears that shape the entire way we approach life. An immoral act or fantasy—behavior—is a sin in itself. But such behavior always arises from desires and beliefs that dethrone God. Whenever I do wrong, I am loving *something besides God* with all my heart, soul, mind, and might. I am listening attentively to *some other voice*. Typically (but not always!), immoral actions arise in connection with erotic desires that squirm out from under God's lordship. But immorality results from many other motives, too, and usually arises from a combination of motives. We saw some of this in describing Tom. Erotic motives, the "feel good" of sex, played an important role. But other motives—"I want a wife"; "If I'm good, God owes me goodies"; "I'm angry because God has let me down"—interconnected with his eroticism. Many co-conspirators play a role when Tom starts rummaging in the gutter of "I want to look at a naked Playmate" and "I need sexual release now." Many other lusts join hands to give a boost to sexual lust. It's worth digging, both in order to understand yourself and in order to minister wisely to other people. As our understanding of sin's inner cravings deepens, our ability to know and appreciate the God of grace grows deeper still. Consider a handful of typical examples to prime the pump.

### a. Angry Desires for Revenge

Sexual acting out can be a way to express anger. I once counseled a couple who had committed backlash adulteries. First they had a big fight, full of yelling, threats, and bitter accusations. In anger the man went out and slept with a prostitute. Still burning with anger, he came home and gloated about it to his wife. In retaliatory anger, the woman went out and seduced her husband's best friend. Did they get any erotic pleasure out of those acts? Probably. But was eros the driving force? No way. Though it's not always so dramatic, anger often plays a role in immorality: A teenager finds sex a convenient way to rebel against and to hurt morally upright parents; a man cruises the Internet after he and his wife exchange words; a woman masturbates to fantasies of former boyfriends after she and her husband argue. In all these situations, the redemption of dirtied sexuality can happen only alongside the redemption of dirtied anger.

### b. Longings to Feel Loved, Approved, Affirmed, to Be Given Romantic Attention

Consider the situation of an overweight, lonely, teenage girl with acne, whose enjoyment of sex as an act is minimal or even nil. Why then is she promiscuous, giving away sexual favors to any boy who pays her any attention? She barters her body, not in service to erotic lust, but in order to feed her consuming lust for romantic attention. When boys say sweet things and pledge their faithful love, she might even know inside that they are lying. She knows that they are merely using her as a receptacle for their lust, but she temporarily blocks out the thought. She engages in sex anyway—because she's hooked on "feeling loved." Ministry to such a young woman does her a disservice if we concentrate only on the wrong of fornication and do not help her to understand the subtler enslavement of living for human attention. Sex can be an instrument in the hands of nonsexual lust. Both evils must find the mercies and transforming power of Christ.

### c. Thrilling Desires for the Power and Excitement of the Chase

Some people enjoy the sense of power and control over another person's sexual response. The flirt, the tease, the Don Juan, the seducer are not motivated solely by sexual desires. Often evil erotic pleasure is enhanced and complemented by deeper evil pleasures: the chase, the hunt, the thrill of conquest, the rush that comes with being able to manipulate the romantic-erotic arousal of another. There is a kind of sadistic pleasure driving through such sexual sins. These people like to see others get aroused, "fall" for them, and squirm. They may become indifferent to a willing sexual partner once that particular chase has ended. Repentance and change for seducers will address lusts for perverse power and excitement, as well as lusts for sex.

### d. Anxious Desires for Money to Meet Basic Survival Needs

Sex makes lots of money for lots of people. As in the previous cases, eros may be one factor. But in money-making sex, pleasure plays second fiddle to mammon. There are also more subtle situations. A single mother in our church was in very tight financial straits. She found herself strongly tempted by her sleazy landlord's offer of free rent in exchange for sexual favors. If she had fallen, sexual desire might have been non-existent. In fact, she might have fornicated despite feeling active repugnance, shame, and guilt in the act. To God's glory, she opened up her struggle to a wise woman. In a variety of appropriate ways the church was able to come to her aid with care and counsel. One aspect of care for her came from the deacons (who didn't even know what had almost happened): "Know that you will not end up on the street. We are your family. If you get stuck, if you wonder where the money will come from for rent, or groceries, or a doctor's bill, don't think twice about asking for help." Interesting, isn't it? Mercy ministry to financial needs played a significant role in reducing a woman's vulnerability to one particular sort of sexual temptation.

### e. Distorted Messianic Desire to Help Another

Certainly there are pastors and priests who are sexual predators, but that's not the only dynamic of sexual sin in the ministry. I've dealt with a number of situations that involved the very impulses that make for ministry—run far off the rails. For example, a pastor feels deep concern for a lonely young widow or divorcée. He wants so much (too much) to help her and comfort her. She so appreciates his wise, Scriptural counsel. He's such a role model of kindness, gentleness, communication, attentive concern. But life is still very hard and lonely for her. He starts to console her with hugs. They end up in bed. The motives? Sexual, yes. But more significant in the early going was a warped desire to be helpful, to be admired, to make a real difference, to be important, to "save" her. When anyone who is not the Messiah starts to act messianic, it gets very ugly very fast. When you minister to a minister who has committed sexual sin, you might find that sex was only the poisoned dessert. The poisonous entrée might have been a very different set of deceitful desires, desires arising more from the mind than from the body (Eph. 4:22; 2:3).

### f. Desires for Relief and Rest amid the Pressures of Life

Sexual sin often serves as a kind of "escape valve" from other problems. When steam pressure gets too high in a pressure cooker, it blows off steam. That's a metaphor for what's often true with people, too. Consider a man who faces, and mishandles, extreme pressures in his workplace. He's part of a team facing a drop-dead deadline for a major project. They've been running behind. He's had a month of eighty-hour work weeks. He's harried, driven, preoccupied, worried, worn out. Every day his boss applies more pressure, more panic, more threats. There's been vicious infighting on the project team: who's responsible for what task, who's to blame for what glitch, who gets credit for what achievement. All along, he isn't casting his real cares on the God who cares for him; he isn't "anxious for nothing" (Phil. 4:6, NASB), but anxious about lots of things. After two straight all-nighters, just under the wire, they finish the project. They made it. He made it. Success. Finally he has a free night, with no deadlines, no jungle of intramural combat, no tomorrow to worry about. But after a month of living "stressed-out," he feels no relief. He finds no satisfaction in achievement. So he surfs the Internet, revels in pornography, forgets his troubles. What's going on with him?

Erotic sin is part of his picture, but there's lots more. Every deviant motive—every lust of the flesh, lie, false love—is a hijacker. It mimics some aspect of God. It usurps some promise of God. About two-thirds of the Psalms present God as "our refuge" amid the troubles of life. Amid threat, hurt, disappointment, and attack, God protects, cares, and looks out for us. Our friend has faced troubles: people out to get him, threats to his job, intolerable demands, relentless weeks. But he's been finding no true refuge during this frenzied month. Now, in a spasm of immorality, he takes "false refuge" in eroticism. His erotic behavior serves as a counterfeit rest from his troubles. Psalm 23 breathes true refuge: "Even though I walk through the valley of the shadow of death, I will fear no evil, for you are with me." This man pants after false refuge: "After I've walked through that godforsaken valley of the shadow of death, I will fear no evil, because the photograph of a surgically enhanced female wearing no clothes is with me." A false refuge looks pretty silly when exposed for what it really is.

Sexual sin is one expression of a deeper war for the heart's loyalty and primary love. Learning to see more clearly is a crucial part of your sanctification journey. Teaching others to have eyes open to the deeper battles is a crucial part of wise pastoral ministry. Jesus Christ looks better and better the more we see what he is about. He is not simply in the business of cleaning up a few embarrassing moral blots. Deepening the battle deepens the significance of the Savior. He alone sees your heart accurately. He alone loves you well enough to make you love him.

### 5. It's a *Subtler* War

A newcomer to war imagines that the first battles are the hardest battles. When you're first coming out of the morass of an adulterous relationship, of being betrayed by a spouse's adultery, of promiscuous fornications, of having experienced rape or molestation, of a homosexual lifestyle, of an obsession with Internet porn, it can seem as though your troubles will be over if you can only get past the particular bad behavior.

Those battles are hard. But will your troubles be over? That's not how life works. That's not how sanctification works in the clean-up from sexual dirt. In fact, in some ways it's the opposite. The more obviously destructive sins can be "easier" to deal with. The subtler sins can be more stubborn, pervasive, sneaky, and elusive.

Consider a metaphor for this. Many computer and video games send you out on a quest, a sort of pilgrim's progress. You proceed through level after level, facing test after test, until, say, at Level 50 you've run the race and won. Level 1 starts you out with easier challenges. The tasks are clear-cut. The enemies are slower, more limited in their abilities, more obvious in their approach, not so smart. With some practice, you learn to accomplish your task and blow away your attackers. Level 2 gets a little harder. Each successive level gets harder still. The

tasks get trickier. The enemies are wilier, stronger, quicker, more numerous. The skills you need are subtler and more varied. If you ever arrive
at, say, Level 40, it's because you've died often, but you learned something each time, and you kept coming back. You've come a distance in
the right direction.

The struggle with sexual sin (as with any other sin) has a certain similarity to those video games. There is typically a front-and-center issue,
and the "front lines" of the current battle move from the more overt sins
to subtler sins.[8] Let's work out the metaphor.

### a. High-Effort, High-Cost Sins

Think of consenting sex (adultery, fornication, homosexuality, prostitution) and criminal sex (rape, child abuse) as the Level 1 sins. These are
the obvious evils. I don't mean that such sins are easy to break or easy
to change. But they are relatively easy to see. Easier to recognize as
wrong. Easier to know when you're doing wrong, once your conscience
starts to see straight. And such sins are usually harder to do and harder
to get away with. Think about that. You have to do a lot of scheming
in order to arrange a liaison. You have to hide things from people who
love you, who would be unhappy if they found out what you've been
doing. You have to tell consistent and increasingly complex lies in order
to get away with it. You have to lie to your own conscience to persuade
yourself that everything's okay. Because these actions involve actual sexual relations with other people, those partners may blow your cover, or
blackmail you, or slip up, or report you. These sins can catch up with
you very quickly, taking you down in an instant. They can destroy your
reputation. Destroy family relationships. Destroy finances. Destroy
health by a sexually transmitted disease. Even send you to jail. In other
words, these sins take a lot of work and can bite back hard. If you're
willing to seek mercy and change, it's easier to set up meaningful barriers against the high-effort, high-cost sins.

Jesus Christ often begins his work of mercy and renewal by dealing
with such high-handed sins. Often the dramatic first steps of sanctifica-

---

[8] The video game metaphor captures a progression of different *kinds* of battles we face. It does not capture how in real life we also "regress" and may have to fight an old battle over again. It also does not
capture that in real life the subtler sins are actually present all the way through. But they don't tend to
come front-and-center when some other struggle is more overt and decisive for that moment.

tion shake off overt evils. Oily-rag people make leaps and bounds into the garden of light. There are adulterers who repent and *never again* have sexual relations with anyone who is not their own wife or husband. It is entirely possible to have lived an immoral life for many years, with a string of lovers, and then to make such a complete break with that sin that you will never be immoral again—in the Level 1 sense. That does not always happen. And it's never a snap of the fingers. And you may still face ongoing consequences. And believers do fall back into such sins. But grace and change can be as easy to see and as powerful as the sin once was. Accountability relationships can really help. The Scriptures openly and frequently speak to the obvious sins to bring transformation. (By doing this, God also familiarizes us with how the subtler versions of sin and love work, teaching us how to see more of life for what it is and can become.)

### b. Lower-Effort, Lower-Cost Sins

Let's say you've done some growing. You've put away overt evils. No immoral liaisons. By grace you've worked and fought your way to a Level 8 battle. Pornography was around before, but now it's the biggie. In some ways, pornography is a tougher problem than adultery. In one sense, it's "not as bad," because it doesn't involve an accomplice or victim. But it's harder to get rid of. Harder to set up protective barriers against. Why is this? Pornography is easier to do and easier to get away with. The necessary deceit is not as complicated. It doesn't take much work for you to do the sin. Adultery usually takes a lot of effort, both to arrange and to cover your tracks. But pornography? The gap between temptation and sin can be a matter of seconds. Three clicks of the mouse and you're there. A few dollars at an airport magazine shop. A remote control in your hand to check out what's on cable TV. And who's to know? No one. Pornography use is harder to discover. Unless you fail to erase it off your computer. Or you spend so many hours online late at night that friends and family get suspicious. Or someone walks in on you. Or you get depressed and grouchy because you feel guilty. Or your relationships slowly fray and alienate because of your preoccupation, defensiveness, and hiding. The consequences are shameful—but usually not as disastrous as with the interpersonal sins.

So pornography is both "not as bad" as adultery, and yet harder to defeat because it's easier to do and not as devastating. Christ is merciful here, too. Lots of people have broken with pornography and never gone back. You learn the joys of righteousness, the deeper pleasures of a clear conscience and honest relationships. You learn to say no to yourself. You get more interested in good things. You care about people, and sin just doesn't have as much room to insinuate itself into your heart. Some practical tools can help, too. A friend who will look you in the eye, ask a direct question, and expect an honest answer can help you. You can set up Covenant Eyes software (www.covenanteyes.com) to monitor your Internet use and email a report to a friend.

### c. No-Effort Sins

Let's say you've put pornography and immoral sexual relations aside. The acted-out sins no longer draw you. Are there no more enemies to fight? Now we're up to Level 16: mental tapes. This is an even subtler problem. You don't even have to *do* anything. No effort, no expense. You aren't having sexual relations outside of marriage. You aren't cruising the Internet. But you have a theater and library in your own mind. It's all stored there: memories, images, stories. At your mind's fingertips are things you did, experiences you had, people you watched or read about. You don't have to tell any lies or arrange anything. You just open a door in your mind. You can't get caught—except by the Searcher of hearts, before whose eyes all things are open and laid bare, him with whom we have to do. Because he sees us on the inside, and because he's merciful both inside and out, grace is available here, too.

Sometimes the battle with mental tapes stalls because you actively cherish and nurture old memories. But when you actually start to fight, you wish you could push ERASE and obliterate the collection of old videos. But the erase button on memories doesn't work on request. It's a subtler battle, learning to say no inside your mind, and yes to your Father who is right at hand. The point is clear. The enemies get subtler. They aren't as "bad" outwardly. But they're "worse" when it comes to getting rid of them, because sins are so easy to arrange and not so immediately self-destructive.

I've chosen examples from the active sins. But there is an analogy for those who experienced the dark splash of evil as the victim of another's sin. In some ways, it can be "easier" to deal with an abusive relationship (Level 1). Hard as it is to get away, it can be done. The problem is clear-cut and definable. Like adultery, the wrongdoer can be caught in the act. Violence can be intercepted. The action steps are obvious. Friends will help you. The law can help protect you: police intervention, a restraining order, criminal charges against the offender. You can flee. When you aren't in the same room, the person can't hurt you anymore. There are places to live where you are safe. But how do you deal with the memories (Level 16)? Memories aren't as "bad" as being abused, but they can be harder to get rid of. They inhabit the room of your mind. Or, how do you deal with the fact that you are primed to interpret anyone's irritation at you as a threat of imminent violence (Level 24)? How do you deal with the subtle fears that you now bring to all relationships, apprehensions so automatic that you don't even know you're doing it (Level 40)? Those motions of your soul are almost invisible, but they are pervasive, hard to intercept, and highly corrosive to developing future trust and love. The themes of safe refuge, peace, and watchful care run deep in the Psalms. God is trustworthy at every level. Psalm 23 means one very good thing at Level 1, something still richer at Level 16, and wonders beyond wonders at Level 40. The significance of the Lord's kindness is not exhausted at the more obvious levels. The Psalms go deep, deeper, and deepest, the more you bring complex, honest experience onto the table.

### d. Sins That Come Looking for You

Let's say you've left adultery and pornography behind, and you simply don't go there. You're closing and locking the door on mental tapes. But how about those situations where you aren't looking for sin, but sin is looking for you? Let's call that Level 24. In this battle the insurgents are trickier. An invitation to lust can sneak up and attack you in ways that no actual human being can. Our culture has many "acceptable" predators. Have you ever been blindsided by a lewd image or suggestion that you were not looking for, but that was looking for you? The fashion industry, entertainment industry, advertising industry, and sex industry know their business well. They are looking to find you, to snag your heart, to shape your identity, your goals, your worries, your spending. We live in a culture of visual media, where such ambushes are increasingly common:

- You're on the Internet, searching for an out-of-print theology book. A slightly mistyped web address pipes hardcore porn onto your screen. Or, you open an email that looks like it's for real, but it turns out to be well-disguised spam spewing gutter words in bold, colorful print. Or, you recognize that an email is spam and delete it, but you can't avoid reading the filth on the subject line. You feel splashed with sewer water. You weren't looking for sin; you didn't linger; but you're dirtied anyway.

- In the grocery store, a handsome, charming young man starts to flirt suggestively with you, a mature, married woman with well over a hundred thousand miles on your odometer! Is there an answering flutter inside you?

- You hear that a certain movie is worth watching, but get blindsided. A lewd scene was gratuitously inserted to avoid a G rating. Or, you find yourself feeling deep empathy for a couple committing adultery because their respective spouses are portrayed so unfavorably.

- You're driving down the highway when, suddenly, you see a twenty-by-sixty-foot billboard advertising beer, featuring a nearly undressed lady. Wouldn't it be wonderful if there were nothing inside answering back to her call, if that ad created the same indifference as the neighboring billboard, advertising a 5.25 percent mortgage rate? No one ever came under church discipline or was sued for divorce for looking twice at a billboard of a mostly naked lady. But that's where the ambush occurs.

- You've learned to deeply trust and love your God and a circle of dear friends, after torturous experiences many years ago. You've learned not to shrink from new people. Your new boss generally treats you reasonably, but his appearance, voice, and mannerisms bear an uncanny resemblance to the person who once betrayed you. Where that person was cruel,

your boss is only irritable and sarcastic on occasion. His sins
are 1 percent of what you once experienced; but that's where
today's battle erupts.

You can have a lot of light growing in your life, good latticework in place,
gardens of healthy sexuality. But wherever there's still a broken lattice, an
oily stain, then an inner spark or inner flinch can answer to what comes
at you. Redemption proceeds exactly in such places. You face things that
whisper the very things that once shouted in your life. And Christ speaks
loud and clear, so that at this level, too, you learn to choose well.

### e. Sins So Atmospheric They Seem Like Who You Are

Sometimes lust is so subtle it doesn't even seem like lust—until you think
about it, unmask it, pull it toward the light: Level 40. For example, have
you ever used sexual attraction criteria in sizing up a person? It can be
a largely unconscious operation. Subliminal radar explores, notices, reg-
isters on the wavelength of mildly sexualized desire. It's a quiet current
trending in the direction of lust. You're subtly aware of a body's shape;
of the cues communicated by posture and gesture; of the messages
expressed through clothing, hairstyle, makeup, scent, tone of voice. This
subtle attentiveness correlates to the heart's erotic attraction: "Is this person desirable to my eyes, worth further exploratory interest?" Perhaps
this thought process rarely surfaces into conscious awareness. Perhaps
you almost as instinctively say no, resisting the impulse to convert its
intentions into a conscious lewd look. But the very existence of such
atmospheric erotic intentionality subtly stains you. It is yet another
aspect of our battle with darkness.

    When you see sin's subtlety, you realize how much our lives hang
upon sheer mercy from God. He is utterly aware of thoughts and intentions of which we may be wholly unaware. Mercy extends here, too.
"Who can discern his errors? Declare me innocent from hidden
faults. . . . Let the . . . meditation of my heart be acceptable in your sight,
O LORD, my rock and my redeemer" (Ps. 19:12, 14).

    Is it possible to alter the subtle tendencies that pattern how you look
at people? Yes. The Holy Spirit is about this business. But he takes time
with us and works with us over time: a lot of walking on the paths of

light, a lot of needing God and loving God, a lot of receiving his mercies, a lot of learning to genuinely love people. But you can grow wiser even at this subtlest of levels. You can increasingly view each human being as a sister or brother, a mother or father, a daughter or son, not as a sexual object. Your gaze and intentions can become more and more about the business of caring and protecting.

### f. Truly Changed, Truly Changing, and Still at War

All this—from Level 1 to Level 40—is the arena of sanctification. In heart, soul, mind, and might we are being conformed and transformed into radiant purity. A heightened view of our war brings with it a heightened view of the significance of our Jesus Christ. One of the deep truths of sanctification is that you get "better" and "worse" at the same time!

You truly shine more brightly as you move toward the light. You hold onto God more steadily. You're more loving and joyful. You're more trustworthy. More teachable. You give to people rather than use them. But brighter light also exposes more dark corners, pockets of unconscionable and once unimaginable iniquity. As we have seen, sin is not only the worst things I ever did. It's also an atmospheric narcissism: "Is that person pleasing to the sexual impulse that animates my desires?" John Calvin captured well the historical wisdom of the church regarding these things:

> The children of God [are] freed through regeneration from bondage to sin. Yet . . . there still remains in them a continuing occasion for struggle whereby they may be exercised; and not only be exercised, but also better learn their own weakness. In this matter all writers of sounder judgment agree that there remains in a regenerate man a smoldering cinder of evil, from which desires continually leap forth to allure and spur him to commit sin.[9]

A "smoldering cinder of evil." A restless inner motion of sin. Jesus' first beatitude is first for a reason. Awareness of an impoverished need for mercy is the opening motion of living faith. The better I know my Christ, the better I know my need for what he alone is and does.

When you understand your subtle sinfulness, you will never say of any

---

[9] Calvin, *Institutes*, 3.3.10.

human being, "How could he do that?" or "Can you believe she did that!" We are fundamentally more alike than different. You may never have been an adulterer, fornicator, homosexual, or consumer of pornography. But you know with all your heart that no temptation overtakes anyone that is not common to everyone (1 Cor. 10:13). And grasping the subtlety of the battle helps you to grasp the true subtlety and scope of the work of our Savior. "Remember me, O LORD, according to Your lovingkindness."

## 6. Remember the Goal

We've looked at many varieties of sexual darkness. The war is longer, wider, deeper, more subtle than we might imagine. It is no accident, therefore, that the height, depth, length, and breadth of the love and work of Jesus is more wonderful than we understand at first. What is God after in remaking our lives? Is his purpose merely that we would just stop sinning? That we would become more involved in religious activities? Yes, stop sinning. Yes, use the means of grace. But neither is an end in itself. The point is to become more like Jesus.

Jesus loves God. He lives out a head-on, honest relationship with his Father. Whether in pain or joy, whether needy or exultant, whether looking at the weather or looking at the people out to hurt him, whether considering God's love or considering God's wrath, Jesus talks it all out with God his Father. He needs God, thanks God, trusts God, serves God. The Psalms aren't merely "devotions" for him. When Jesus talks and acts, he brings life to God and brings God to life. That's what God intends the means of grace to accomplish. As you stop sinning, that's how you live instead.

The way Jesus works as a person is the diametric opposite from how the oily rag works. When you're living in sexual sin or swamped in unredeemed sexual sufferings, you live in your own head. Sin pulls you into an in-curving, self-absorbing inertia. You shut God out. The universe becomes all about you. Suffering tends to have the same effect, as we return evils for evils. But Jesus suffers in the exact opposite way, opening out to God in his times of need. Jesus teaches life lived in God's direction. He teaches you how to talk out everything that matters with the One whose opinion most matters, the only One who can do something about it all.

In the same way, Jesus loves people. He notices others. He stops. He helps people where they most need help. He answers real questions. He inverts hostile questions. He relentlessly leads people to think about the two decisive life-or-death questions: "Whom are you living for? How are you living?" He's dedicated to the true welfare of others. He protects and promotes the sexual purity of others (even when interacting with notoriously immoral women). He attacks oppressors and tenderly bends toward the helpless. He dies willingly, the innocent for the guilty.

The way Jesus loves is the diametric opposite from how sexual sin works. Whether flagrant or atmospheric, whether physical or imaginary, sexual sin is hate. It misuses people. Jesus' love treasures and serves our sexual purity. We misuse God's gift of sexuality when we do not treasure and serve the sexual purity of others. We degrade ourselves and degrade others. As Jesus starts to rearrange how you treat people, you are becoming a qualitatively different kind of person. Let me give two simple examples.

First, *you learn to see and treat all people in wise, constructive ways.* In principle, for the Christian, every person of the opposite sex fits into one of three categories: either family member, or spouse, or threat. (Every person of the same sex fits into one of two categories: either family member or threat.) "Family member" is the controlling category. In general we are to view and treat people as beloved sisters and brothers, mothers and fathers, daughters and sons, grandmothers and grandfathers. The lines are clear: anything that sexualizes familial relationships is wrong. True affection and fierce protection go hand in hand. The notion of incestuous sexuality is abhorrent before God. In marriage, one sister, Nan, becomes my wife, and I become her husband. All our sexuality belongs rightly and freely to each other. The notion of treacherous sexuality—infidelity—is abhorrent before God. A third group of people falls into the category of threat. Males and females who prove unfamilial in their intentions are threats. Again, the lines are clear: nothing sexualized, so flee seduction, whether in person or in imagination. The notion of an invitation to immoral sexuality is abhorrent before God. Love is radically free to be fiercely faithful.

Second, *good sexual love is simply "normal."* Sometimes the idealized view of good sex can sound overheated, even when we prize and protect marital sexuality. Sometimes we may get the idea that good sex is a gymnastic, ecstatic, romantic, ravishing bliss of marital passion! Sorry to disillusion you. But much of good sex is just . . . well, normal, everyday. Think about it. Most people in the history of the world have lived in one-room huts, where the kids sleep in the same room with their parents! Countless families have lived with only curtains for room dividers, your mother-in-law in the far corner, your wife's younger brother sleeping on the couch. Or they've lived in tents, as nomads. Not much sound-proofing or major privacy operative in that housing arrangement! Not much in the way of gymnastics or sound effects is possible unless you have no children. That's not to say that a married couple with children shouldn't get away for a weekend, or close the door, or do things to make sex special. Nothing wrong with some high-wire encounters that bring a little extra spice.

Think of the analogy with food, another of life's very redeemable pleasures. Occasionally you pull out all the stops for a memorable feast with all the fixings. But in normal life, you eat a lot of healthy breakfasts. In the redemption of sex, lots of normal things flourish. How about courtesy? Basic kindness and patience? How about humor—pet names, teasing, irony, private jokes? Good sex is not *that* serious! How about mercy? How about a shower, shave, and being relaxed? How about a fundamental willingness to be available to another, simply to give? How about conversation? How about quiet, slow, leisurely time together? Basic love goes a long way toward making good sex good. It's great when the Richter Scale tops out at an earth-shattering 8.1. But in normalized good sex, you'll also enjoy the 3.1 temblors that hardly rattle the teacups.

Get your goals straight. It heightens the significance of your Savior. He alone restores you to practical love for God and to the practical love appropriate for each of your various kinds of neighbors. He alone makes daily life shine with visible glory.

## 7. Get Down to Today's Skirmish in the Great War

We've talked about the war, the direction of the journey, the destination. The final word in restoring joy to your life as a sexual being is to get down to business. And your business has three parts.

First, *where is today's skirmish?* Your battle in the area of sex will always be fought one step at a time; no one wins this war all at once. "Today's trouble" (see Matt. 6:34) is where you find God's aid. Where are you tempted, now? Tom had to figure out how to refight his Friday nights so that he wouldn't keep coming out a loser. How about you? Where is today's choice point?

Second, *what one thing about God in Christ speaks directly into today's trouble?* Just as we don't change all at once, so we don't swallow all of truth in one gulp. We are simple people. You can't remember ten things at once. Invariably, if you could remember just *one* true thing in the moment of trial, you'd be different. Bible verses aren't magic. But God's words are revelations of God from God for our redemption. When you actually remember God, you do not sin. The only way you ever sin is by suppressing God, by forgetting, by tuning out his voice, switching channels, and listening to other voices. When you actually remember, you actually change. In fact, remembering is the first change.

Here's a simple example. God says, "I am with you" (e.g., Gen. 26:24; Isa. 41:10; Hag. 1:13; Matt. 28:20). Those are his exact words. How does taking that to heart utterly change the script of *your* sexual darkness? What if you are facing a temptation to some immorality? For starters, with these words in view you realize that nothing is private, no secrets are possible: "I am with you." "I . . . am . . . with . . . you." Say it ten different ways. Slow it down. Speed it up. Say it out loud. Say it out loud back to him: "You are with me, Lord." You'll probably find that you immediately need to say more, like, "Help me. Have mercy on me. I need you. Make me understand that you are with me." You will find that the competing voices, sly and argumentative, will become more obvious. To the degree that you remember that your Lord is with you, then what those other voices say will sound devious, tawdry, hostile to your welfare. How did they ever sound so appealing! The contrast, the battle of wills, the battle between good and evil, will be more evident. Your immediate choice—Which voice will I listen to?—will become stark. Remembering what's true does not chalk up automatic victory. It's not magic. Your battle will heat up. But we do secretive things only when we're kidding ourselves. Every time you remember that you are out in public, then you live an out-in-public life. "I am with you" means you're *always* out in public. In order to sin, you'll have to drown out the voice of reality, put your fingers in your ears, and switch to the fantasy channel, the lie channel, the death channel. And even if you switch channels and sin by high-handed choice, you will *still* be in broad daylight before

God's searching eyes. You can shut your eyes and plug your ears, he's still right here. You'll never get away.

And you only have to open your eyes, listen, and turn around in order to find help. After all, he who *loves* you says, "I am with you."

"I am with you" means that the person who can help you right now knows and is watching. In fact, he is watching over you to protect you. He will help you escape darkness, because he has transferred you into the kingdom of the Son whom he loves.

What if you face a different struggle today? What if you feel overwhelmed with aloneness and fear, buried under your hurt, abandoned and betrayed? "I am with you." "I am with you." Again, when you really hear that, and take it to heart, you *know* you are not alone. You *are* safe. Manipulative or violent lust betrayed you; steadfast love never betrays you.

Or what if you're overwhelmed by the grime of past failures? "I am with you." God is not shocked by the ugliness of your past. He came to die for the worst of sinners (as Paul twice refers to himself—1 Tim. 1:15-16). Whatever your struggle, "I am with you" changes the terrain of battle.

Third, *put trouble and God together. Start talking, and start walking.* We began to do this in the previous paragraphs. It was impossible simply to identify choice points and then to offer promises and revelations of God without starting to capture the honest human responses: faith's need for God, and constructive love for others. You must fiercely pursue God. He must be to you what he says he is and do for you what he says he will do. You are not yet what you shall be, but you are growing toward it, step by step in real life. How will you treat people today? Will love contain and express your sexuality well? Or will evil squander and warp your sexuality, treating others as sex objects?

Walking in the light is not magic. When you see the fork in the road more clearly (today's skirmish) . . . , and when you see and hear your Lord more clearly (something he says) . . . , then you start talking, start needing, start trusting, and then you start making the hard, significant, joyous choice to love people rather than use them.

Go into action in today's battle. That's our final word. It gets us down to where our Savior is going into action. It's where our Father is making us more fruitful. It's exactly where the Spirit of life is changing us into his image of light and delight.

# CHAPTER 5

# Homosexual Marriage as a Challenge to the Church: Biblical and Cultural Reflections

R. ALBERT MOHLER, JR.

The question of homosexual marriage presents the church with a monumental challenge. Advocates for homosexual marriage are pressing their case and, even with significant legal and political barriers in place, have framed the issue so that those who hold to a biblical concept of marriage are put on the defensive, and advocates of same-sex relationships are portrayed as agents of liberty, progress, and inevitable cultural evolution.

For the church, the very concept of homosexual marriage strikes at the heart of our biblical and theological foundation. According to the Christian tradition, marriage is not merely a social arrangement between two persons but a God-ordained institution through which the Creator's glory is demonstrated to the cosmos. The covenant fidelity at the very center of marriage is a picture of God's purpose in the creation of the world and the redemption of the church.

In essence, the term "homosexual marriage" is a tragic oxymoron. In any previous era, those two words would be seen as mutually exclusive. The fact that homosexual marriage is even an issue for public debate demonstrates that we are a civilization in crisis, because a great many barriers must be breached in order to put this question on the cultural agenda. Firewalls, traditions, habits, and convictional practices must fall before marriage can be redefined and utterly transformed by the inclusion of same-sex relationships. At the root of this development is an attitude of moral rebellion that reflects a suspicion of authority, a confusion about the order of creation, and a rebellion against God's design for human sexuality.

As Christians, we are charged with the difficult task of compassionate truth-telling. This has never been easy—just ask the apostles—but it is particularly difficult in a time of cultural ferment and sexual revolution. Compassionate truth-telling requires the church to speak from its deepest convictions while demonstrating the love of Christ—speaking truth that will be heard as a hard message while demonstrating the love of Christ through the very act of telling the truth. Compassionate truth-telling means, not only the accurate presentation of biblical truth, but the prayerful and urgent hope that the individuals to whom we speak will be transformed by that truth and respond to the grace of God in Jesus Christ.

The challenge of compassionate truth-telling means that we must think strategically and carefully about how these issues should be addressed, both in terms of individual conversations and in the larger context of public debate. We must ensure not only that we *think* rightly about these things as ordered by Scripture, but that we *speak* rightly about controversial issues as well. We cannot address homosexual marriage as an isolated issue but must place it in the larger context of the Christian worldview and of the great story of God's purpose in creation and redemption.

The Christian worldview affirms the unity of the good, the beautiful, and the true—known as the "transcendentals"—in the transcendent, self-revealing God. Thus, the Christian worldview understands the good, the beautiful, and the true as being established in the very character of God. At the same time, these transcendentals—the good, the beautiful, and the true—are, in reality, the same thing. Each is rooted in the beauty of God, in the reality of his character, and in the glory of his holiness.

In its confusion, the world wants to separate the good from the true, the true from the beautiful, and the beautiful from the good. In isolating and separating the transcendentals, the secular picture of the world becomes fractured and disoriented. Thus, this confusion can produce tragically problematic arguments for why the false may be beautiful, the ugly may be true, and evil may be good.

We understand the source of this confusion, of course. The Christian doctrine of sin, rooted directly in the Genesis account of the Fall, explains that the consequences of sin lead directly to this kind of disorientation and confusion.

Christians must resist the temptation to speak the truth in a manner that falls short of the good, the beautiful, and the true. We betray the truth when we speak of it with an ugly spirit, or attach it to base arguments or mean-spirited impulses. We must reunite what the secular world has divided and present Christian truth in all of its power, its beauty, and its goodness.

With all that in mind, how shall we approach issues related to homosexual marriage? I have grown increasingly convinced that most of our approaches focus on what homosexuals would have to rethink in order to see this issue with clarity and understand the error of their lifestyle and social agenda. We often assume that the real issue is what kind of people homosexuals would have to be in order to hear our message and receive its truth. While this is an important consideration, I am convinced that the more urgent challenge for the church is to clarify our own self-identity and our understanding of the gospel. What kind of people must *we* be, if we are to address the challenge of homosexual marriage with faithfulness and Christian love?

I would suggest seven principles that can serve as a framework for a Christian response to the challenge of homosexual marriage. Each of these is deeply rooted in biblical truth, and each is pointed to the challenge of addressing homosexuals with compassionate truth-telling.

1. *We, as Christians, must be the people who cannot start a conversation about homosexual marriage by talking about homosexual marriage.*

We simply cannot start with the issue of homosexual marriage. Instead, we must gain some conceptual altitude over this immediate question and understand the larger issues at stake. We must look at the big picture, and we must understand that starting with the issue of homosexual marriage will lead us nowhere, for we will have already surrendered the most critical issues at stake.

Working backwards from the immediate challenge of homosexual marriage, we have to ask some very basic questions, and we must find those answers in the theological resources of the Christian worldview. We must consider the purpose for which God created the entire universe. The Bible answers this question with clarity: the entire cosmos was created for the glory of God. Thus, we must reconceive every single question in terms of how God's glory will be most clearly manifested in his creation. Any moral question, any issue dealing with the good, the beautiful, and the true, will come back to the question of how God's glory is made visible in his creation. The end for which all things were made is the glory of God, and every atom and molecule of the universe is directed to God's glory. Every single creature, every inanimate object, and, most importantly, every single human being, was made for the glory of God.

We must understand that the right ordering of all things will be the order that demonstrates God's glory most profoundly in his creation. With that established, we can then work backwards from creation and understand that human dignity and the purpose of human life are rooted in the fact that we are made in the image of God. Alone of all creation, human beings bear the *imago Dei*. Theologians through the centuries have debated exactly what this means, but at the very least it means that human beings are alone able consciously to know and to glorify God.

The rest of creation also exists for God's glory, but the animals are completely unaware that they are created for that purpose. Human beings stand in an entirely different relation to this question, for we understand that God, in making us in his image, has invited us to know him and has commanded us to seek his glory.

This understanding of humanity stands in direct opposition to the materialistic naturalism that prevails in the secular world. The evolutionary worldview conceives all of life as a product of an accidental meeting of space, time, and energy. According to this worldview, human beings are nothing more than chemical machines whose greatest purpose is the replication of genes and the reproduction of the species. If this portrait of humanity is accurate, morality is nothing more than an artifact of the evolutionary process—habits that may lead to more efficient reproduction. This is a tragically reduced and corrupted view of human nature, but it stands at the foundation of the sexual revolution and the culture of moral relativism.

Genesis 2 will help us understand how God's glory is displayed in creation. Significantly, Adam did not declare his need for a mate, nor did he even understand his masculinity prior to God's act in revelation. It was the Lord God who said, "It is not good that the man should be alone; I will make him a helper fit for him" (Gen. 2:18). From this point, the text moves to the creation of woman—but not directly.

As Genesis 2 unfolds, the text moves from the Lord's declaration of Adam's need to a narrative about Adam's responsibility to name each of the creatures. Adam had the opportunity to review the animal kingdom in its entirety, "but for Adam there was not found a helper fit for him" (Gen. 2:20).

Only at this point are we told of the creation of the woman. The Lord God caused a deep sleep to fall upon Adam, and in the midst of his sleep he removed one of Adam's ribs and closed up its place with flesh. With this rib, the Lord God made the woman and brought her to Adam. Adam immediately recognized that this indeed was the perfect complement for him. "This at last is bone of my bones and flesh of my flesh; she shall be called Woman, because she was taken out of Man" (Gen. 2:23).

Significantly, it was the Creator who declared Adam's need for a complement—a "helper suitable for him." This was not the result of Adam's self-recognition. This was no dawning consciousness that came upon Adam; it was his Creator's declaration.

With the creation of Eve, humanity was completed and perfected in the distinction between male and female. Gender is a part of the goodness of God's creation. The distinction between male and female is not a matter of evolutionary differentiation nor mere social convention, but an essential component of God's purpose in creation. The Lord God has shown his glory in making a distinction between man and woman. Human beings cry out for completion and companionship. It is not good that we should be alone. We may come to this self-awareness, but our need was first declared by God, who made provision for us, not only in the gift of gender but in the institution of marriage. In Genesis 2, we have the absolute declaration of God's glory in the rightness, the perfection, and the complementarity of man and woman, male and female.

Moving on from Genesis 2, the Bible reveals a comprehensive understanding of human gender and sexuality. The institution of marriage stands at the center of this picture, and the family unit becomes the arena for God's glory to be displayed in the receiving and raising of children. The relationship between the man and the woman—even the authority of the husband in the institution of marriage—is affirmed throughout the text of Scripture. We are not self-defining creatures, nor are we autonomous moral agents. We are creatures who are fully accountable to our Creator. Our purpose is to display his glory, and we cannot discuss the issue of homosexual marriage without returning to this touchstone of creation, in order to be reminded about the very purpose of gender and the institution of marriage.

The perfect institution of marriage was revealed when the Lord God declared, "Therefore a man shall leave his father and his mother and hold fast to his wife, and they shall become one flesh" (Gen. 2:24). This one-flesh relationship is physiological, anatomical, emotional, and absolutely glorious. In the covenant of marriage, the man and the woman are drawn together so that there is completion—a picture of God's glory painted in miniature. This one-flesh relationship, solemnized and protected in the covenant of marriage, is the very foundation of human civilization. This is the nonnegotiable foundation of everything Christians understand about human life, sex, gender, and the entire complex of issues related to embodiment and sexuality. In reality, it's all there in Genesis 2.

With all this in mind, we can see genuine grandeur in the gift of gender. This gift brings a necessary awareness of our humility as human beings. As men, we must admit our need for a wife—the gift God gives us in a woman. Similarly, women must admit their need for a husband, and the necessary completion of their sexuality in the man. Even for men and women given the gift of celibacy, and for those who by other circumstances are unmarried, marriage remains the defining institution for understanding masculinity and femininity and the arena of human sexuality.

With marriage come many goods, privileges, and responsibilities. Of course, these include pleasure, protection, intimacy, and procreation. Each of these falls into its proper place as God's design for husband and wife comes together in covenantal fidelity. The female is drawn to the male, the man is drawn to the woman, and husband and wife are united in the holy covenant of marriage, living together and receiving all the goods of marriage even as they fulfill all of its responsibilities, until they are separated by death.

This stands at the very center of creation. Armed with God's revelation in the Bible, we have no excuse for failing to know this truth. As a biblical people, we are entrusted with the stewardship of this truth. Even for those without God's written revelation, general revelation—found in the very structure of creation and accessible to all persons—tells the story of God's intention in gender. It is surely no accident that every civilization has found its way to marriage—*heterosexual* marriage—as basic to the social structure. In a very real sense, marriage is the foundation of civilization.

Pitirim Sorokin, founder of the department of sociology at Harvard University, made very clear that marriage stands at the center of civilization and is what he called the "civilizational essential." Without marriage, no social structure larger than marriage can be sustained. There can be no community, no culture, no enduring patterns of human life. Even where there have been aberrations such as polygamy or other forms of wrongly construed marriage, these have been noteworthy precisely because they *are* aberrations, and because they have been culturally transient. None of these experiments has lasted through time. God's glory will be demonstrated one way or another, and the persistent and universal endurance of marriage has been a demonstration of God's glory throughout human experience.

*2. We must be the people who cannot ever talk about sex without talking about marriage.*

The moment Christians accept that we can talk about sex without talking about marriage, we abandon the high ground of the Christian worldview and surrender the question at stake. From the very beginning of every conversation about sex, we must emphasize that Christians cannot talk about sex without making clear its connection to marriage.

The moral credibility of the Christian church is very much at stake in the debate over homosexual marriage. If Christians allow a low estimation of marriage, and if we accept the breaking of marital vows and the violation of marital covenants, we destroy the very foundation of our moral capital in the debate over homosexual marriage.

We must hold to a culture of marriage because we know that God's glory is displayed in this institution and because we know the power of human sexuality. Sex is so powerful, and sexual desire is so easily corrupted, that we must point to marriage as the institution God has designed in order for sexuality to be enjoyed, appreciated, and fulfilled.

According to the Christian worldview, sex makes sense only within the context of marriage. Sex outside of marriage is an insult to the Creator's design and a display of human arrogance. Unsatisfied with God's provision for us in marriage, human sinfulness is displayed in our demand for autonomy—for our "rights" as creatures—and in our rejection of the Creator's purpose.

Marriage becomes the touchstone for our understanding of why sexual sins are so inherently sinful. We understand that adultery is sinful precisely because it robs God of his glory by desecrating a covenant made in his name. Marriage is intended to be a display of covenant fidelity, which points to the faithfulness of the Creator and the character of the covenant-making God. The New Testament goes so far as to present the relationship between Christ and his church in the metaphor of the bride and the bridegroom. Adultery is so abhorrent precisely because it lies about what covenant faithfulness is supposed to be.

Similarly, fornication (premarital sex) is understood to be sin precisely because, in this practice, the creature is demanding *a part* of what marriage represents while rejecting the entirety of the marital covenant. But God will not allow his good gifts to be separated.

Throughout the Bible, sexual sins are revealed in their inherent sinfulness precisely because each of these sins—whether incest, or bestiality, or homosexuality, or lust—is a desire for something less than God's completion in the covenant of marriage, and for something less than purity in our reception of God's gift.

Christians simply cannot talk about sex without talking about marriage. We are the people who have to talk about covenant faithfulness because we serve the covenant-making God. We must talk about male and female with constant reference to marriage. We must talk about the relationship between Christ and his church, the gifts of intimacy and fidelity, and the reality of order within the institution of marriage, simply because the Bible so clearly puts marriage at the center of human existence. A genuinely Christian response to the challenge of homosexual marriage would go back to marriage itself and to the gift of gender, demonstrating the rightness and the perfection of marriage as a picture in miniature of the kingdom of God. Every marriage, every domestic household, is to be a little picture of the kingdom of God in the right ordering of all things and in the creatures' grateful reception of the Creator's gifts. This little picture—this little domestic portrait that centers in the covenant of marriage—presents a picture more powerful than anything the world can ever distort. The existence of *just one faithful marriage* demonstrates the fatal falsity of any other ordering for human sexuality.

3. *We must be the people who cannot talk about anything of significance without acknowledging our absolute dependence upon God's revelation—the Bible.*

We must admit this right at the outset: Christians do not claim to be smart enough to figure out everything on their own. Without the Bible, we would be as lost and blind as anyone else. Had God not given us his gift of revelation, we would be utterly confused about sexuality and every other important dimension of life. Put bluntly, everything we know about sex we know from the Bible. The order of creation does give us a basic knowledge about gender, as well as pointers toward the institution of marriage. Nevertheless, the authoritative and perfected knowledge of these things is revealed only in the Bible. We cannot compete with secular specialists in terms of sexology. We do not approach these questions as secular anthropologists, sociologists, physicians, or psychologists. Our expertise is a biblical expertise, because our knowledge is a biblical knowledge.

The gift of God's revelation explains why Christians have something distinctive to say. Our particular expertise is established solely in our knowledge of what God has revealed in the Bible. We do not speak with authority on issues related to human sexuality because of our personal experience; nor can we base our claims upon scientific expertise, popular opinion, or sociology. Everything we know about love and marriage is a *revealed* knowledge.

The Bible contains not only incredible portraits of marriage as God's institution, it also includes teaching passages that set down specific commands and instructions related to sex and marriage. In humility, we must confess that we are not able to come up with the idea of marriage on our own; we are entirely dependent upon revelation. As the apostle Paul explained, the law is our teacher.

The order our Creator has placed within the universe is not merely an observable structure, however; it is also a structure of order and command. The Bible does not present humanity with a multiplicity of optional sexual lifestyles. Marriage is not presented as a multiple-choice equation or a puzzle to be assembled in accordance with individual desire. Instead, the Bible presents a mandate. Receiving God's revelation about marriage also requires that we admit our obligation to *obey* God's command.

Human sinfulness requires that we be protected from ourselves. The Bible's commands limit and constrain our sinful predilections. As the Lord said to Israel, "I have set before you life and death, blessing and curse. Therefore choose life, that you and your offspring may live" (Deut. 30:19).

In Scripture, we are given a clear understanding of how God's glory is to be displayed in creation. In particular, we are shown how marriage is to function in the coming together of the man and the woman in a holy covenant that protects our health, our holiness, and our wholeness, even as it displays God's glory. Thankfully, human beings are not left to devise our own sexual codes and relational structures. We have been addressed by our Creator in the Holy Scriptures, and, in the end, the only choice is between obedience and disobedience.

The Bible's verdict on homosexuality is clear and unequivocal. Though revisionist scholars have done their very best to turn the biblical text on its head and to undermine its authority, the Scripture resolutely resists such reductionism and rejection. Homosexual advocates have attempted various interpretive maneuvers in order to subvert the plain teaching of Scripture. Some have gone so far as to argue that the sin of Sodom and Gomorrah was not homosexuality but inhospitality (a claim effectively rejected in Jude 7). Others have argued that the apostle Paul's clear teaching about homosexuality in Romans chapter 1 has nothing to do with homosexuality as it is experienced today. They insist that Paul, who condemned homosexuality in no uncertain terms, simply had no conception of our modern "discovery" of sexual orientation and committed homosexual partnerships. Others have argued that Paul's warnings in 1 Corinthians 6:9-10 related only to those who would commit homosexual rape or would force nonconsensual sexual acts.

Our task is simply to allow the text to speak. There can be no question that the Bible comprehensively and candidly identifies homosexual acts—and even homosexual desire—as sin. Put plainly, if the Bible does not speak clearly to the issue of homosexuality, it does not speak clearly to anything. Constrained by Scripture, Christians must be the people who speak this truth with compassionate honesty.

Like Paul, our concern must be to see all sinners—including homosexual sinners—come to terms with the awful reality of their sin, and then turn in repentance to embrace the grace of God through the gospel of Jesus Christ. Listen to the urgency of Paul's warning: "Do you not know that the unrighteous will not inherit the kingdom of God? Do not be deceived: neither the sexually immoral, nor idolaters, nor adulterers, nor men who practice homosexuality, nor thieves, nor the greedy, nor drunkards, nor revilers, nor swindlers will inherit the kingdom of God" (1 Cor. 6:9-10). Could there be a more direct warning than this? Can we doubt Paul's urgent concern for those trapped in these sins? We must model his courage in declaring this truth without compromise or evasion.

Speaking about homosexuality, Paul was as candid as the language of his day would allow—even using the terms related to both the active and the passive participants in homosexual acts. Paul was not telling the Corinthians what they wanted to hear. His message was as politically incorrect in the context of first-century Graeco-Roman culture as our biblical worldview is politically incorrect today.

Paul's concern is a gospel concern, for he urgently desires to see sinners saved by the grace of the Lord Jesus Christ and transformed by the power of God. He warns that those who give themselves to such sins will not inherit the kingdom of God.

We must note that homosexuality is not the only sin identified in this text. As in Romans 1, Paul's point is the universality of human sinfulness. But we sin in the particular rather than in the general, and these catalogs of specific sins are necessary so that we would see ourselves and our sin in the mirror of God's Word.

Some Christians find homosexuality more *distasteful* than sinful. Too many Christians try to deal with the issue of homosexuality by dismissing it with disgust. Leon Kass, chairman of the President's Council on Bioethics, is a major moral philosopher of our times. He describes what he calls the "yuck factor" as an attitude of disgust that lacks any substantial moral argument. The "yuck factor" is an interesting observation about the public mind, but it is implausible and unhelpful as a moral principle. Christians must go beyond mere disgust and point with gospel passion to the objective biblical truth about the sinfulness of homosexuality. We cannot trust the "yuck factor" because human beings have demonstrated time and again that we can overcome any amount of disgust if we are determined to rationalize misbehavior. The fallen human mind is a moral computer of infinite rationalization, a fact that underlines again why we are so utterly dependent upon the authority of Scripture.

I was thirteen years old when I first heard the word *homosexual*. I heard it on the radio during a lunchtime news report while staying at my grandparents' home. Paul Harvey simply used the word in the course of his reporting. As a thirteen-year-old boy, I didn't know what a homosexual was, and my curiosity was immediately aroused.

After lunch, I asked my grandfather, a kind and generous-hearted man—but a man of few words—to tell me what a homosexual was. He responded, "Boy, if you ever use that word again, you won't sit down for a week—you understand me?"

Well, I understood that I had asked the wrong person to answer that question! But of course, his non-answer simply increased my curiosity. Thankfully, my father, a wonderful Christian man who took it as his responsibility to speak plainly and succinctly to a thirteen-year-old, described to me in simple terms what homosexuality was all about. My father based his argument and explanation on the Bible. I trusted my father, but I trusted his trust in the Bible even more.

Where would we be if we did not have the Bible? As Paul tells us in Romans 2, we cannot trust our conscience. Corrupted by sin, the conscience arbitrarily excuses and condemns us in a continuous cycle of rationalization and self-deception. Even though the law of God is written in the structure of the universe, we have corrupted that knowledge and we no longer see what was so evident in Eden.

We cannot say anything of significance about homosexual marriage or anything else without absolute dependence on the Bible. Do we acknowledge legal, sociological, anthropological, cultural, political, and various other dimensions to this issue? Of course we do. Nevertheless, everything we understand about human sexuality is directly derived from the knowledge God has given us in the Bible. The Reformation principle of *sola Scriptura* applies even to sex.

4. *We must be the people with a theology adequate to explain the deadly deception of sexual sin.*

The church of the Lord Jesus Christ, standing on the authority of Scripture, must have a theology adequate to explain how God's glory can be so pervasively denied and how God's design can be so utterly corrupted as it is in the advocacy of homosexual marriage. How is it that humans miss this point so entirely?

In reality, there is only one sufficient explanation for sexual brokenness, and this is the very essence of sin. In Genesis 3, the Bible presents the truth of the Fall and its consequences. Sin is the one category indispensable to our explanation of the human problem. We cannot possibly reach a correct diagnosis of the human condition without getting to the very heart of what sin is and what sin means.

In Romans 1, Paul describes human sinfulness as an effort to suppress the truth in unrighteousness (v. 18). Thus, at the center of human sinfulness is an ambition to rob God of his glory and to hide the truth from ourselves, even as we give ourselves to lawlessness and moral anarchy.

As Paul sees it, the human race is involved in a massive exercise of self-deception, suppressing the truth and hiding it even from ourselves. We are all without excuse in this, says Paul, because God has revealed his laws even in the very structure of the universe (vv. 19-21). Nevertheless, "Claiming to be wise, they became fools, and exchanged the glory of the immortal God for images resembling mortal man and birds and animals and reptiles" (Rom. 1:22-23). Rather than accept the truth, we have exchanged the glory of God for various forms of idolatry.

As Paul makes clear, God's verdict is devastating:

> Therefore God gave them up in the lusts of their hearts to impurity, to the dishonoring of their bodies among themselves, because they exchanged the truth about God for a lie and worshiped and served the creature rather than the Creator, who is blessed forever! Amen. For this reason God gave them up to dishonorable passions. For their women

exchanged natural relations for those that are contrary to nature; and
the men likewise gave up natural relations with women and were consumed with passion for one another, men committing shameless acts
with men and receiving in themselves the due penalty for their error.
(Rom. 1:24-27)

Can there be any doubt that this text speaks precisely about homosexuality? As a matter of fact, this important text speaks not only about
the sinfulness of homosexual acts, but about the corrupted nature of
homosexual desire. The language about women who "exchanged natural relations for those that are contrary to nature" and "men likewise,"
who "gave up natural relations with women and were consumed with
passion for one another," indicates that homosexual desire is itself a per-
version of the divine intention.

The devastating nature of God's righteous verdict on human sinfulness is made clear with specific reference to the sexual sins detailed in
this text. The formula repeated three times in this text (plus v. 28), "God
gave them up," is one of the most chilling words of judgment anywhere
in the Bible. The utter finality of this formula stands as an irrefutable verdict on the nature of homosexuality.

This text should not function as an intellectual "trump card" for
Christians to use in argument, but rather as a foundation for revealing
the universal and pervasive sinfulness of humanity. Paul's purpose is to
show that our human rebellion against God is the very essence of sin,
and according to Romans 1, homosexuality is the chief illustration of
that truth. Rebelling against God's design for sexuality is the primary
exhibit of human sinfulness in action.

Again, we must acknowledge that homosexuality is not the only sin
listed by Paul in this important chapter. As a matter of fact, Paul follows
with a catalog of human sinfulness that encompasses all of us. By the
time he mentions gossips, slanderers, haters of God, the insolent, the
haughty, and the boastful, much less those disobedient to parents (vv.
29-30), he has included every single human being who ever lived. When
speaking to homosexuals about the truth of God revealed in this passage, we must make clear that it not only indicts homosexuals for the
sin of homosexuality, but every other sinner for every sin ever committed. Nevertheless, the specific reference to homosexuality here helps us

understand the depth of sexual brokenness and sexual sin. We dare not miss this point or ignore Paul's message.

An important dimension of Paul's argument deals with the issue of idolatry. It is worth noting that the specific forms of idolatry common to the Graeco-Roman world, and to other ancient cultures, centered in exaggerations of human sexuality and fertility. A quick look at most museums of antiquity will reveal cases filled with figurines characterized by exaggerated genitalia. Many are explicitly pornographic, as the power of sex has been transformed into an idol and object of worship. This is an insight of inestimable theological significance.

When Christians address homosexuals and homosexual advocates with the reality that the Bible clearly condemns homosexual behavior as sin, we must acknowledge that we are sexual sinners speaking to other sexual sinners. Armed with the Bible's profound understanding of human sinfulness, we understand that sin corrupts every dimension of human existence. The doctrine of total depravity affirms that the entire human being—including sexual desire and the emotions—is utterly corrupted and disoriented by sin and its consequences.

Christians have often sinned against homosexuals by arguing that homosexuality is simply a "chosen" form of behavior and lifestyle. Clearly, participation in homosexual behavior is a matter of choice, but the underlying desire is often not experienced by homosexuals as a matter of choice at all.

The biblical understanding of sin helps us to understand that every human being is a sexual sinner and every profile of individual desire is corrupted by sin's effects. Even as our bodies show the effects of sin as we age, decay, and die, our affections show the corruption of sin because we desire what should not be desired. The church of the Lord Jesus Christ must stand before the world and acknowledge that we often do not even understand our own desires and inclinations.

When speaking of homosexuality, we must acknowledge that the pattern of male and female homosexuality is often different. We must understand that female homosexuality is often directly traceable to the misbehavior of men. Males have often acted toward women with such violence, anger, and rejection that they can no longer trust men to meet their needs for intimacy.

Is a woman who resorts to lesbianism for such reasons responsible for her sin? Of course she is, but we must understand that all of us are inclined to lie to ourselves as we rationalize our misbehavior. This is true not only for homosexuals but for all human beings. As a matter of fact, sin is so deceptive that we no longer even understand *why* we desire *what* we desire. The Scripture clearly identifies lesbianism as sin, but we must understand that this pattern of sin often follows an experience of sin at the hands of others. This does not excuse the sinner, but it helps us to understand why this sin can become such a deeply rooted part of an individual's self-understanding.

Male homosexuality is usually a very different reality. The male sex drive—more essentially physical and genital—can be corrupted in so many different ways. There is no man who will be able to stand before God on the Day of Judgment and say, "I was only interested and aroused by righteous and holy desire." Each of us is a sexual sinner, and the male pattern of sexual sin includes corrupted desire, confusing arousal, and perverse thoughts.

No man, not even the most committed heterosexual husband, will be able to say on the Day of Judgment, "My sexual affections, my sexual arousal, was always, from the very beginning, only directly toward that which was holy—the covenant of marriage and the wife that I was given." Every man struggles with a corrupted affection, and that corrupted affection, given the reality of the male sex drive, is often directed toward a desire for fulfillment entirely at odds with the glory of God. Every man bears a different sexual struggle, but every man is engaged in a sexual struggle, and this should give us an attitude of sympathy as we address homosexuals with the truth.

When homosexuals say, "I did not choose this," they are often speaking the only truth they know. The homosexual movement tells homosexuals that their arousal is their destiny. This is a slander against God. We must learn not to trust our sinful affections and erotic interests, but to submit all of this to the objective authority of God's Word. By God's grace, we must all come before the throne of Christ and pray that God will order our affections, our passions, and our erotic interests to his glory. We must say that to ourselves, even as we say it to the homosexual. All of us stand under the same need for forgiveness and with the same accountability before our Creator. We must not sin against our homosexual neighbors by describing their pattern of sin as something they have arbitrarily chosen in terms of desire. We must declare God's verdict that every single homosexual act is sin and that homosexual desire is itself sinful, but we must speak with compassionate honesty even as we seek to understand this reality.

*5. We must be the people with a theology adequate to explain Christ's victory over sin.*

If we must begin with a theology adequate to explain the deadly deception of sin, we must also present a theology adequate to explain Christ's victory over sin. By the grace of God, we are not left where Romans 1 ends. The Bible presents the transforming grace of God as demonstrated, accomplished, and applied through the cross of our Lord Jesus Christ.

After Paul had reviewed his catalog of sin and warned that those who give themselves to such sins will not inherit the kingdom of God, he turned to the church and reminded Christians, "Such were some of you. But you were washed, you were sanctified, you were justified in the name of the Lord Jesus Christ and by the Spirit of our God" (1 Cor. 6:11).

This text declares that Christians, saved by the grace of God, are those who have come out of these patterns of sin, who have been justified, and whom the Holy Spirit progressively conforms to the image of the Lord Jesus Christ.

This message of transformation by the grace of God—the presentation of atonement and redemption in full biblical glory—stands in stark contrast to the message homosexuals are given by the secular world. Therapists, sexologists, physiologists, and sociologists say to homosexuals, "This is who you are. Just claim your identity as a homosexual man or woman and press for full rights in the normalization of your lifestyle." Psychologists and psychiatrists have removed homosexuality from lists of mental disorders, effectively normalizing homosexuality in the human experience.

Christians have no right to excise homosexuality from the Bible, but our ultimate purpose is to move from the diagnosis of sin to the power of the gospel. We are the people who know that Christ has won the victory. The church is the redeemed people of God who understand that God's redeeming love, made manifest in the cross of Jesus Christ, offers genuine transformation, reconciliation, and the forgiveness of sins. The substitutionary nature of Christ's atonement affirms that Christ has paid the penalty for sin in full, suffering and dying in the place of sinners, and his accomplished work is the very foundation for our confidence as we promise salvation and healing to those who will call on Christ's name.

The God of the Bible is not only clear in judgment, but powerful to save. The church must declare without reservation the Bible's doctrine of regeneration. This is not a self-help program or a mere sexual recovery program—it is a comprehensive program of transformation as the dead are made alive. The old things have passed away even as all things become new. Christians alone have a theology adequate to explain this.

While we proclaim the gospel's saving and transforming power, of course, we must also acknowledge that sin has enduring consequences, even in this life. An analogy might be useful at this point. Consider a man who has sinned by driving under the influence of alcohol. One night, sinfully drunk and recklessly irresponsible, this man drives right into a wall at high speed. His body is broken, but his life is saved as he is taken to the hospital and receives emergency treatment. He recovers from the accident, but he will forever walk with a limp.

Let us follow this man as he comes to faith in Christ. The grace of God transforms him, reordering his affections as he gains victory over alcoholism. Regeneration has produced a new man. "The old has passed away; behold, the new has come" (2 Cor. 5:17)—but he still walks with a limp.

That limp does not disqualify him from displaying the glory of God. As a matter of fact, he may see his limp as an opportunity for witness: "I want to tell you who I was in order to tell you who I now am by the grace of God. You see, this limp is a part of my story. It's an important part of how I came to know the Lord Jesus Christ and how he changed my life."

In reality, every one of us limps. Throughout our lives, until the day of our glorification, every one of us will limp. We must look to the moment of our future glorification (Rom. 8:30) as the moment of our release from every limp. On that day, every tear will be wiped away, every injury will be fully restored, everything will be made right, and everything will be made whole. Everything and every redeemed person will then perfectly display the glory of God. We are the people with a theology adequate to explain this, and thus we can offer a sin-sick world the only genuine means of personal transformation.

We know better than to say that people cannot change. We also know better than to believe that people can change themselves. As Jonathan Edwards made clear, we sin in our affections, and we do not even understand why we love the things we love and desire the things we desire. This is why we are so dependent on the work of Christ in our lives and the continuing work of the Holy Spirit in reordering our affections. This is no easy process, but it is real and it is enduring.

Is our purpose to make homosexuals into heterosexuals? The answer to that question must be both yes and no. We must urge all sinners to repent and abandon their sin, but convincing homosexuals to think of themselves as heterosexuals is not the same thing as salvation. We must show homosexuals their need for salvation and transformation. We can promise that this power of transformation will, by God's grace, lead to a reordering of their lives, and we must also explain that it will require a turning away from the sins of their past.

I want to speak honestly to those who are struggling with homosexual affection. You must know that this is sin, and you must recognize that your affections are corrupted by sin. Like all of us, you are a sinner in the midst of a sinful world, but don't let anyone tell you that you can't change. Becoming heterosexual is not salvation, but the miracle of regeneration and sanctification will produce, by God's grace, the right affections in your heart. Knowing what God has declared to be objectively right and objectively wrong, we must direct ourselves—whether our sinful sexual profile be heterosexual or homosexual—toward the objective glory of God as revealed in his Word. We must claim the promises of God and seek God's glory in every dimension of our being.

Do we want homosexuals to find heterosexuality? Yes, as much as we want liars to become tellers of the truth and adulterers to be faithful; as much as we want the disobedient to become obedient and the proud to be humble. Thankfully, God provides for us even what he requires of us. The grace to be humble is given to the proud, *if* the proud heart leans only on Christ. Similarly, the grace to fulfill God's purposes for human sexuality will be given even to those who find their hearts full of sinful sexual desires. By the grace of Christ, homosexuals and heterosexuals alike can be transformed so that we actually begin to desire what God wills for us to desire.

This is what the church is all about. We are the people who gather together to exult in the grace of God and to proclaim the cross of the Lord Jesus Christ as the answer to human sinfulness. We come together to hold each other accountable to the Word of God and to rejoice in what God is doing in us until the very day that we die. We come together in the assurance of the resurrection and glorification that is to come. Like the apostle Paul, we are convinced that "he who began a good work in [us] will bring it to completion at the day of Jesus Christ" (Phil. 1:6).

*6. We must be the people who love homosexuals more than homosexuals love homosexuality.*

This is a tough challenge. We have to be the people who, because we are possessed by a passion to see God's glory in his creation, love homosexuals more than they love their sin. This means that our love has to be tenacious. This will also require that we come to know and establish relationships with those struggling with homosexuality. Armed with an awareness of both the problem and God's provision, we have no right to believe that homosexuals are beyond the grace of God or that any individual is beyond the hope of redemption and transformation.

Every sinner loves his sin, but the church must love sinners more than sinners love their sinfulness. This is precisely how Christ has loved us, and we must love other sinners even as Christ has loved us.

We cannot allow a homosexual to reduce his identity to being a homosexual. We live in an age of identity politics when people say, "What I do in my sex life is who I am—period!" We are the people who know that this is nonsense. Sex is a part of who we are—a vitally important and powerful part—but it is only a part of the total human being. Our sexual desires and sexual practices are genuine pointers to our inner reality and our relationship to God, but sexuality is not the end of the story.

Christians must be the people who refuse to put the period at the end of the sexual sentence. We cannot allow homosexuals to be isolated as a class of persons who are beyond the grace of God and exist in some special category of human sinfulness. We must be the people who say to homosexuals, "I am going to love you even more than you love your sin, because in this same way I was loved until I came to know the Lord Jesus Christ. Someone loved me more than I loved my sin, and this is how I came to know my Savior."

Our doctrine of salvation must be accompanied by a strong doctrine of the church. The *ecclesia*—the purchased people of God—are a covenanted community gathered in mutual accountability to the Word of God. In the bonds of Christ, we are to love each other even more than we love ourselves. Even in the process of church discipline, our purpose is not only to protect the integrity of the people of God but to love persons into obedience and conformity with the Word of God. The common life of the church is really all about this mutual accountability, mutual encouragement, and exhorting each other to faithfulness to the authority of God's Word. The church sins when we deal with these issues wrongly, unscripturally, and superficially.

It is easy to detect a sense of fatigue setting in among Christians in America who are tired of arguing, debating, and speaking the truth about homosexuality in the midst of a fallen and rebellious culture. This may be an understandable response to the difficulty of our task, but it is also evidence of sin. We are now coming to a point of cultural crisis, and the church is called to faithfulness as we declare God's truth with a boldness never summoned before. The church must demonstrate even *more candor, more courage, and more truth-telling.* We must demonstrate more genuine compassion as we reach out to a civilization that is literally falling from within. Even as civilization falls, the church of the Lord Jesus Christ must stand as the people of God, determined to keep its wits as it shows the love of God and seeks the glory of Jesus Christ, in season and out of season.

*7. We must be the people who tell the truth about homosexual marriage and thus refuse to accept even its possibility because we love and seek the glory of God for all.*

We must love homosexuals so much that we refuse to accept the very concept of homosexual marriage. The normalizing of homosexual behavior through the radical reformulation of marriage will take the sinfulness of homosexuality to a new level of moral rebellion. God's glory demonstrated through marriage and the covenant that he created will be corrupted so utterly that idolatry will be institutionalized and the truth will be suppressed in radical unrighteousness.

Why is the issue of marriage so preeminent in the biblical worldview? Why is marriage an issue of such urgent attention? It is so preeminent and so urgent simply because marriage as God intended and established it is a norm that declares to all creation that *everything* else falls short of God's intention. Compared to the divine standard of marriage, every disordered sexual passion is revealed to be disordered. Therefore, if your ambition is to normalize sexual misbehavior, you must "denormalize" marriage. So long as it remains the norm, the institution of marriage represents the repudiation of every sinful sexual lifestyle. It stands as a monument to the only right ordering of human sexuality and relatedness.

For the Christian church, marriage is far more than a legal contract, a matter of constitutional interpretation, or a political or sociological issue of debate. It is a deeply *theological* matter.

We have no guarantee that this culture will not crumble or that this society will somehow find a way to apply brakes to our headlong rush into moral rebellion. Nevertheless, our love of neighbor as commanded by Christ must compel us to do all within our power to assure that marriage is recognized in this culture as God intended and designed it to be.

In the end, the church may be the last people on earth who really know what marriage is. This knowledge of marriage may in fact become one of the missiological manifestations of the church in this fallen world.

Should we have political, cultural, legal, sociological, and constitutional concerns about the concept of homosexual marriage? Of course we should, and we should engage these issues in public debate in a way that demonstrates Christian candor and genuine understanding. But we can win the political and constitutional battles and still lose the war. Our greatest concern must be spiritual and theological, not political and procedural.

The church must gather its wits, summon its convictions, and speak the truth about marriage before a fallen world. We must exult in marriage, even as we winsomely, happily, humbly, and honestly point to marriage as the metaphor of Christ's relationship to his church. We must bear witness to God's love in the right ordering of marriage as husbands and wives come together in purity, giving themselves devotedly to each other and lovingly receiving all the gifts God intended in marriage.

Christian couples must also recognize that our marriages are crucial tests of Christian discipleship, even as others denigrate marriage as a mere cultural contrivance. We must demonstrate God's glory as we raise our children to admire marriage and to aim themselves for sexual purity and the eager embrace of marriage as God's gift. The happiest people on earth should be Christians, who find their happiness in receiving God's gifts, and who can point to marriage as a paramount display of the glory of God. As the bride of Christ, the church cannot fail to speak courageously and eagerly about marriage without forfeiting our own identity and insulting our Savior. We must be the people who by God's grace know what marriage is and why it matters.

We must be the people who cannot talk about homosexual marriage simply by talking about homosexual marriage. We must be the people who cannot talk about sex without talking about marriage, and the people who cannot talk about anything of substance or significance without dependence on the Bible. We must be the people who have a theology adequate to explain the deadly deception of sin, as well as a theology adequate to explain Christ's victory over sin. We must be honest about sin as the denial of God's glory, even as we point to redemption as the glory of God restored. We must be the people who love homosexuals more than homosexuals love homosexuality, and we must be the people who tell the truth about homosexual marriage and refuse to accept even its conceptual possibility, because we know what is at stake.

May the church of the Lord Jesus Christ be led by our Savior to be faithful in the face of this great challenge.

# Part 3: Men and Sex

# CHAPTER 6

## Sex and the Single Man

MARK DEVER, MICHAEL LAWRENCE, MATT SCHMUCKER, SCOTT CROFT[1]

A merican men are spending a greater percentage of their lives single. There are many reasons for this, including divorce and longer life spans. Yet more and more men are also choosing to delay marriage. The median age at first marriage for a man has risen sharply from a low of just under 23 in 1960 to its current high of over 27 in 2004.[2]

This lengthened period of singleness brings great challenges to Christian men as they seek to live for the glory of Jesus Christ. In this chapter, we will consider a theological foundation for sex, some practical reflections on physical intimacy, and then suggestions for a biblical relationship between a man and a woman prior to marriage.

### Singleness
#### MARK DEVER

The first thing to say about sex and the single man is, there should be none! If you are not married, the Bible clearly teaches that you should refrain from any sexual contact. Sex should not be experienced outside of marriage.

Sadly, heeding the Bible's instruction is becoming more and more of a problem in our day, not only because people are marrying later, but

---

[1] At the time of writing, the four authors have been married for 22, 14, 16, and 5 years, respectively, and so bring the experience of both singleness and marriage to the topic of this chapter.
[2] U. S. Census Bureau, "Estimated Median Age at First Marriage, by Sex: 1890–Present," http://www.census.gov.

because our culture values marriage less and less. A recent Associated Press report said that people decreasingly view "marriage" as an indicator of adulthood. Researchers have

> found that completing an education was most valued with 73 percent of those surveyed calling it an "extremely important" step in achieving adulthood.
>
> The remainder of the transitions followed: being employed full-time, 61 percent; supporting a family, 60 percent; being financially independent, 47 percent; living independently of parents, 29 percent; and being married, 19 percent . . .
>
> Those younger than 30 were the least likely to rank being married or having children as important criteria for being an adult.
>
> Grant Lammersen, a 27-year-old San Franciscan, said it's true that his generation feels less pressure to get married and have kids—perhaps, he said, because so many of their parents are divorced.
>
> "I don't think those factors are important in defining yourself as an adult," said Lammersen, who is single and works in commercial real estate.
>
> When it comes to marriage and even buying a house, he said, "There's more of an attitude that 'It'll happen when it happens.'"[3]

If you are a single man, it is worth asking yourself, do you have an "It'll happen when it happens" attitude? Is this a Christian attitude? Is it indicative of what God calls Christian men to be?

Of course, not all unmarried men are single for the same reason, or have the same outlook on their singleness. Some men have been married, but in God's mysterious providence, either through death or divorce, they are now single again. If this describes you, you may thank God that he has given you whatever joys you have known through marriage in the past. You may be content in being single again, or you may desire to remarry. And of course, biblically, you may or may not be free to remarry.

Other single men have never been married, and some of these men have been called to a life of singleness (1 Cor. 7:7-8). If this describes you, we praise God for you and your selfless service, and we pray that your local church is serving as your family. Other single men have never been married, but they want to marry. Every such man's calling now is to

---

[3] Martha Irvine, "New Survey Says Americans Put Adulthood at Age 26," *Associated Press*, Chicago, May 8, 2003.

remain sexually pure, to grow in godliness, and to actively pursue marriage. If you desire to be married, do not just wait until it "happens." Your role is not passive. If you are not called to celibacy, get married!

Of course, the desire to be married is no guarantee that it will happen. And for that, I have no great answer. If you find that your efforts toward marriage remain unfulfilled, I can simply tell you that we have a loving God, and that he calls us all to be fruitful in whatever state we are in right now. We are to serve him with whatever he gives us: "Each one should use whatever gift he has received to serve others, faithfully administering God's grace in its various forms" (1 Pet. 4:10, NIV). Ultimately, our object of satisfaction—whether single or married—should not be our spouse; it should be Christ. There will be no single Christians in heaven. It says in Revelation, "One . . . spoke to me, saying, 'Come, I will show you the Bride, the wife of the Lamb.' And he carried me away in the Spirit to a great, high mountain, and showed me the holy city Jerusalem coming down out of heaven from God, having the glory of God" (21:9-11). Christian reader, we will all be married to Christ on that day! In the meantime, single men must learn to live out their sexuality in a way that prepares them for that ultimate wedding day.

## A Theology of Sex
### MICHAEL LAWRENCE

As we explore the topic of sex and the single man, we need to begin by establishing a theology of sex. Now, when you think of sex, theology is probably not the next thing that comes to mind. Morality might come to mind, or a list of do's and don'ts. After all, sex is an activity, and whether you are a Christian or not, your sexual activity is going to be governed by some set of moral rules. As we have already said, the biblical standard for your sexual behavior is that sexual intercourse is reserved for the marriage relationship that exists exclusively between one man and one woman so long as they both live (cf. Gen. 2:24; Ex. 20:14; Lev. 20:10; Mark 10:6-12; 1 Cor. 6:12–7:9).

The problem is not that men—whether single or married, Christian or non-Christian—do not understand this standard or are unaware of it. The problem is that too many of us do not live up to it. Why? Well, on the one hand, our culture finds this standard hopelessly antiquated and unreasonable, and many of us have been influenced by our culture. Our culture reasons that such restrictions on personal pleasure and freedom might have made sense before the advent of birth control or the ability of women to support children on their own. In those days, sex was the prize that women controlled, and the only way to win it was through the commitment of marriage. A *quid pro quo* was in place: the privilege of sex in return for the promise to provide and protect. But in our day and age, the argument runs, why should sex be quarantined on the reservation of marriage? The ill effects of sex outside of marriage can be dealt with painlessly, so why should two consenting adults not feel free to enjoy something that is obviously pleasurable and good? Besides, it's cheaper than dinner and a movie, and loads more fun.

On the other hand, our bodies agree with our culture's assessment. So even as Christian men, we engage in all sorts of physical intimacy with women, from "making out" to "hooking up" and everything in between. Often, we justify our sexual activity on the basis of the commitment level of the relationship. The more commitment that is present in the relationship, the more sexually involved we allow ourselves to be. One of the most common things I hear in pre-marriage counseling is couples saying they managed to refrain from physical activity until they got engaged. At that point, all the internal restraint they had felt suddenly disappeared, and they found themselves struggling—sometimes failing—to stay out of bed.

Have we misunderstood God's standard? Does increasing commitment legitimize increasing levels of sexual intimacy even outside of marriage?

This is precisely where a theology of sex becomes important, and a theology of sex requires far more than a list of do's and don'ts. As it turns out, sex is not the arbitrary reward you get for getting married, and sexual intimacy is not tied to a sliding scale of commitment. Rather, sex has a God-given theological meaning and purpose that transcends "my" experience and opinions about it.

According to the first chapter of Genesis, God created men and women in his own image. "So God created man in his own image, in the image of God he created him; male and female he created them" (Gen. 1:27). What this means is spelled out in the following verses. Like God, men and women are to exercise dominion over the earth; they are to be creative as they bring order and productivity to God's creation. They are

also to live in fruitful relationship with one another. This is the clear implication of God's command to "be fruitful and increase in number" (Gen.
1:28, NIV). The point is made even more explicitly in Genesis 2. In the
middle of God's perfect creation, God plants a garden, literally a paradise
(vv. 1-14). Then God places the man he has made in this paradise of par-
adises and gives him a task (v. 15). He commands the man to tend and
protect this garden. Almost immediately after he gives the man this basic
calling for his life, God declares for the first time that something is not
good: It is not good for the man to be alone (v. 18). So God creates
woman and brings her to the man. And the man is no longer alone. Adam
takes one look at Eve and says, "This at last is bone of my bones and flesh
of my flesh" (Gen. 2:23). We then learn that we are witnessing the first
marriage, as Adam and Eve are united and become one flesh (v. 24).

The Bible teaches us that marriage is a covenant that establishes a
relationship between a man and a woman who have no natural obligations to each other, as a parent and child have, but who voluntarily take
on the permanent obligations and commitments of a family relationship.
Before two individuals marry, they are not related; they are not one flesh.
But in marriage, those two individuals voluntarily become related in a
union so close, intimate, and permanent, that the only language for it is
the language of the family, the language of flesh and blood. Our ability
to form this kind of covenant relationship is part of what it means to be
created in the image of God. Just as Christ is united to his people in such
a way that he is the head and the church is his body (Eph. 5:23, 30), so
God created us to reflect his image as we relate to another person in a
covenantal one-flesh union. To be one flesh does not mean to become
one person. A husband and wife remain distinct people. But it does mean
that as a result of the covenant of marriage, a husband now relates to
his wife as if she were a part of his own body, caring for her and protecting her just as he cares for and protects himself.

Now if marriage is a covenant, then that covenant must have a sign,
something that makes visible the invisible reality of this one-flesh union.
This is the way all covenants work in the Bible. When God covenants
with all of creation not to destroy the world again by flood, he puts the
rainbow in the sky as a sign. When God covenants with repenting sinners in the New Covenant, he gives us the sign of baptism, in which he
visibly portrays the invisible reality of our being buried with Christ,

being cleansed from sin, and being raised to newness of life in Christ. And so it is with the covenant of marriage. Once married, a man relates to every other woman in the world as if she were his sister or his mother—people you do not have sex with. He relates to this one woman as his wife, uniting to her in a one-flesh relationship of mutual love, loyalty, and intimacy. The sign of that unique covenant relationship is the physical act of becoming one flesh in sexual intercourse.

What this means is that the intimacy and pleasure of sex is not the reward we receive for getting married. That would be like saying baptism is the reward we receive for becoming a Christian. No, sex is the sign of the marriage covenant itself. And to engage in sex is to call God as witness to hold us accountable for our covenantal commitment. So regardless of whether it makes sense to our culture or to our bodies to reserve sex for marriage, and regardless of whatever lesser commitments we have made to a woman, as Christians we must realize that having sex outside of marriage makes a mockery of the covenant God instituted and to which he is witness.

The rest of this chapter will be spent explaining what this means for men, and specifically for single men. But let me make two observations at the outset.

## Sexual Intimacy and Relational Commitment

To begin with, as I mentioned above, many assume that sexual intimacy and relational commitment are connected on a sliding scale, in which the greater the commitment, the greater the liberty a couple has to engage in physical intimacy. You can see this in Fig. 6.1, "Typical Slope of Physical Intimacy," where the slope of intimacy gradually increases from no physical intimacy all the way to intercourse as commitment levels increase from no commitment to the ultimate commitment of marriage. Of course, Christians are more likely to follow the lower dotted line, in which intimacy is delayed longer. And these days, non-Christians are more likely to move much more quickly to intimacy, as the top dotted line indicates.

Yet if sexual intimacy is the sign of the marriage covenant itself, rather than the reward for increasing levels of commitment, then the graph should look more like Fig. 6.2, "Biblical Slope of Physical Intimacy," in which the line moves in one big step, from the physical intimacy that is appropriate with a sister/mother to the physical intimacy that is appropriate with a wife. After all, every woman a man is in relationship with is either one or the other. Biblically speaking, there is no in-between area here, where a woman is sort-of-a-sister, or sort-of-a-wife.

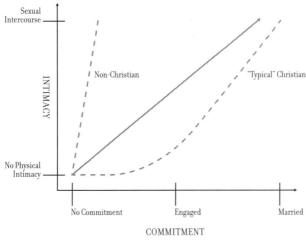

Fig. 6.1

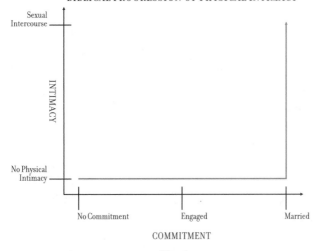

Fig. 6.2

Now I expect some readers are wondering, "Are you saying couples should refrain from kissing or holding hands until married?" I am not trying to draw a new set of boundaries that should not be crossed. That misses the point. Rather, I am suggesting that all of us need to rethink the purpose and meaning of physical intimacy between a man and a woman, and I think the best way I can make this point is to look at it practically, from the other side of the marriage vows. All of the things that dating couples engage in physically, short of intercourse, married couples engage in too. The only difference is that the married couple has a name for this activity. They call it foreplay. So while the unmarried couple console themselves by saying, "This is okay, because it is not sex," the married couple says, "This is great, because it is part of sex." The fact is, God not only created sexual intercourse, he created all the things that lead up to sexual intercourse too. And they are all linked together. Foreplay is a one-way on-ramp onto the highway of sexual intercourse. In our cars, we are not meant to slow down on an on-ramp, and we are not meant to go backwards. That is not what on-ramps are designed for. They are meant to get the car up to speed. So it is with foreplay. God designed foreplay to get a man and a woman up to speed. And it works. So if you are not married, what are you doing on the on-ramp? It is not meant to be a place where you hang out in idle, revving your engines, but not going anywhere.

## Masturbation

The other issue I want to briefly touch on is masturbation. This is an issue many men deal with, and the theology we have laid out addresses it. Many single men think of masturbation as an outlet for pent-up sexual desires, and they assume this issue will fall away once they get married. Many men also assuage their consciences by telling themselves that the Bible nowhere explicitly condemns masturbation. Well, it is true the Bible does not speak directly to masturbation. But it does speak to some other things. First, it teaches that lust is wrong (Matt. 5:27-30). Does a man masturbate without lust? Second, as we have seen, the Bible teaches that the sexual act is not meant to be experienced alone or for selfish reasons. It is meant to bind a man to his wife in a covenant relationship, so that every time they have sex they renew that covenant. Masturbation perverts God's covenant-making and -renewing intent. It teaches people mentally, physically, and emotionally to satisfy themselves. This is why marriage does not solve the problem of masturbation. Masturbation is easier than sex with one's wife, because it is not really about sex. It is about a man's lazy, self-centered desire to satisfy himself, rather than give himself to and for his wife.

How much better to reserve physical intimacy for the place and context for which God designed it: as the sign of the covenant relationship God has established between a man and his wife. Inside marriage, sex is like a good steak dinner. It not only tastes good, but it is good for you and builds up a marriage. Outside of marriage, sex is like candy. It may taste good, but it does not last, and a steady diet of it will make you sick—sick in your soul and sick in your relationships with women.

## Physical Intimacy and the Single Man
### Matt Schmucker

I have been married for sixteen years and have four children. Here are several questions I want you to consider:

- Do you think it would be acceptable or unacceptable for me, a married man, to have sex with a woman who is not my wife?
- Do you think it would be acceptable or unacceptable for me to kiss, caress, and fondle a woman who is not my wife (something short of intercourse)?
- Do you think it would be acceptable or unacceptable for me to have a meal with a woman not my wife and engage in extended conversation about each other's lives (likes/dislikes/struggles/pasts)?

If you answered "unacceptable" to three out of the three, or even two out of the three questions—"yes, it would be unacceptable for you as a married man to do those things"—I want to suggest that a double standard may exist in your mind. Many people who answer "unacceptable" with regard to me, as a married man, would *not* say "unacceptable" for the single man.

## Four Reasons Not to Have Any Physical Intimacy with Any Woman to Whom You Are Not Married

Let me give you four reasons why physical intimacy with a woman—at any level—to whom one is not married is potentially fraudulent, dangerous, and just as unacceptable for a man *prior* to marriage as it is *after* marriage.

### 1. We Are Made in the Image of God

First, as we have already seen, we are made in the image of God, and everything we are and do images, or represents, *God*. Therefore, we should be careful in what we do with our bodies. This is particularly true for the Christian, who has been united to Christ who is the perfect image of God. As Paul writes:

> Do you not know that your bodies are members of Christ himself? Shall I then take the members of Christ and unite them with a prostitute? Never! Do you not know that he who unites himself with a prostitute is one with her in body? For it is said, "The two will become one flesh." But he who unites himself with the Lord is one with him in spirit. Flee from sexual immorality. All other sins a man commits are outside his body, but he who sins sexually sins against his own body. Do you not know that your body is a temple of the Holy Spirit, who is in you, whom you have received from God? You are not your own; you were bought at a price. Therefore honor God with your body. (1 Cor. 6:15-20, NIV)

Now to the male reader who says, "Lying with a prostitute is a black-and-white issue, and of course I would never do that," allow me to reply: You are missing the point. Being bought at a price by God should compel you to honor him with everything you have and with everything you are, including your body. You are an image-bearer. And if you are a Christian, you are a name-bearer. Are you bearing well the image and name of a holy God by the way you conduct your relationships with the opposite sex?

### 2. We Are Called to Protect, Not Take Advantage of, Our Sisters in Christ

Second, Christian men are called to protect their sisters in Christ, not take advantage of them. Consider 1 Thessalonians 4:3-6 (NIV):

> It is God's will that you should be sanctified: that you should avoid sexual immorality; that each of you should learn to control his own body in a way that is holy and honorable, not in passionate lust like the heathen, who do not know God; and that in this matter no one should wrong his brother or take advantage of him.

Where the NIV says, "no one should wrong his brother or take advantage of him," the NASB says, "no one should defraud." Defraud means "to deprive of something by deception or fraud."

What do I mean by defrauding in this context? Simply put, a man defrauds a woman when, by his words or actions, he promises the benefits of marriage to a woman he either has no intention of marrying, or if he does, has no way of finally knowing that he will. The four authors of this chapter often speak on this topic because we know that brothers in Christ in our church and yours are defrauding (taking advantage of) sisters in Christ, and as the apostle James says, "My brothers, these things ought not to be so" (James 3:10).

Executives from the corporate giants Enron and WorldCom were recently on trial for fraud. They had painted a picture of business health, growth, and prosperity when in fact it was all false. The single men in our churches must be encouraged to ask themselves, "In your relationships with single women, are you painting a false picture and committing fraud?" What may be considered innocent—holding hands, putting an arm around her in the pew, some "light" kissing, long talks over Starbucks coffee—all send the message to a sister that reads, "You're mine." Single men must be careful here. A Christian woman is first and foremost a sister in the Lord. I trust none of us would do anything inappropriate with our own flesh-and-blood sisters. How much more a sister in the Lord! She may or may not become the man's wife. But she will always be a sister. Her heart, the "wellspring of life" (Prov. 4:23, NIV), must be guarded as if it were the man's own!

Statistically speaking, a single man should recognize that any single woman with whom he speaks will probably be someone's wife, and he will probably be someone's husband—maybe each other's, maybe not. So there should be no difference in standards of physical intimacy between the single man's conduct with a single woman and my standards as an already married man. Single men must conduct themselves in a way that will not result in embarrassment or shame in the future.

### 3. We Need to Guard Our Eyes and Hearts and Bodies for Marriage

Third, single men need to guard their eyes and hearts and bodies for marriage. "For God did not call us to be impure, but to live a holy life" (1 Thess. 4:7, NIV). A person will not fully know how critical this is until marriage, but trust us old married guys and know that what is done with the eyes, heart, and body *before* marriage matters. Too many times we have seen a Christian man and woman fall in love, get engaged, and then discover, during pre-marriage counseling, that their past relationships are no small factor. Too often, past physical relationships become impediments in the marriage bed.

We do not want a brother standing at the altar on his wedding day looking at his beautiful bride only to imagine behind her the boys and men who took advantage of her and robbed her of the trust and confidence that she now needs for her husband. We do not want a sister standing at the altar on her wedding day looking at her handsome groom only to imagine behind him a string of relationships with girls and women he failed to honor, and knowing that images in his head from pornography use and past flings may stick with him for a long time.

If I have just described you, you may have a painful road ahead of you, but our God is a great deliverer. The grace of God displayed in the shed blood of Christ on Calvary is more than sufficient not only to forgive you of past sins but to fit you for offering the comfort you have received to others, whether you eventually marry or not. If you have failed or are failing in this area, then remember your calling and resolve to stop now and prepare yourself for marriage. Guard your eyes and heart and body.

### 4. We Need to Make Good Deposits in the Marriage Bank

Fourth, we need to make good deposits in the Marriage Bank. What do I mean? The wedding day is the formal ceremony used to charter, if you will, a new bank, the Marriage Bank. Both deposits and withdrawals will be made at this bank. Men will make deposits with their actions of holy living, faithfulness, gentleness, compassion, strength, prayerfulness, and washing their wives in the Word. And wives will draw on those deposits. They draw trust, confidence, and faith. What most men do not understand is, although the Marriage Bank is not officially open till the wedding day, deposits can be made early. The husband who goes into the workplace among attractive, unbelieving women may find that his wife will be tempted to doubt his fidelity because of how he treated her when she was not his wife. Or, he will find she trusts him because he was so careful to protect her when she was not his wife—emotionally, spiritually, and physically. To the single reader, then, let me encourage you to live now in light of the future you desire. Treat all women in a way that ensures, when doubt arises, that the one woman you do marry will be able to draw confidence and faith from the pre-marriage deposits you made through prayerfulness and holy living.

In short, single men must know now that what they do prior to marriage is not inconsequential to what happens in marriage. They will reap what they sow. So they must decide now to sow well. The short-term pleasures of physical intimacy outside of marriage must not be allowed to damage the prospects for long-term joy inside marriage.

## What Does a Biblical Relationship Look Like?
### Scott Croft

Given this biblical theology of sex and marriage, what does a healthy, biblical dating or courting relationship look like in practice?

The attempt to answer that question has brought about a literary flood over the last several years, with different works bearing different levels of usefulness. A few examples include *Boundaries in Dating; Boy Meets Girl; I Kissed Dating Goodbye; I Hugged Dating Hello; I Gave Dating a Chance; Her Hand in Marriage; The Rules: Time-Tested Secrets for Capturing the Heart of Mr. Right;* and *Wandering Toward the Altar.*

These volumes can be divided into two groups. One group generally supports the method of "dating" and attempts to instruct readers how to date in a "Christian" way. The other group rejects the current dating method altogether as biblically flawed. It advocates an alternative system, which most describe as "courtship." In my reading, the book on this topic that seems the most sound theologically and practically is called *Boy Meets Girl,* by Joshua Harris[4] (he is also the author of *I Kissed Dating Goodbye*).

What is the difference between courtship and dating, and is one more biblical than the other? I will provide a working definition of each, describe how the two methods are broadly different, and then recommend why one method is fundamentally more biblical than the other.[5]

## Defining Courtship and Dating

Let's begin by defining courtship. Courtship ordinarily begins when a single man approaches a single woman by going through the woman's father, and then conducts his relationship with the woman under the authority of her father, family, or church, whichever is most appropriate. Courtship always has marriage as its direct goal.

What then is dating? Dating, a more modern approach, begins when either the man or the woman initiates a more-than-friends relationship with the other, and then they conduct that relationship outside of any oversight or authority. Dating may or may not have marriage as its goal.

## The Differences Between Courtship and Dating

What are the differences in these two systems? For our purposes, there are three broad differences between what has been called biblical courtship and modern dating.

### 1. The Difference in Motive

The first difference lies with the man's *motive* in pursuing the relationship. Biblical courtship has one motive—to find a spouse. A man will court a particular woman because he believes it is possible that he could marry her, and the courtship is the process of discerning whether that belief is correct. To the extent that the Bible addresses premarital relationships at all, it uses the language of men marrying and women being given in marriage (see Matt. 24:38; Luke 20:34-35). Numbers 30:3-16

---

[4] Joshua Harris, *Boy Meets Girl* (Sisters, Ore.: Multnomah, 2000).
[5] If after reading the chapter, you have unanswered questions, you can find the notes for my six-week Sunday school class on courtship and dating at www.capitolhillbaptist.org.

talks about a transfer of authority from the father to the husband when a woman leaves her father's house and is united to her husband. The Song of Solomon showcases the meeting, courtship, and marriage of a couple—always with marriage in view. I am not advocating arranged marriages; rather, I am pointing toward the biblical purpose for why young men and women associate with one another. These passages do not argue that marriage should be the direct goal of such relationships so much as they assume it.

Modern dating, on the other hand, need not have marriage as a goal at all. Dating can be recreational. Not only is "dating for fun" acceptable, it is assumed that "practice" and learning by "trial and error" are necessary, even advisable, before finding the person that is just right for *you.* The fact that individuals will be emotionally and probably physically intimate with many people before settling down with the "right person" is just part of the deal. Yet where is the biblical support for such an approach to marriage? There is none. How many examples of "recreational dating" do we see among God's people in the Bible? Zero. The category of premarital intimacy does not exist, other than in the context of grievous sexual sin.

The motive for dating or courting is marriage. The practical advice I give the singles at our church is, if you cannot happily see yourself as a married man (or woman) in less than one year, then you are not ready to date.

## 2. The Difference in Mind-set

The second major difference between biblical courtship and modern dating is the *mind-set* couples have when interacting with one another. What do I mean by that? Modern dating is essentially a selfish endeavor. I do not mean maliciously selfish, as in "I'm going to try to hurt you for my benefit." I mean an oblivious self-centeredness that treats the whole process as ultimately about *me.* After all, what is the main question everyone asks about dating, falling in love, and getting married? "How do I know if I've found the one?" What is the unspoken ending to that question? "For me." Will this person make me happy? Will this relationship meet my needs? How does she look? What is the chemistry like? Have I done as well as I can do? I cannot tell you how many men I have counseled who are courting a wonderful woman and are terrified to commit, worrying that as soon as they do, "something better will come walking around the corner." Selfishness is not what drives a biblical marriage, and therefore should not be what drives a biblical courtship.

Biblical courtship recognizes the general call to "do nothing out of selfish ambition or vain conceit, but in humility consider others better than yourselves" (Phil. 2:3, NIV). It also recognizes the specific call that Ephesians 5:25 gives men in marriage, where our main role is sacrificial service. We are to love our wives as Christ loved the church, giving himself up for her. That means loving sacrificially every day. Biblical courtship means that a man does not look for a laundry list of characteristics that comprise his fantasy woman so that his every desire can be fulfilled, but he looks for a godly woman as Scripture defines her—a woman he can love and, yes, be attracted to, but a woman whom he can serve and love as a godly husband. In other words, modern dating asks, "How can I find the one for me?" while biblical courtship asks, "How can I be the one for her?"

### 3. The Difference in Methods

Third, and most practically, modern dating and biblical courtship are different in their *methods*. And this is where the rubber really meets the road. In modern dating, intimacy precedes commitment. In biblical courtship, commitment precedes intimacy.

According to the current school of thought, the best way to figure out whether you want to marry a particular person is to act as if you are married and see if you like it. Spend large amounts of time alone together. Become each other's primary emotional confidantes. Share your deepest secrets and desires. Get to know that person better than anyone else in your life. Grow your physical intimacy and intensity on the same track as your emotional intimacy. What you do and say together is private and is no one else's business, and since the relationship is private, you need not submit to anyone else's authority or be accountable. And if this pseudo-marriage works for both of you, then get married. But if one or both of you do not like how it is going, go ahead and break up even if it means going through something like an emotional and probably physical divorce.

Such is the process of finding "the one," and this can happen with several different people before one finally marries. In the self-centered world of secular dating, we want as much information as possible to ensure that the right decision is being made. And if we can enjoy a little physical or emotional comfort along the way, great.

Clearly, this is not the biblical picture. The process just described is hurtful to the woman that the man purports to care about, not to mention to himself. And it clearly violates the command of 1 Thessalonians 4:6 not to wrong or defraud our sisters in Christ by implying a marriage-level commitment where one does not exist. It will have a damaging effect on the man's marriage and hers, whether they marry each other or not.

In a biblical relationship, commitment precedes intimacy. Within this model, the man should follow the admonition in 1 Timothy 5:1-2 to treat all young women to whom he is not married as sisters, with absolute purity. The man should show leadership and willingness to bear the risk of rejection by defining the nature and the pace of the relationship. He should do this before spending significant time alone with her in order to avoid hurting or confusing her. He should also seek to ensure that a significant amount of time is spent with other couples or friends rather than alone. The topics, manner, and frequency of conversation should be characterized by the desire to become acquainted with each other more deeply, but not in a way that defrauds each other. There should be no physical intimacy outside the context of marriage, and the couple should seek accountability for the spiritual health and progress of the relationship, as well as for their physical and emotional intimacy. Within this model, both parties should seek to find out, before God, whether they should be married, and whether they can serve and honor God better together than apart. The man should take care not to treat any woman like his wife who is not his wife. Of course he must get to know his courting partner well enough to make a decision on marriage. However, prior to the decision to marry, he should always engage with her emotionally in a way he would be happy for other men to engage with her. In all these ways, a biblical relationship looks different than a worldly relationship. If this is done well, Christian women will be honored, even as they are pursued. Christian wives will be honored. And God will be glorified.

## Conclusion
### MARK DEVER

Some of these ideas will seem obvious to some readers, and revolutionary to others. We have heard objections to parts of this teaching, but none that have caused us to doubt the wisdom of it. And we increasingly hear wonderful testimonies.

I talked recently with an unmarried friend in his mid-thirties who had just finished listening for a third or fourth time to a 9Marks Ministries interview with Joshua Harris, Al Mohler, Scott Croft, and myself on dating.[6] He said that he was beginning to think he had wrongly approached finding a wife. (He also said his age was leading him to the same conclusion!)

Not too long after that, I was in a seminary bookstore, and a young couple came up to me and announced they had become engaged soon after hearing this same interview. They simply wanted to thank me. The young man in particular said that such marriage-focused teaching on male-female relationships had shown him his responsibility and had given him courage.

And now we pray that you, our unmarried readers, will not despair, but that you will be blessed as you pray, study God's Word, discern God's will, seek godly counsel, and either pursue finding a godly wife or embrace a life of celibacy. We also pray that our married readers and church members generally will better know how to counsel and encourage our single brothers and sisters in Christ as they approach God's wonderful gift in marriage.

How true the words of Solomon: "He who finds a wife finds a good thing and obtains favor from the LORD" (Prov. 18:22).

---

[6] Available at www.9marks.org.

# CHAPTER 7

# Sex, Romance, and the Glory of God: What Every Christian Husband Needs to Know

C. J. MAHANEY[1]

A smile crossed the king's face as he dipped his quill into the inkwell one last time. With firm, smooth strokes the final lines flowed freely onto the parchment.

Pushing back from his writing desk, he sighed with satisfaction. The project had gone very well. This was some fine work. Rising from the chair and lifting his hands to heaven, Solomon the son of David offered thanks to the Lord. Here, complete at last, was his greatest song, one of the most important pieces of writing he had ever done. With satisfaction he lowered his eyes to the finished work spread out before him. Today, we call it the Song of Solomon.

It's about sex.

In his lifetime, Solomon would produce 3,000 proverbs and more than 1,000 songs and hymns. The son of a legendary king, and a great king himself, he would be esteemed in Scripture as the wisest man who had yet lived. And his "Song of Songs" is nothing less than an explicit and unblushing celebration of sex within marriage.

To Solomon, this may have been simply a deeply personal reflection on love. But really it was much more than that. Because one day, as we know, it would be counted among the perfect and infallible words of Scripture, inerrantly inspired by the Holy Spirit, and intended by

---

[1] The material in this chapter can be found in expanded form in my book, *Sex, Romance, and the Glory of God: What Every Christian Husband Needs to Know* (Wheaton, Ill.: Crossway, 2004).

God as a primary source of guidance for mankind until the return of the Son.

That's right, gentlemen. Solomon's Song of Songs is an entire book of the Bible devoted to the promotion of sexual intimacy within the covenant of marriage. It's an eight-chapter feast of unbridled, uninhibited, joyous immersion in verbal and physical expressions of passion between a man and a woman.

Not a couple of verses. Not a chapter or two. God didn't consider that enough. He decided to give us a whole book!

But can the Song of Solomon really be about sex? Isn't the Bible about, well, spiritual stuff? It sure is. And as we'll see, sexual intimacy within marriage has profound spiritual significance.

## Real People, Real Bodies

Let's put ourselves back in King Solomon's study for a moment. As husbands called to lovingly lead our wives, we need to try to understand this book of the Bible. And when you want to understand what a section of Scripture really means, you have to start with what the original writer actually meant. So let's briefly consider this book through Solomon's eyes.

When Solomon was writing his Song, what do you think he had in mind? The question is important because some Christians see Solomon's Song as a book of symbolism. Men more godly than I, and a lot smarter, have believed that this book of the Bible, if it's about marriage at all, is only about marriage in a secondary way. They see all its talk of love and longing as primarily symbolic of the relationship between Christ and the church, or Christ and the soul of the individual believer.

Maybe that's how you see Solomon's Song. If so, please understand: While I don't share that view, I'm not attacking or ridiculing you or anyone else. But I am going to try to persuade you otherwise!

Marriage does, of course, point to a greater reality: the unique relationship that will exist forever between Christ and the church. But there are five reasons why I think the primary purpose of the Song of Solomon is exactly what it appears to be: to celebrate and promote intimacy and the gift of sex between a man and woman in the context of marriage.

### 1. Solomon's Topic Was Obviously Sex

Just look at all the sensual and erotic language in this book! It certainly *looks* like it's about physical and emotional passions between a real man and a real woman. When Solomon was at his desk writing the Song, do you think he had in mind some symbolic, spiritualized relationship between God and his chosen ones? I don't.

### 2. The Bible Never Suggests That the Book Isn't Primarily About Sex

No New Testament writer (or Old Testament writer) suggests that this book ought to be understood primarily as an illustration of spiritual realities. This compels me to read Solomon's Song according to the plain meaning of the words.

### 3. God's Relationship with Man Is Not Sexual

The Song is full of erotic phrases, yet our relationship with God is never portrayed in the Bible as erotic. The church certainly *is* the Bride of Christ. But although the marriage between Christ and his Bride will be many unimaginably wonderful things, it will not involve sexuality. Will it be extraordinarily and supernaturally intimate? Yes. Infinitely rewarding and fulfilling? Absolutely. But not physically erotic.

When describing our relationship with God, or when communicating our passion for him in prayer or worship, it's right to use a vocabulary of love. But this language should never include anything erotic. "God is spirit, and those who worship him must worship in spirit and truth" (John 4:24).

### 4. Spiritualizing the Book Doesn't Work

When many of the passages from Solomon's Song are viewed as symbolic statements, the results can get very strange.

"Let him kiss me with the kisses of his mouth! For your love is better than wine" (1:2). Now that sounds an awful lot like a particular woman saying she wants to be kissed by a particular man. But some commentators say that this verse is actually about a spiritual yearning for the Word of God.

"My beloved is to me a sachet of myrrh that lies between my breasts" (1:13). There are commentators who somehow find in this passage a reference to Christ appearing between the Old and New Testaments. Guys, I'm no scholar, but I don't think so!

"Your stature is like a palm tree, and your breasts are like its clusters" (7:7). Again, one commentator—a godly and sincere person, I have no doubt—suggests that "breasts" here refers to the nurturing effect that sound biblical teaching has upon the church. You know, that idea never occurred to me. When the man says to the woman that her breasts are like fruit on a palm tree, seems to me he's talking about . . . her breasts!

Spiritualizing the Song of Solomon just doesn't make sense. What's worse, it denies to us the powerful impact that God intends for it to have on our marriages.

### 5. We Need Instruction on Sexuality

If marriage is immensely important to God (and it is), and if sex is a marvelous gift from God to married couples (which it is), it's entirely appropriate for God to tell us in Scripture how to understand and enjoy it.

Would God leave us, his most beloved creatures, on our own when it comes to something as powerful and universal as sexuality? Would he give us such a gift without also giving guidance? Where is a Christian couple supposed to look for a model of God-glorifying sexuality? If not to Scripture, where? To Hollywood? Pop culture? Pornography?

We must not—*cannot*—take our sexual cues from the sinful impulses of ourselves or others. And we don't have to. God has not left us in the dark. Scripture illuminates the path of marital intimacy. The Song of Solomon shines brightly, showing us the way to the best sex we can possibly experience.

So I trust my point is clear. I don't believe the Song of Solomon is allegory, or typology, or drama, or an elaborate diary entry. I agree with the biblical commentator Lloyd Carr: "The lover and the beloved are just ordinary people."[2]

Tom Gledhill, in his commentary, puts it this way: "The two lovers are Everyman and Everywoman."[3] That's encouraging. The Song's

---

[2] Lloyd Carr, *The Song of Solomon* (Downers Grove, Ill.: InterVarsity Press, 1984), 49.

[3] Thomas Gledhill, *The Message of the Song of Songs* (Downers Grove, Ill.: InterVarsity Press, 1994), 23.

about your marriage and mine. These eight chapters of Scripture can speak to us, and in doing so, make a dramatic difference in our lives, for the glory of God.

## Communication and Creativity

There is a clear lesson at the heart of Solomon's Song, a truth that threads through the entire book. I have sought to weave that same thread into this chapter. It is a truth that should be emblazoned on the heart of every husband. If you remember nothing else from these pages, remember this:

> *In order for romance to deepen, you must touch the heart and mind of your wife before you touch her body.*

This, gentlemen, is a truth that can change your marriage. Nothing kindles erotic romance in a marriage like a husband who knows how to touch the heart and mind of his wife before he touches her body.

Too often we reverse the order. We touch her body prematurely and expect that she will respond immediately and passionately. Normally that's not how it works.

Let's begin now to examine Solomon's Song in greater detail, studying specifically how these lovers model the use of communication to first touch one another's heart and mind. After that, as we seek to apply the lessons of the Song, we will explore how, through study and planning, we can develop the creativity to lead our wives well in this area. Through this combination of *communication* and *creativity* we can unlock the passion already present in our wives and cultivate a fresh and growing passion for the rest of our life together.

### Communication: The Language of Romance

They call it "intercourse." But the word doesn't refer just to sexual union. In fact, the first couple of definitions in my dictionary don't refer to sex at all. They basically involve human communication and interaction of every kind, especially the exchange of thoughts or feelings. It's only when you get to about the third definition of the word that any direct reference to sexuality appears.

On this point, the dictionary echoes the authoritative teaching of Scripture. A clear lesson from Solomon's Song is that speech and sex are intimately connected. Duane Garrett writes of the lovers in the Song:

> They relish their pleasure in each other not only with physical action, but with *carefully composed words*. Love is, above all, a matter of the mind and heart and should be declared.
>
> The lesson for the reader is that he or she needs to speak often and openly of his or her joy in the beloved, the spouse. This is, for many lovers, a far more embarrassing revelation of the self than anything that is done with the body. But it is precisely here that the biblical ideal of love is present—in the uniting of the bodies and hearts of the husband and wife in a bond that is as strong as death. Many homes would be happier if men and women would simply speak of their love for one another a little more often.[4]

I believe genuine romance, such as we find modeled in the Song, is meant to be a growing reality within every Christian marriage, not a dimming memory. And I am convinced that a key to consistent growth in romance is found in the regular use of "carefully composed words."

You communicate with words every day, don't you? For many of us, our days revolve around giving and receiving short bursts of information, whether in person or through some form of technology. Often the success of our careers depends on how good we are at coming up with words that communicate clearly, creatively, and with purpose.

So why do so many of us go home at the end of the work day—home to our wife, the most important person in the world to us—and suddenly *stop* communicating clearly, creatively, and with purpose? It's no mystery. We can all be selfish and lazy. So let us heed Duane Garrett's words: We could have a happier home if we would simply speak of our love for our wives . . . even a *little* more often.

Husbands, it is our privilege, joy, and God-given responsibility to romance our wives . . . *really* romance our wives. As we look to the Song for guidance in romance, we are immediately struck by the obvious, central role played by language.

---

[4] Duane Garrett, *Proverbs, Ecclesiastes, Song of Solomon,* The New American Commentary (Nashville: Broadman & Holman, 1993), 379.

## CAREFULLY COMPOSED WORDS

Let's look at one of the most remarkable features of the Song of Solomon—how the lovers speak to one another. Solomon's Song contains the finest examples of carefully composed, romantic words I know of:

> [He] How beautiful you are, my darling!
>   Oh, how beautiful!
>   Your eyes are doves.
> [She] How handsome you are, my lover!
>   Oh, how charming!
>   And our bed is verdant. (1:15-16, NIV)

> [He] You have stolen my heart, my sister, my bride;
>   you have stolen my heart
> with one glance of your eyes,
>   with one jewel of your necklace.
> How delightful is your love, my sister, my bride! . . .
> You are a garden locked up, my sister, my bride;
>   you are a spring enclosed, a sealed fountain.
> Your plants are an orchard of pomegranates
>   with choice fruits. . . .
> You are a garden fountain,
>   a well of flowing water
>   streaming down from Lebanon. (4:9-10, 12-13, 15, NIV)

> [She] . . . at our door is every delicacy,
> both new and old,
>   that I have stored up for you, my lover. (7:13, NIV)

This is miles away from simple chit-chat, or practicalities like kids, carpools, and church meetings. This is a category of communication set apart from the stuff of daily life, reserved for a unique and wonderful purpose. It is highly intentional, creative, provocative, erotic language. Its purpose is to arouse romantic passion—to inflame, slowly and intentionally, all the while honoring and delighting one's spouse.

The whole book resonates with this sort of exotic, extravagant verbal foreplay between the lovers. Long before they begin to enjoy one another's bodies, they excite one another's minds with tender, creative speech. They model for us what it means to *feel* sexual passion and to *articulate* that passion.

The best sex begins with romance, and the best romance begins with the kind of speech we read in the Song of Solomon. It begins with "carefully composed words."

CREATIVE COMPLIMENTS

In the language of these lovers is a variety of expressions that you just don't hear too much anymore. Not only is it poetic. It's a kind of poetry rooted in Hebrew culture one thousand years before Christ. To learn and properly apply the lessons of Solomon's Song, we need to examine what these odd-sounding phrases really mean. Here's an ideal example.

> Your neck is like an ivory tower.
> Your eyes are the pools of Heshbon
>     by the gate of Bath Rabbim.
> Your nose is like the tower of Lebanon
>     looking toward Damascus. (7:4, NIV)

In Solomon's day these were, without question, tender and heartfelt expressions of deep admiration for a woman's physical beauty. And that is how they would have been received. A woman hearing those lines would have understood them to mean something like, "Your nose is lovely, a feature perfectly suited to the rest of your face. It adorns your face the way a tower gives breadth and character to the horizon. It transforms and compliments you wonderfully."

So let's not make the big mistake of simply parroting such phrases. If you try telling your wife that her nose is kind of like a big stone tower, it probably won't arouse the specific passions you had in mind.

Here's another passage. The man speaks to his beloved, saying,

> I liken you, my darling, to a mare
>     harnessed to one of the chariots of Pharaoh. (1:9, NIV)

The phrase, "My darling," establishes a tone of tenderness and admiration right from the start. He then uses an analogy that we can thoroughly misinterpret. In commenting on the use of the word "mare," one writer suggests the woman must have had very large hips, suitable for childbearing. Another indicates she is no doubt a fast runner! But more accomplished scholarship reveals the beauty and the vibrant sexual overtones of this high compliment.

It seems that in Solomon's day mares were never used to pull the king's chariot, but only stallions were so used, and always hitched in pairs. Yet in this picture, a mare has been harnessed to the chariot *alongside* a stallion. This puts the stallion into a frenzy of galloping desire. So this analogy has nothing to do with comparing her to a horse. Instead, it declares the overwhelming sensual impact she makes upon him. Her very presence drives him wild!

Here is a magnificent passage, packed with carefully composed words carrying a potently erotic intent:

> How beautiful you are, my darling!
>> Oh, how beautiful!
>> Your eyes behind your veil are doves.
> Your hair is like a flock of goats
>> descending from Mount Gilead.
> Your teeth are like a flock of sheep just shorn,
>> coming up from the washing.
> Each has its twin;
>> not one of them is alone.
> Your lips are like a scarlet ribbon;
>> your mouth is lovely.
> Your temples behind your veil
>> are like the halves of a pomegranate.
> Your neck is like the tower of David,
>> built with elegance;
> on it hang a thousand shields,
>> all of them shields of warriors.
> Your two breasts are like two fawns,
>> like twin fawns of a gazelle
>> that browse among the lilies.
> Until the day breaks
>> and the shadows flee,
> I will go to the mountain of myrrh
>> and to the hill of incense.
> All beautiful you are, my darling;
>> there is no flaw in you. (4:1-7, NIV)

These verses begin with a declaration of the beauty of his beloved. But generalities are not enough for him, nor should they be for us. In this passage alone he praises seven different parts of her body, using clear and complimentary analogies. This is some serious creativity!

"Your eyes behind your veil are doves" speaks of her gentleness and tenderness. You see, he has studied her eyes. He has thought about what he sees in them. And he has made an effort to express that to her in terms that will bring her joy.

In describing her hair as "a flock of goats descending from Mount Gilead," he evokes the image of a distant hill, completely covered with black-wooled goats moving toward its base, so the entire hill seems alive. In Solomon's day, this was a reference to thrilling, state-of-the-art special effects!

Her teeth are white and fresh, like newly shorn and bathed sheep that glisten in the sun. Best of all, "each has its twin"—no missing teeth! Three thousand years ago, that was a big deal.

He goes on to praise in specific, compelling, poetic terms, her lips, mouth, and temples. The word he uses for her mouth suggests that he finds her very speech a thing of beauty. One's words reveal one's heart. So here he is seizing an opportunity to honor her for godly character.

Gazing lower, he speaks in tender and radiant language of her neck and breasts, declaring with breathtaking delicacy and understatement his unmistakably erotic intentions. He then ends this love poem where he began, assuring her that, in his eyes, she is "all beautiful . . . no flaw." Perfection itself.

And note this well, gentlemen. Throughout the passages in which one lover describes the body of the other—for the woman in Solomon's Song also compliments her man—there are both beauty and brilliance. In these phrases, the most private emotions about the most intimate parts of the lover's body are expressed appropriately, romantically, erotically, and tastefully. There is no medical language, no crudeness, and no profanity anywhere in the book. Every word is tender and sensual, and carefully composed to produce appropriate and passionate arousal.

## INTENTIONAL EXAGGERATION

In the man's description of his beloved, notice that we have very few clear statements of fact. We know she had no missing teeth—a real plus—but there's little else we can really nail down. The overall description we have of this woman is filtered almost exclusively through the man's impressions of her. He even goes so far as to call her flawless.

Now, is he lying? Is he flattering her? Does he need glasses? Not at all. He is not describing so much *what* she looks like, but *how* he feels about her. There is a huge difference.

So many Christian husbands and wives have been deeply influenced by the fashion and advertising industries that we may have a challenge really understanding these descriptions. To a certain extent we have been conformed to this world, and it is compromising our ability to understand truth clearly. When we read these statements, we make the error of applying them culturally, not biblically. But as romance is biblically cultivated, these really can be very apt and accurate descriptions.

When the man says, "All beautiful you are, my darling; there is no flaw in you" (4:7, NIV), and when he calls her "my perfect one" (6:9), what's going on is very clear. He is lavishing high praises upon his beloved in an effort to communicate her effect on him. These are expressions of his heartfelt evaluation of her. They are not based on cultural criteria. Others may not share his assessment of her beauty. But he doesn't care. This is how he sees her, and together they rejoice in that assessment.

The same is true of the woman's view of her man (see 5:10-16). She describes him in a way that few men could ever hope to deserve. Yet these are statements of integrity because they represent her personal assessment of him, an assessment informed by her exclusive, passionate love for him.

What we see in these compliments is simply a purified and well-articulated form of something universally common to lovers: They view their beloved as uniquely special. You *should* be special in her eyes, just as she should be special to you—uniquely set apart, outrageously exceptional, with a value far above that of any other person, a value that others might even see as "inaccurate."

There is, and should be, a marked difference between an emotional description of one's beloved and an objective, factual description. A man may say to his wife, "My darling, you are five-feet seven-and-one-half inches tall, of medium build, with a birthmark on your left shoulder blade, and you are mildly allergic to shellfish." In this, he may be entirely accurate, but he will not be telling her how much she means to him. And he certainly won't be adding any fuel to the fires of romance.

## LEARNING THE LANGUAGE

Now, a lot of us think we're doing pretty well if once in a while we say, "That dress looks nice on you, dear," or "Hey, are those new earrings?" But I trust we're seeing from Scripture that the standard is far, far higher. By all means, tell her when you think she looks nice, but recognize the world of difference between a simple compliment (however sincere) and phrases describing your appreciation and passion for her.

But I can hear you now: "C. J., if I can't quote Solomon, how do I generate my own carefully composed words? I'm not a poet. I don't even like poetry. And I'm definitely not Shakespeare."

Well, neither am I. Where I grew up, if a guy revealed that he was interested in anything vaguely poetic, he would have been beaten up. Poetry was, by definition, effeminate and revolting. Real guys played sports. We talked about sports. And we read sports. Not poetry, and definitely not Shakespeare.

Just a few years ago, in fact, out of arrogance and deep ignorance, I said in passing from the pulpit, "Shakespeare was a bum." One horrified literature teacher in our church very kindly offered to help me. A little while later, I spent an evening with a group of friends, including this teacher, watching a video of *Henry V*. As I watched, I came to understand something: it was really me who was the bum. Here was highly poetic speech, which I had once scorned, but it was incredibly powerful stuff, and not feminine in the least.

Solomon, too, was definitely masculine. Far from scorning carefully composed words, I should accept the lesson of Solomon's Song and learn how to use them. Poetic language is a gift from God that can help me promote godly romance with my wife!

So let's try to bring this home a little. How many times in the past week or month have you spoken to your wife in ways that she found to be romantically and perhaps erotically arousing?

Now, what are the things that would hold you back from doing this on a regular basis? What are the issues in your own heart that would prevent you?

Let's try a few on for size. Maybe one of them will fit you.

*"I'm not sure it really matters to her."*

Wrong. Remember: thanks be to God, our wives aren't wired like men. The spoken word can be as alluring, provocative, and enticing to your wife as any visual stimulation you experience with her.

*"I don't think I can come up with anything creative."*

It might not be the easiest thing you've ever done. But if you will humble yourself and seek him for it, God is eager to give you that simple but effective phrase to say to your wife. The first such phrase will begin to break down the barriers of pride and self-absorption that hinder you. The second phrase will be easier. Then you're on your way.

*"It just seems silly."*

But it doesn't have to. Find what's genuine and works for you and your wife. Again, don't let the poetry aspect turn you off. What sort of language appeals to both of you and comes naturally?

After I taught this material in our church, one man showed me a line he had written: "Honey, to me, you are like freshly shucked corn in a trough surrounded by hungry hogs." Now, this didn't quite fit my cultural background, but I was immediately able to encourage him. "If your wife is romanced by this, fantastic! If this speaks her language, and encourages her, and helps her understand your passion for her, then Solomon would be very pleased with you."

The point is, guys, you don't need to be a Shakespeare or a Solomon. You don't need to imitate some specific style. But you should definitely follow the example given to us in the Song—by carefully composing words of a romantic and erotically suggestive nature that will express your love for her. As you do this, you and your wife will be drawn into a deeper and more satisfying relationship.

What changes, even something small, can you make *this week* to begin cultivating and expressing your passion for your wife?

Now, some of you may be more comfortable, creative, and effective when you communicate in written form. By all means, do so! But however you do it, I think you'll find that after a little practice with carefully composed words, they will begin to come more easily. As you build the habit of delighting your wife with your words, the phrases can become more spontaneous.

Recently, Carolyn and I were in a mall while on vacation. We intentionally separated for a while, and as the time drew near for us to meet up again, I began searching the crowds for her. Finally, I caught sight of her. She approached and I embraced her. I said, "Love, I just want you to know that whenever I'm searching for you in a crowd, you are the only one who appears in color. The rest of the world is black and white to me."

These spontaneous words didn't come from any unique gifting in me. I think they were inspired by my study of the Song of Solomon. Words like these are far more effective than, "Hey, uh . . . you look nice." So believe me, God is eager to help you grow in this area. That's why there's hope for every husband. Even those who call Shakespeare a bum.

### Creativity: Learning, Leading, and Loving

Communication, as we've seen from the Song, is vital to the promotion of romance. We've also noted how, in order for your words to ring true—to *be* true—they can't be patched together from convenient, one-size-fits-all phrases. All true romance is custom-designed. To produce phrases and actions designed especially for your wife, you must study her and then creatively apply what you have learned.

In this section, we're going to get very practical about how to touch the heart and mind of our wives by creating and carrying out tailor-made plans for romance. But before we can creatively plan, we must first learn to study our wives.

Now, after that Shakespeare story, it will come as no surprise that when I was growing up, I hated school and studying. Well, I hated *most* studying. But I loved two local sports teams: the University of Maryland Terps—specifically, the basketball team—and my beloved Washington

Redskins. Somehow I acquired an impressive body of knowledge about these teams, even as I continued to get lousy grades in school.

Why was that kind of learning so easy for me, when formal education was so hard? What made the difference?

Passion.

No secret there. What we love, we want to learn about. And what we love to study, we come to love even more. That's just the way God has wired us. I loved the Terps and Skins, so learning about them and growing in my zeal for them was a totally natural process.

I still enjoy following those teams, but my strongest passions now lie elsewhere.

My highest and greatest love will always be reserved for God, for when I was his enemy and worthy of his righteous wrath, in his great mercy he sent his only Son to live a perfect life and die a perfect death in my place. But after my love for God, nothing compares to the passion I hold for Carolyn, my wife.

It has been my privilege to be a student of Carolyn since before our engagement. As I have studied her—seeking to learn what pleases, excites, honors, encourages, refreshes, and helps her—my love for her has only increased.

And as I study her, I love to find new ways to please her. So I constantly keep my eyes and ears open for ideas to record. I've been known not to hear my name called at a doctor's office because I was furiously scribbling information from a magazine article.

In my PDA I keep track of good getaway spots, ideas for dates, and many other bits of useful information. I know what to record because I have studied Carolyn—her life, her preferences, and her responsibilities—and have learned what makes her tick, romantically speaking. And I learned a long time ago that, no matter how amazed or impressed I am by an idea or thought, I almost certainly will forget it if I don't write it down. These notes are my building blocks for creating and cultivating a more romantic marriage.

To learn how to touch *your* wife's heart and mind, you must study her. Here are two lists that may be helpful. You can probably add to them.

Do you know how to surprise and delight your wife in specific ways in each of the following areas?

- Sex
- Clothing sizes, styles, and stores
- Jewelry
- Health
- Exercise
- Books and magazines
- Movies
- The arts
- Sports
- Food
- Music
- Entertainment
- Places to visit
- Intellectual interests
- Hobbies
- Vacations/Getaways
- And, of course, sex

Do you know how your wife is faring in each of *these* areas?

- Theological knowledge
- Practice of the spiritual disciplines
- Growth in godliness
- Spiritual gifts that can be used to serve others
- Local church involvement[5]
- Children
- Parents
- In-laws
- Friends
- Personal retreats
- Fears
- Hopes
- Dreams
- Disappointments
- Temptations

---

[5] On the vital topic of the local church, I strongly recommend Joshua Harris's *Stop Dating the Church!* (Sisters, Ore.: Multnomah, 2004).

How much of this information do you have readily available to you, preferably in written form? How much do you really know about your wife in each of these areas?

## Processing and Planning

Studying our wives and gathering information, of course, is only step one. We must not confuse being *informed* with being *transformed*. Transformation doesn't just happen automatically or effortlessly. It is the fruit of application and action.

This is precisely where most men fail, including me. And it should be no mystery why, gentlemen. We have a tendency to be lazy and selfish. Genuine growth involves grace-motivated work, even extended effort. Our information gathering must be followed by detailed planning and follow-through. Romance is what you know about your wife specifically *applied*.

Here is a practice I've been observing for years and have found immensely helpful. You might want to consider trying it . . . or create your own practice. The important thing is that you have some pattern you observe on a frequent, regular basis. Otherwise, all your efforts to learn about your wife will have little actual effect.

Every week, on Sunday evening or Monday morning, I get away to the local Starbucks. The heart of this time is when I define what is most important for me to accomplish during the next seven days. (I do this with respect to all my roles, but here we'll just focus on my marriage.)

With respect to Carolyn, I identify no more than three important goals I can accomplish *that week*, and I plan them into my schedule. These may be a date night, a surprise I can bring her, a scheduled time to discuss an issue I know is important to her, or something else.

Outwardly, it appears there's nothing special going on. I'm just another bald guy in a coffee shop communing with a piece of technology, a wrinkled sports page by my side. But I assure you, great fruitfulness flows from these times, regularly and faithfully invested. This is how the things that are most important in my life are defined and protected. This is how mere information leads to actual transformation.

This is where hope and desire begin to become reality. Without some practice like this, I simply would not be able to touch my wife's heart and mind before I touch her body.

## Making It All Happen

Time and energy, lovingly invested, *will* increase romance, which *will* increase marital intimacy. But what, exactly, should you plan for?

Ultimately, any detailed answer to that question must come from you. But in general terms, there *are* specific things that for most marriages, most of the time, can bring about genuine romance. Here are seven practical ways that I hope you will find helpful in touching her heart and mind before you touch her body.

### 1. Date Night

Time away from the routine busyness of life is essential for the cultivation of romance in any marriage. A regular date night provides a couple with a reliable, peaceful oasis in the middle of a busy world.

At this point, three of our four children are married. But I've been practicing the priority of a weekly date night since before any of them were born. (That's right. I said weekly.) If you have small children, I recognize that challenges can exist. Certainly there is the matter of child care, an area in which you should bear the burden of finding a solution if one is not readily available. But also, the maternal instincts of many mothers of small children can kick in hard, leading a mother to think that it's more important for her to be with her children than to take a regular date night to grow closer to her husband.

If that is your situation, let me encourage you to lead with love. These are critical years for you to invest in your marriage relationship. If you have small children, your wife is even more in need of your care and attention during this season.

If you do not have a consistent date night now, my first recommendation is . . . do it! Do whatever it takes to establish a regular date with your beloved. And let me suggest that you take the plunge. Unless it's simply impossible, go ahead and make your date night a weekly event, starting right now!

Now guys, date night is not about running errands or visiting the local mega-hardware store together. A date night is intentional. It has a goal and a purpose. The main goal is not so much to *relax with* each other, as to *relate to* each other.

Sure, there's a place for the relaxation-oriented approach to dates once in a while. But don't let that become your standard fare on these critical evenings. Over a period of months, you ought to be able to look back and see that your date nights have been drawing you together as a couple, not simply giving you an opportunity to get out of your home and relax at the same time.

And date nights don't have to be expensive. A date can simply be a few hours together—walking in a park, looking into one another's eyes while sitting in a coffee shop—and talking about anything and everything, from the boringly practical to the strikingly romantic.

One more important point, gentlemen. Our date night is my joy, privilege, and responsibility to plan. When Carolyn and I get in the car I don't want to have to turn to her and say, "So, uh, where'd you like to eat?" I want to show her that she is important enough to me that I have planned ahead.

## 2. *Phone Calls*

I try to speak with Carolyn from the office at least once a day. These don't have to be long conversations. I'll pick up the phone in a spare moment and call her just to say, "Hi, love. I just wanted to hear your voice. Is there anything I can do for you?" (Be sure to listen to her answer, guys.) And when our conversation is over, I may wrap it up with something like, "I love you with all my heart and I can't wait to see you in a few hours. Bye."

Calls like this can have a transforming effect on Carolyn. They allow me, in a matter of just a few moments, to touch her heart and mind.

## 3. *Notes, Cards, Letters, and Email*

The written word can be even more powerful than the phone call. How many times have you driven to the store, looked through perhaps dozens of greeting cards, and ended up with either no card or one that was less than ideal? Wouldn't that time and energy be better spent in a quiet place crafting your own words? Let's depend less on greeting cards and more on God's grace to help us express ourselves romantically.

## 4. Gifts

Romance can be communicated quite effectively through small gifts. They don't have to be expensive, but they shouldn't be exclusively practical, either. Giving your wife a dust buster or a waffle iron might serve her or make her life a little easier, but it does not qualify as romancing her.

Too many men try to make up for a lack of daily romance with the occasional extravagant gift, as if to apologize for the past and offer an excuse for the future. I would argue against the large, occasional, and expensive gift in favor of the small, frequent, and thoughtful (although, if possible, both are recommended!).

Buying perfume and clothing for Carolyn has been a joy for me over the years, as well as an adventure. When I present these gifts to her, I am always careful to remind her that she need feel no obligation to keep or wear them, and she knows I mean this (yes, I give her the receipt, too). I am thankful that romancing my wife has little to do with my fashion sense, and everything to do with the effort I make to express my feelings for her.

By the way, don't rule out flowers. At one point, I thought that for Carolyn flowers had run their course. I don't understand this at all, but flowers still have an impact on her. A dozen roses, or a large bouquet, are not necessary. A single flower speaks volumes.

## 5. Music

If you are gifted musically, what a difference that can make. Play for your wife. Sing her a love song. *Write* her a love song!

But gentlemen, please exercise sober judgment about where you are gifted and where you aren't. If, like me, you are not gifted musically, please don't even try. In fact, if you decide to delight your wife with your nonexistent musical gifts—you didn't read it here!

## 6. Getaways

I'll make this point again: time is absolutely necessary to the cultivation of romance and God-glorifying sex. Much time. Unhurried time. Undistracted time. While a date night creates an oasis in the middle of a busy week or month, a getaway creates an oasis in the middle of a year. When was the last time you took your wife away for at least two nights?

When Carolyn and I go away, we usually like to get out and do lots of things. We try new restaurants and search out interesting, off-beat locales to explore. But however much we see, and whatever activities we get involved in, I'm always careful to keep our focus primarily on one another. The heart of each of these events is our time alone together: talking, reading, making love, and taking long walks.

Is there a place your wife has been wanting to visit? What activities do you enjoy together? What's keeping you from making those plans? What's keeping you from saving the money for this very worthy investment?

### 7. Surprises

Here's a question to ponder during your weekly planning. "At this point in our life together, what would my wife define as a welcome surprise?" I ask myself that question all the time. I'll start writing some ideas, and maybe not come up with very much, but somehow it gets the gears turning. Then the next day in the shower I get an idea, then another one three days later while driving. Or I might overhear a conversation in a store and it triggers a thought.

Every time I get an idea, I write it down. And it all begins with a simple commitment to try to surprise my wife. As a result, Carolyn lives with the constant and delightful tension that I am always planning some sort of surprise for her.

Surprises make a huge and very romantic statement of your care. You can surprise her with any of the things I've mentioned—a phone call, a letter, a song, a gift, a getaway, or a date—or get creative and make up a whole new category!

But here's a recommendation. Don't "surprise" her on Valentine's Day, or her birthday, or an anniversary. Sure, plan something for February 14. But a true surprise is unexpected.

So, in calling my wife each day—in writing her notes or buying her gifts or taking her on dates—I'm not just blindly following some recipe for a happy marriage topped off with good sex. Rather, I've studied what the Bible says, especially in Ephesians 5, about what it means to be a husband and a godly leader in the home, and I've tried to come up with practical ways to make my marriage actually be what the Bible says it should be. The result is the seven recommendations you have just read. For me, and quite often for others, these things work.

If they work for you, great. But if not—and you certainly don't have to emulate them—create your own! What matters is that you are learning, leading, and loving your wife with creativity and intentionality. Because if you are not intentional in planning for creative romance, it just won't happen.

## Is It Still Obvious?

Think back with me for a moment. There was a time when it was obvious to everyone that you were uniquely passionate about your wife. You couldn't stop thinking about her. You constantly talked about her and to her. You were always eager to spend time with her, going out of your way to delight and surprise her, and you regularly spent serious money on her.

Is your passion for your wife still obvious to everyone? Is it obvious to her?

Here's a way to find out. If you have children living in the home, ask your beloved this one simple question:

*Do you feel more like a mother or a wife?*

The answer may well speak volumes. In my book (of the same name as this chapter) I'm able to elaborate further on this and the other points made here. But suffice it to say that she certainly *can* feel more like a wife than a mother (or homemaker, employee, or professional). Whether she does, however, is primarily up to you.

Yes, the Bible calls us to a high, godly standard, guys. But it's one we definitely can reach by God's grace. We must touch the hearts and minds of our wives before we touch their bodies. As our words and actions touch their hearts and minds, much will be transformed—our wives will be transformed, our marriages will be transformed, and you will discover a marvelous and growing sexual passion, all for the glory of God.

How will you begin this glorious process? How will you touch your wife's heart and mind?

## The Gift of Marital Intimacy

Here it is, gentlemen. Time to talk about sex. For there comes a point when we have studied and planned . . . when we have spoken our tender and provocative words of love . . . when we're ready to move beyond verbal foreplay. So let us prepare once again to learn from Scripture—where, beyond such foreplay, the lovers in Solomon's Song definitely do move.

As this man and woman enter into lovemaking, they do not hold back, nor does Scripture refrain from recording intimate details of their mutually delightful encounter. Far from a mechanical recitation of "who touched who where," we read of the extravagant indulgence of all five senses. Touch, taste, smell, sight, and hearing are put to full use. Solomon's Song teaches us that lovemaking is intended by God to be an elaborate and pleasurable feast of the senses—a holy immersion in erotic joy.

So let's be inspired by this powerful piece of poetry—by the romantic, the sensual, the erotic, and the tasteful but specific descriptions of the physical relationship enjoyed by these two lovers. Solomon has given us the divine perspective on the gift of sex. Let's explore that perspective, that with our wives we might experience its transforming effect.

### Kissing

There are numerous references in Solomon's song to kissing. At one point the man declares, "How beautiful is your love, my sister, my bride! How much better is your love than wine, and the fragrance of your oils than any spice! Your lips drip nectar, my bride; honey and milk are under your tongue" (4:10-11).

There was clearly some serious kissing going on here. The man delights in the kisses of his beloved—deep, long, passionate kisses. The "honey and milk" mentioned in this verse are symbols of fruitfulness, satisfaction, and pleasure. He's a skillful kisser, too, so the enjoyment is mutual. His bride says of him, "His mouth is most sweet" (5:16).

These two are obviously very familiar with each other's lips and mouths. They revel in the touch, tastes, and scents associated with their kissing. Their kissing is erotic, sensual, enjoyed, and apparently prolonged.

In many marriages today, however, kissing is often neglected and can all too easily become routine. If your kisses rarely get much more passionate than a handshake, there is huge room for improvement.

So I suggest you take inventory. How often do you kiss? How long do you kiss? How passionate is your kissing? Ask your wife what she thinks of your kissing. What does she like or dislike about it? How does it compare with what is described here? How does it compare with your past kissing? How can you improve?

Don't assume that kissing is a thrill that belonged mainly to some earlier point in your marriage. Kissing between a husband and wife is a unique expression of their passion for one another, and a unique means of cultivating fresh passion. In light of the divine encouragement found in the Song, let's purpose to explore this rich gift of kissing.

### Touching and Caressing

Sexual touching and caressing of many kinds are found throughout the Song. "Your stature is like a palm tree, and your breasts are like its clusters. I say I will climb the palm tree and lay hold of its fruit. Oh may your breasts be like clusters of the vine" (7:7-8).

Touching and caressing are to be an ongoing part of the marriage relationship. How I touch Carolyn will certainly depend on where we are and what we're doing. But if she's near me, I'll almost certainly be touching her in some way, even if it's simply holding her hand.

A few years ago, after returning from a busy overseas trip that was full of meetings and responsibilities for both of us, Carolyn and I took an overnight together near our home. As we were checking out of the hotel, the man at the registration desk commented, "I noticed you two yesterday, and I've watched you today. You remind me of a couple of high school sweethearts."

Now it wasn't as if Carolyn and I had been doing anything inappropriate. We actually get those "sweetheart" comments with some regularity. When we respond that we've been married since 1975, it can open the door to a more meaningful conversation. What a great opportunity it gives us to testify to the grace of God in our lives!

Gentlemen, I want to encourage your frequent, imaginative touching of your wives (as appropriate given your level of privacy). Touching your wife in a variety of creative ways is not just a warm-up to your next sexual encounter. When practiced regularly as a genuine expression of affection, love, and passion it contributes to a closeness and intimacy that can help fuel your romance and sex life well into the future.

So talk to your wife about what she thinks makes for appropriate and pleasurable touching, in public and in private. In this process you may need to lead diligently, graciously, and with love. Do whatever is necessary to get beyond any embarrassment arising from pride that might be associated with such a subject. The two of you need to be able to discuss these topics openly and honestly. The better you learn how to touch her heart and mind, the better the two of you will be able to communicate freely and really learn how to love one another more and more.

*Ultimate Intimacy*

In chapters 4 and 5 of the Song, Solomon gives us a glimpse of ultimate physical passion as this couple prepares to come together for sexual intercourse. The restraint that has characterized the book to this point no longer applies. The time has come for sexual union.

Their encounter begins with the woman inviting the man to come and enjoy her love. "Awake, O north wind, and come, O south wind! Blow upon my garden, let its spices flow. Let my beloved come to his garden, and eat its choicest fruits" (4:16).

In the next verse, the man eagerly responds. Even here, the poetry is discreet and restrained, bursting with passion yet completely devoid of vulgarity. "I came to my garden, my sister, my bride, I gathered my myrrh with my spice, I ate my honeycomb with my honey, I drank my wine with my milk" (5:1).

Myrrh, spice, honeycomb, honey, wine, milk—he likens her sensual delights to the most extraordinary luxuries available in that culture. Nine times he employs the word "my," as one by one he claims her "choice fruits" as his own possessions. She is his, fully, completely, and without reservation.

Then, at the end of verse 1, we find this ringing affirmation of sexual indulgence within marriage: "Eat, friends, drink, and be drunk with love!" Here, as elsewhere in the Song, Solomon employs a "chorus," which stands outside the narrative as a witness and commentator. The chorus encourages the couple to enjoy lovemaking to the fullest, to be intoxicated with one another in their love. With God as Author of Scripture, can there be a clearer expression of the divine approval and encouragement of sexuality within marriage?

Let this chorus remind you that, when you make love to your wife, the two of you are not alone. God is present, and he is pleased when you and your wife find erotic satisfaction in one another. Indeed, he encourages you with the same unqualified approval with which they were encouraged: "Be drunk with love."

Many passages of Scripture liken the experience of sexual intimacy to intoxication. (No hangover, either!) When was the last time you and your wife drank deeply enough of one another's sensual joys to come to that place of sweet, godly drunkenness?

## Mutual Fulfillment

Because this is a chapter for men, we need to talk briefly about how selfishness can show up during lovemaking in a way that's unique to us. Unless you just got married last week, you're surely aware that effective lovemaking—the kind that really serves your wife—is not instinctive.

I'm talking, obviously, about that extremely common tendency for husbands to find satisfaction in lovemaking sooner than their wives. Does the Bible have anything to say about that? You bet.

If I am living in obedience to 1 Corinthians 7:3-4, I will take my thoughts captive during lovemaking, disciplining my body in order to focus primarily on giving to my wife sexually, rather than only receiving from her. ("The husband should give to his wife her conjugal rights, and likewise the wife to her husband. For the wife does not have authority over her own body, but the husband does. Likewise the husband does not have authority over his own body, but the wife does.") Indeed, any married person who rightly sees these verses as commands from God will bring to the marriage bed a servant's mind-set that places primary emphasis on the sexual satisfaction of his or her spouse.

Are you a skillful and unselfish lover? Don't assume you know what your wife likes, or what arouses her. She is aroused differently than you are. You must discover what arouses her—and what does not—by engaging her in extended conversation.

Making love is not simply a technique. It's a key part of the marriage relationship. A couple that enjoys great sex, as biblically defined, is a couple that has good, open, honest communication about lots of things, including sex.

You need to lead your wife into conversations where you can ask very intimate, personal questions. Any reluctance we may have in this area, guys, is simply due to our pride, and the solution is simply to humble ourselves—before God and our wives. We need to approach our wives with an attitude of genuine interest, an attitude that says, "I want to be an unselfish lover. How can I serve you through this gift from God?" "What can I do, or what do I do, that arouses you prior to and during the sex act?" "Is there anything I sometimes do that you'd rather I not do?"

As lovers, many of us have plateaued, but none have arrived. We can all improve. To really find out what brings pleasure to your wife, you have to ask her.

### Realistic Expectations

Now, just to set the record straight, I'm not promising that this chapter will turn your every sexual encounter with your wife into a sweating, shouting frenzy. I *am* confident that a consistently God-glorifying approach to marital intimacy can improve any couple's sex life significantly. But let's keep in mind that we're human, with human limitations. Moreover, eventually all of us will find that age is more of an issue than it used to be.

On the subject of sexual expectations, Douglas Wilson has pointed out that while some meals are steaks, and some are macaroni and cheese, both are enjoyable.[6] That's wise counsel. So let your expectations be realistic, and enjoy.

Enjoy the humorous moments, too. More than once I've found myself in a situation where all I want to do for the next minute or so is stay very, very focused on what my wife and I are doing *right now*. But

---

[6] Douglas Wilson, *Reforming Marriage* (Moscow, Ida.: Canon, 1995), 83.

then this leg cramp shows up out of nowhere. Now, a cramp has a way of demanding your full and complete attention. So in about five seconds I go from the heights of sexual enjoyment to incapacitating agony. I want to keep my attention on Carolyn, but suddenly all my attention is on my leg. I want to keep my hands on her, but *they* have to go to my leg, too.

What do we do? We laugh like crazy. And hope the kids don't hear.

So you see, ultimately, sex is not a matter of performance. We've talked a lot about getting better at sex, but I'm not suggesting for a moment that your marriage should become a multi-decade quest for the ideal set of orgasms. While I do want to please my wife whenever we make love, sex is not primarily a goal-oriented activity. It's an event, an experience. It's about expressing passion to my wife, and receiving her expressions of passion for me. If a couple is living with a biblical under-standing of and attitude toward sex, then every experience can be enjoyable and glorifying to God.

## The Love Behind the Sex

We close where we began, learning once more from the Song of Solomon.

It's remarkable how Solomon's language, while obvious in its intent, is never biologically specific in a way that is either vulgar or clinical. As a result, while we can clearly say that the Song features some pretty provocative stuff, and that sexual intercourse is definitely included in the subject matter, we cannot point to a specific phrase and say, "Yes, look, right here, in *this* verse the language clearly indicates that they are engaged in sexual intercourse."

But that fact is itself full of meaning. Although sexual intercourse is certainly an ultimate expression of a married couple's erotic encounter, it is *not* the outstanding central feature of the Song. The book is not *about* the act of sexual intercourse. Rather, it is about the remarkable nature of the couple's overall relationship—in all its romance, yearning, desire, sensuality, passion, and eroticism.

These two desperately desire to be together, *but not simply so they can experience sexual gratification.* They want to be together because they are in love, and the sex they enjoy with one another is an expres-sion of that love. Their mutual attraction is not primarily hormonal. It is primarily relational.

Five times in Solomon's Song, the man calls his beloved "my sister, my bride," or "my sister, my love." She refers to him as "my beloved" and "my friend." Their love is comprehensive and complete; they love one another on multiple levels. As a married couple, they have great sex *because* they love one another so completely, not the other way around.

In a strong Christian marriage that glorifies God, a couple's enjoyment of one another takes place on a long continuum of romantic affection and expression. Toward one end are things like "companionship" and "fellowship." Toward the other end of the continuum are things like "playful intimacy" and "really serious sex." But exactly where one category begins and the other ends isn't always clear. That's because solid Christian marriages are not primarily about one category or the other. They're about the entire continuum: the relationship itself.

This chapter has focused on the romance-and-sex end of the continuum—but without disconnecting it from any other aspect of the marital relationship. That's what Solomon did in the Song. That's what you should be doing, too, by God's grace. Because it's all about touching her heart and mind before you touch her body.

# Part 4: Women and Sex

# CHAPTER 8

## Sex and the Single Woman

CAROLYN MCCULLEY

I received a rude awakening recently at a spinning class. (Yes, I'm a single woman, but don't panic—this isn't a class for practicing spinsters! It's a sweaty, unglamorous, long ride on a stationary bicycle.) It was 7 A.M., and after riding for an hour, everyone was wide-awake and engaging in small talk.

"I'm scared to death of the teenage girls these days," the instructor announced as she wiped down her bike.

"I know exactly what you mean!" chimed in another forty-something woman. "They're completely predatory these days. It's incredible!"

"My son is being stalked—there's really no other word for it—by this fifteen-year-old girl," the instructor continued. *"Fifteen!* She calls him night and day, sends him the most suggestive instant messages, and then—get this!—she stood at her back door *completely* naked, waving to him across the yard. I was so angry! And she's not the only one. Other girls chase my son just as strongly, though maybe not so crassly."

Most of the class participants were women in their late thirties to early fifties—outspoken, athletic women whose conversations had never indicated that any of them shared my Christian faith. The occasional serious male cyclist joined us when the weather was bad, but on this morning it was all women, with an unexpected kind of girl talk. I listened with serious concern—troubled at the reports I was hearing of life in twenty-first-century high school.

Normally I'm not shy about joining such conversations, but this time I was actually shocked into silence by their tales. I left that class burdened to pray for my instructor, her son, and his female "stalker." For days I kept thinking about what I'd heard—especially the reactions of these parents, women who were probably proponents of and participants in the sexual revolution of the 60s and 70s. Now, only one generation later, they are dismayed by the effects of that "revolution."

## The Tipping Point

Pollster and analyst Daniel Yankelovich has been studying American values for more than 50 years. In a recent interview with the *Washington Post Magazine,* he said that during the 1960s and 70s, Americans underwent the kind of dramatic transformation of social values that usually occurs over generations.[1] But for their children, technology introduced a darker, uglier dimension as first the home VCR and then the Internet made pornography easily accessible and even acceptable to some. This has had a profound, and perhaps unexpected, effect on young women that has not been ignored by feminists themselves.

"I think the tipping point came three or four years ago with the first generation to grow up with the Internet," says feminist author Naomi Wolf. "They were daughters of feminists. The feminist message of autonomy got filtered through a pornographized culture. The message they heard was just go for it sexually. . . . The downside is we've raised a generation of young women—and men—who don't understand sexual ethics like: Don't sleep with a married man; don't sleep with a married woman; don't embarrass people with whom you had a consensual sexual relationship. They don't see sex as sacred or even very important anymore. That's been lost. Sex has been commodified and drained of its deeper meaning."[2]

This disturbing trend now has the attention of mainstream media. I've noted a number of articles in recent months about the "hook-up" culture even among middle schoolers. It's as though parents who work as journalists are just now discovering what their children are actually doing in our sex-saturated culture.

---

[1] April Witt, "Blog Interrupted," *The Washington Post Magazine,* August 15, 2004, 17.
[2] Ibid., 16.

We really shouldn't be surprised when we consider sex and the single woman in twenty-first-century American culture. There are only two portraits of the single woman in popular media. One is the current pop icon, surgically augmented with a low fabric-to-flesh wardrobe ratio, usually sporting a vulgar phrase on her bust or bum, and unabashed in her sexual aggressiveness. The other is the forlorn result of the pursuit of sexual freedom—the confused waif whose self-centered ruminations are the fodder for the fictional characters on television (Ally McBeal) or in movies and literature (Bridget Jones).

I don't make these comments as though I'm standing outside of our culture, lobbing in the critiques. I grew up a feminist. I even have a women's studies certificate to accessorize my journalism degree from the University of Maryland. As I didn't become a Christian until I was thirty, I assumed nothing much could shock me about mainstream culture. But now—when I read articles about the spreadsheets college women keep about their sexual activities, or when I watch how the Christian men I know struggle to avoid the parade of barely dressed women before them at a mall or restaurant, or when I have to turn over all ten women's magazines at the grocery checkout because my nieces can now read their soft-porn headlines—I find I am more than shocked; I am deeply grieved. *This* is what feminism has done to improve the standing of women? It's a very poor trade-off, indeed.

As conservative commentator Danielle Crittenden writes in *What Our Mothers Didn't Tell Us: Why Happiness Eludes the Modern Woman*:

> Indeed, in all the promises made to us about our ability to achieve freedom and independence as women, the promise of sexual emancipation may have been the most illusory. These days, certainly, it is the one most brutally learned. All the sexual bravado a girl may possess evaporates the first time a boy she truly cares for makes it clear that he has no further use for her after his own body has been satisfied. No amount of feminist posturing, no amount of reassurances that she doesn't need a guy like that anyway, can protect her from the pain and humiliation of those awful moments after he's gone, when she's alone and feeling not sexually empowered but discarded. It doesn't take most women long to figure out that sexual liberty is not the same thing as sexual equality.[3]

---

[3] Danielle Crittenden, *What Our Mothers Didn't Tell Us: Why Happiness Eludes the Modern Woman* (New York: Touchstone, 1999), 31.

## "You're Not Normal"

Crittenden is right, but I don't see where that revelation is inspiring any counterrevolution in our culture. It's not even possible. The only key to true change is found in the power of the gospel. Christ's redemptive power to break the bondage of sin and restore what sin has consumed is the *only* good news for women. As sex is both God's idea and his good gift to us, Christians should be uninhibited in addressing this topic.

But let me ask a hard question right here. Do we, as committed Christian single women who are by God's grace avoiding sexual immorality, truly *believe* we can address our culture on this topic? I mean, we're the "just say no" camp, right? Wouldn't it be easier to address the sexually broken women around us if we could talk firsthand about the joys of marital intimacy and God's plan for sex within the covenant of marriage?

I've thought this way, to be honest. As a volunteer for a local crisis pregnancy center, I was asked on several occasions how I could handle living without sex. These clients didn't ask me flippantly. They were really concerned they couldn't do the same, as if maybe they would explode from all the built-up pressure. I would assure them God's grace was sufficient, but they remained doubtful.

It's the same with a number of my friends who knew me as an unbeliever. The seriousness of my conversion was quickly established when they discovered now I actually was going to wait until marriage. That commitment then became the litmus test—more so than other aspects of my faith. When an unbelieving client asked me out shortly after my conversion, my colleagues insisted I declare myself and my standards to him. "You have to tell him you're not normal," they said.

*"You're not normal."* You're a Christian single woman called by Scripture to sexual purity and abstinence until marriage, living and working in a sex-saturated society during the week. On the weekends, you fellowship with families in your church, where marriage and family are generally held in high regard. But you don't feel that you fit in either place. After awhile you may start to think it's true; maybe you're really *not* normal.

It's true. You're not normal. But this is good news. If you've repented of your sins and put your trust in the finished work of Jesus Christ and his substitutionary death on the cross for the punishment of your sins, then you're definitely not "normal." Your identity has been reclaimed and reordered by the Lord. You are a Christian, a woman, and a currently single adult. And that's the order of information that's most important about you. Your most important identity is as a Christian, ransomed by God himself. Second to that is your identity as a woman, made feminine and made in God's image. Those two identities will never change. But your status as a single adult could change several times within your lifetime, so that is the least important aspect of your identity.

Unfortunately, we are often parked on the "single" label—and not really trusting God with it. That makes it hard to share the gospel at times, doesn't it? It's hard to be an authentic witness to the lost when bitterness about unanswered prayers for a husband threatens to overwhelm the joy of our salvation.

To be fruitful in our outreach and impact, we need to clearly see our singleness through the lens of Scripture and not our desires. (That doesn't mean they are mutually exclusive, however.) And we need to find a biblical guide for this season. Let's start with what the Bible says about being single.

## The Gift of Singleness

Did you ever notice that it was a single man who wrote the longest passage in Scripture about singleness? It's also the only place in the Bible where singleness is called a gift—and a *good* gift—which may be surprising to some.

Look at 1 Corinthians 7:6-9. As you read this excerpt, please keep in mind that Paul was addressing some specific questions or views that the Corinthian church had previously sent to him—questions that we don't have access to today. Paul begins in verses 1-5 by addressing married people. In fact, he quotes a statement from the Corinthians that he's going to correct ("it's good for a man not to have sexual relations with a woman") and then he turns to singleness in verse 6:

> Now as a concession, not a command, I say this. I wish that all were as I myself am. But each has his own gift from God, one of one kind and one of another. To the unmarried and the widows I say that it is good for them to remain single as I am. But if they cannot exercise self-

control, they should marry. For it is better to marry than to be aflame
with passion.

Here we have Paul calling singleness both good and a gift. But it's
not a gift in the way we might think about it on our birthdays or at
Christmas: "Do I like it? Do I want to keep it? Can I exchange it for
what I really want?" There are several Greek words that could be trans-
lated as *gift* in English. One word denotes a gift presented as an expression of honor. A second euphemistically infers that a gift is more a matter
of debt or obligation. A third denotes a free gift of grace, used in the New
Testament to refer to a spiritual or supernatural gift.[4] This is the word
Paul uses in this passage—*charisma.*

Despite all the modern connotations associated with the word
*charisma,* it means much more than the nuances found in either the
Pentecostal/charismatic theology of spiritual gifts or the functional
"identifying your spiritual gifts" lists common in evangelical circles. As
a gift of grace, it stresses the fact that it is a gift of God the Creator freely
bestowed upon sinners—his endowment upon believers by the operation
of the Holy Spirit in the churches.[5] New Testament scholar Gordon Fee
says that Paul's use of *charisma* throughout this letter to the Corinthians
stresses the root word of *grace,* not the gifting itself. Fee writes:

> Thus, even though Paul has concrete expressions of "grace" in view . . .
> and even though in ch. 12 these concrete expressions are understood
> as the direct result of Spirit activity, there seems to be no real justifica-
> tion for the translation "spiritual gift" for this word. Rather, they are
> "gracious endowments" (where the emphasis lies on the grace involved
> in their being so gifted), which at times, as in this letter, is seen also as
> the gracious activity of the Spirit in their midst.[6]

But for what purpose would God give us this "gracious endowment" of being single? Paul gives us a glimpse a few chapters later, in
chapter 12, verses 4-11:

---

[4] W. E. Vine, *The Expanded Vine's Expository Dictionary of New Testament Words,* ed. John R.
Kohlenberger III (Minneapolis: Bethany, 1984), 476-477.
[5] Ibid., 477.
[6] Gordon D. Fee, *God's Empowering Presence: The Holy Spirit in the Letters of Paul* (Peabody, Mass.:
Hendrickson, 1994), 86.

Now there are varieties of gifts, but the same Spirit; and there are varieties of service, but the same Lord; and there are varieties of activities, but it is the same God who empowers them all in everyone. *To each is given the manifestation of the Spirit for the common good.* To one is given through the Spirit the utterance of wisdom, and to another the utterance of knowledge according to the same Spirit, to another faith by the same Spirit, to another gifts of healing by the one Spirit, to another the working of miracles, to another prophecy, to another the ability to distinguish between spirits, to another various kinds of tongues, to another the interpretation of tongues. *All these are empowered by one and the same Spirit, who apportions to each one individually as he wills.*

Here we see two important points: 1) God is the one who apportions to each of us the gifts that he wills us to have; and 2) each one is given the manifestation of the Spirit for the common good. This means we can rule out worldly ways of evaluating why we're not married—too old, too young, too fat, too skinny, too loud, too tall, too short, and so on. You can look around any of our churches and see plenty of married women who fall into these categories. Ultimately we are single because that's God's will for us right now.

Let's think about that for a moment. We're single because that's God's will for us right now. Is that discouraging to hear? It shouldn't be. That's when we need to remember that our most important identity is not being single; it's being saved. God has done for us something *far* more important than getting us to the wedding altar. The gentle words of my pastor, C. J. Mahaney, are a good reminder: "Your greatest need is not a spouse. Your greatest need is to be delivered from the wrath of God—and that has already been accomplished for you through the death and resurrection of Christ. So why doubt that God will provide a much, much lesser need? Trust His sovereignty, trust His wisdom, trust His love." [7]

One more thought: I've often heard married people say to singles that we won't get married until we're content in our singleness, but I humbly submit that this is not true. I'm sure that it is offered by well-meaning couples who want to see their single friends happy and content in God's provision, but it creates a works-based mentality to receiving gifts, which can

---

[7] C. J. Mahaney, cited in Joshua Harris, *Boy Meets Girl* (Sisters, Ore.: Multnomah, 2000), 213.

lead to feelings of condemnation. The Lord doesn't require that we attain a particular state before he grants a gift. We can't earn any particular spiritual gift any more than we can earn our own salvation. It's all of grace. However, we *should* humbly listen to our friends and receive their input about cultivating contentment—after all, the apostle Paul says that "there is great gain in godliness with contentment" (1 Tim. 6:6); we just shouldn't attach it to the expectation of a blessing.

If you are single again due to divorce or death, I realize it can be challenging to reconcile your current experience with the concept of a gift that God has allowed or even willed, but this is the testimony of Scripture. I trust the expanded definition of "gift" has helped you to understand better your current situation.

## Gifted for the Common Good

So, great! We have this gracious endowment and it's God's will for us. But . . . for what purpose? Paul says that the purpose is for the common good, which by implication means the local church. Now, this doesn't mean that it's for the good of all the rest of the men in our churches that we didn't marry them! We can get a better idea of what Paul is talking about by looking at 1 Peter 4:10. It says, "As each has received a gift [*charisma*], use it to serve one another, as good stewards of God's varied grace." The NIV translates this passage as "faithfully administering God's grace in its various forms."

Ladies, we have to stop here and ask ourselves if being gifted for the benefit of the church is something that's important to us. This passage from 1 Corinthians 12 shows us that singleness gives us a *context* for the other spiritual gifts we may have and is a *resource* to be faithfully administered. But this biblical passage also goes on to give us a *place* to invest our gifts. Verses 14-26 go on to present the analogy of the church as members of a body and emphasize the interdependency of the members. Verse 15 says, "If the foot should say, 'Because I am not a hand, I do not belong to the body,' that would not make it any less a part of the body." Do we ever act like that foot? Are we saying (in thoughts, words, or actions), "Because I am not part of a couple, I do not belong to the body"? We *are* part of the body, and we have a vital function within our churches. Those other members need us, and we need them.

As I've become older, I've grown in my gratitude for my church. Many times I've looked around the Sunday worship service or at my friends in a small-group meeting, and silently thanked God for the fellowship I have there. Not only am I grateful for the wealth of relationships, I am grateful for the grand vision before me. When I think of how much Christ loves his bride, the church, and how in his merciful kindness he has rescued me and made me a part of this body, I am even more grateful for the purpose I find in the church.

Without the context and eternal purpose of the church, singleness can seem like the waiting room of adulthood. *With* the context and eternal purpose of the church, singleness truly is a gift for the common good of others. We can love the bride of Christ by joyfully investing the "firstfruits" of our resources, affections, and time in our churches.

### Proverbs 31 and the Single Woman

So these 1 Corinthians passages help us to have a biblical view of singleness, but there's another place in Scripture where we can find practical application and a role model. Oddly enough, it's in the Proverbs 31 woman—the portrait of the excellent wife! Because of her role, it's easy for single women to glaze over these verses—but they are important to us. This epilogue (vv. 10-31) is a twenty-two-verse acrostic; each line starts with a successive letter of the Hebrew alphabet. It is attributed to the mother of King Lemuel, who instructed her young son through this memory game in both the alphabet and the qualities of a virtuous wife. In other words, she wanted this future ruler to know by heart what to look for in a *single* woman to ensure that he had found someone who would make an excellent wife.

When I considered this for the first time, I laughed out loud. The very passage I often skipped because it was about an excellent wife was the key to understanding my singleness! Here was the guide I needed to understanding my femininity as a single woman and for showing me how to invest this season, this gift, in the church. As I studied the Proverbs 31 woman, the priorities for my life came into focus. The *role* that's described in this passage is that of a wife, but her godly, noble character is what all women should desire. While many translations call her a wife, the original Hebrew word is *ishshah*, or woman. The King

James Version refers to her as "a virtuous woman." The New International Version calls her a "wife of noble character." The English Standard Version calls her "an excellent wife." No matter her role, this woman is virtuous, noble, and excellent. She is commended as "a woman [ishshah] who fears the LORD" in verse 30. These are virtues for all Christian women, whatever our marital status.

The Proverbs 31 woman is a savvy businesswoman with financial assets. She is an encouraging and enterprising wife. She is an affectionate mother. She is a gourmet cook. She is an artful homemaker. She speaks with wisdom. And she cheerfully trusts the Lord for her future. Her example can be applied to all seasons of a woman's life, including singleness. I can't go into detail here,[8] but here is a quick overview of some of those verses and how single women can apply them:

- From verses 14 and 15 we see that we are to cultivate a love for the home even when we're not there very often. These verses say: "She is like the ships of the merchant; she brings her food from afar. She rises while it is yet night and provides food for her household and portions for her maidens." Food from afar isn't a pizza delivery! Because Scripture emphasizes the priority of hospitality, we should see our homes as a place for evangelism to the lost and service to the saints. We don't have to be married to own a home, china, or furniture. We don't have to be married to practice cooking. We don't have to be married to have (most) houseguests. But we do have to be intentional about being home and cultivating domestic skills! Our model is Lydia, who was a successful, single businesswoman in Philippi, and yet who was ready to extend hospitality to Paul upon her conversion (Acts 16:14-15).
- From verses 16-19 we have an example of how to wisely steward finances, professional skills, time, and training. These verses say: "She considers a field and buys it; with the fruit of her hands she plants a vineyard. She dresses herself with strength and makes her arms strong. She perceives that her merchandise is profitable. Her lamp does not go out at night.

---

[8] A more detailed treatment can be found in my book, *Did I Kiss Marriage Goodbye? Trusting God with a Hope Deferred* (Wheaton, Ill.: Crossway, 2004), chapters 4-13 and the epilogue.

She puts her hands to the distaff, and her hands hold the spindle." If the Lord brings a husband to us, these skills and savings would be a blessing. If not, they will support us and give us resources to further the gospel and support the local church. Our challenge is to evaluate all the opportunities before us through the grid of biblical femininity, and the Proverbs 31 woman keeps us from following the worldly model of a career being the ultimate priority.

- From verse 28, we see that we are to be intentional about investing in the next generation. That verse says: "Her children rise up and call her blessed." While we may not have children of our own, the Lord has placed children in our lives. Psalm 145:4 says that "one generation shall commend your works to another, and shall declare your mighty acts." This raises some important questions. Are we participating in the work of evangelizing and discipling the next generation? Are we being faithful to love the children who are already in our lives while we trust the Lord with our desire to be mothers? We don't have to bear children of our own to have the next generation bless us for investing in them.

This is God's portrait of femininity. The Proverbs 31 woman's generous orientation to blessing others stands in stark contrast to what our culture has created and deemed important for modern women. We neither have to emulate the aggressive female sexuality of our culture nor feel excluded from the model of biblical femininity in the church just because we're unmarried.

## Sexual Snares at Work

Speaking of standing in stark contrast to our culture, I think a discussion of sex and the single woman would be incomplete without addressing sexual snares at work. So if you'll allow me, let's take a sidetrack into the pitfalls of our workday worlds.

First, let's be candid. Our office settings or the functions of our jobs can also present specific temptations to sin—snares that we *must* identify and work hard to avoid—but I think the most common is the temptation of sexual sin. Whether it's pornography in our hotel rooms while we travel on business or the allure of a married colleague's attentions, our jobs can be minefields for sexual sin.

Before I became a Christian, the majority of my dating relationships were connected to my job. When I became a Christian, I had to quickly establish boundaries with a married colleague who had often engaged me in banter ranging from flirtatious to vulgar. A few weeks after my conversion, I invited him to my office and explained my new beliefs. I then informed him that I would no longer entertain his attentions because I had been sinfully and selfishly drawing his affections away from his wife. But I wanted him to understand my new convictions and why I saw this as stealing from his wife, and I asked his forgiveness. He was stunned—but unfortunately he never seemed to entirely understand the boundaries I had redrawn that day. Over the years (even after I left this job), he would periodically ask me to lunch and I would always decline, citing that as his wife wouldn't be present I didn't think our lunch would honor her. Maybe he was testing my convictions, but I'm glad to say by God's grace I didn't waver.

As single women, we must be savvy about the emotional connections that can be made on the job. We women were designed by God to be helpers and to make men successful. We can't be oblivious to the fact that our encouragement, support, and promotion of our male colleagues can sometimes misfire in our own hearts—not to mention theirs. I've known many Christian single women who have wrestled with their attraction to unbelieving single coworkers or even married colleagues. We can help each other here by listening carefully as our friends talk about their colleagues. Do our friends light up when talking about one particular person at work? If so, ask questions. It's better to be labeled a little nosy now than later to walk with your friend through the fallout of an immoral relationship or adulterous affair. It's not easy to do this, I know. I remember one friend who seemed a little too delighted when her married male boss called her at home or asked her to work late. She talked about him a lot, so I finally asked her if she was sliding down that slippery slope of adultery. She was shocked when I asked, but I told her that the top of the slope is innocent attraction—and that's where she seemed to be. I wanted her to be aware of gravity's pull. She dismissed my concern then, but a few months later did come back to confess it was more serious. Though she did not overtly sin, she was poised for a spectacular crash-and-burn, and she was glad I asked her about it in time.

Sexual sin isn't always a subtle, slippery slope. Sometimes it's just blatantly there. Another friend of mine recently confessed her temptation in a situation she never thought would appeal to her. While attending a political hearing in another town, she ended up talking to the immensely attractive man next to her. Their discussion made it clear he wasn't a Christian (strike one), but she wasn't sure about his marital status. He had no ring. During the lunch break, he invited her to join him in the building's cafeteria. She accepted, and found herself enjoying his attentions. She knew this wasn't a good idea, but she dismissed her conscience by telling herself it's just lunch. After the hearing concluded, he asked her to return to his hotel with him. By then, the warning bells were going off, but she was still slow to flee sin—tempted by the idea that "no one would know." Except God, of course, who mercifully sent a coworker from this man's office at that very moment. In the course of that conversation with his coworker, this man revealed that he had invited my friend to his hotel room. His coworker asked how this man's wife might react, and the man said his wife wouldn't care because they had an "open marriage." Upon those words, the fear of God entered my friend's heart and she immediately declined any further contact and left. Later, she said she was appalled by how tempted she was to respond to this man's blatant sexual overtures, and she asked for ongoing accountability in this area.

None of us is immune to sexual temptation at work. Just read the newspaper. How many of the accounts of adulterous affairs noted there began on the job? It's a classic story, and we must be mindful that we are not above the same temptations. The Enemy of our souls studies us and knows our weaknesses, and the hunger for a relationship leaves us vulnerable unless we guard against sin and ask God for his grace to overcome. There are some practical steps we can take, however, to avoid sin. Here are a few questions we can ask ourselves in order to evaluate temptation:

- Am I avoiding the appearance of evil on the job? Is it necessary for me to have exclusive lunch meetings alone with a married colleague? Or am I conducting business alone in a hotel room with him, instead of in a public area?

- Am I looking forward to Monday morning because of the attention I might receive from an "off-limits man"—a married man or a single but unbelieving coworker? Or do I "swing by" his office with a question, instead of using the telephone or email, just so I can engage his attention?
- Am I offering my male boss or colleagues the kind of sympathy or emotional support that is more appropriate from a wife?
- Have I allowed myself to become an outlet for the personal troubles of my married boss or colleague? (Warning! Do *not* discuss his marital woes!)
- Do I crave attention and encouragement from an "off-limits" coworker?
- Am I fantasizing about these "off-limits" men? If so, have I confessed this to the appropriate person and asked for accountability?
- Am I taking steps to avoid other sexual temptation, such as canceling the pornography channels in hotel rooms or refusing to buy trashy women's magazines when traveling?

You may be reading these questions thinking that I'm being overly dramatic. Unfortunately, I've learned these warning signs from my own life and the lives of my friends. Our little fantasies and mild crushes are sowing seeds to a craving that demands to be satisfied, and that satisfaction is not honorable before the Lord. But don't forget it's not our sexuality that is dishonorable—it is our lust that is. As Joshua Harris writes:

> Keep this radical but liberating idea in mind: God *wants* you to embrace your sexuality. And battling lust is part of how to do that. Does the idea of embracing sexuality and fighting lust sound contradictory? That's probably because today's culture offers a very narrow definition of what it means to embrace your sexuality. It equates embracing your sexuality with doing whatever feels good. So according to our culture, to deny a sexual impulse at any point is to be untrue to yourself. . . . As Christians, embracing our sexuality looks radically different. We don't obey every sexual impulse—nor do we deny that we have sexual desires. Instead, we choose both restraint and grate-

fulness. For us, sexual desire joins every other part of our lives—our appetite for food, our use of money, our friendship, our dreams, our careers, our possessions, our abilities, our families—in bowing before the one true God.[9]

## Trusting God with a Hope Deferred

Are you discouraged or overwhelmed by this point? I know it can be a temptation for us all to peer into our futures and wonder if any good will come our way. So let's explore what it means to trust God with a hope deferred.

As I stated earlier, our primary identity is in being Christian. Second, it is in being a woman, for that is how God created us. And we see in the creation account in Genesis that God created Eve fully feminine before Adam ever laid eyes on her. So our femininity is not determined by a man's response—nor a lack of response! Our Creator is the one who determined what it means to be a woman, and he has given us plenty of instruction in the Bible as to how this is fleshed out—instructions that transcend marital status. Being single is last of those three identities.

But if we desire to be married, is it wrong to "ask, seek, and knock" for a husband and children? Absolutely not! The Bible tells us these are good gifts from the Lord. The question is, what kind of effort should we invest in those hopes? Should we feel compelled to make this desire our *chief* focus and priority—possibly to the detriment of serving others? Lots of well-meaning people may advise us to do so, but let's consider the stewardship concept that we are exhorted to remember from 1 Peter 4:10. If we're *always* out and about trying to meet men, we come across like a truck with its deer-hunting headlights on high beam—our desperation is nearly blinding! More importantly, there can be bad fruit from living with our "hunting lights" up. We could be called home to heaven tomorrow and all we could say for our time is that we've attended lots and lots of singles meetings looking for a husband. (Please don't misunderstand me. I'm not saying attending a singles ministry meeting is bad. Nor am I saying that any appropriate initiative to meet godly men is wrong. I'm addressing the kind of driven, restless activity

---

[9] Joshua Harris, *Not Even a Hint: Guarding Your Heart Against Lust* (Sisters, Ore.: Multnomah, 2003), 42.

that becomes distracting and undermines our service in our churches and to those around us.)

We don't have many accounts in Scripture of how various couples met and married, but we do have the stories of Rebekah and Ruth to consider. These were women of godly initiative in the fact that they noticed the needs of others around them and they worked hard to meet them. When the Lord decided to introduce them to their future husbands, these two women were serving, not hunting. We can trust God with our desires, even when we don't see any activity and we're not receiving any answers to our prayers. For this reason, I find great comfort in two intimate, poignant accounts of how the Lord blessed single women in the Bible.

The first is from the book of Ruth. Most single women are quite familiar with this narrative and can identify with Ruth. But how often are we more like *Naomi?* Here she was, a widow with a dependent, widowed daughter-in-law, returning to her hometown of Bethlehem after ten years in Moab—and she was facing real poverty and uncertainty about the future. When these women arrived in Bethlehem, they were greeted by the women of that town, who marveled that Naomi had returned to them. But to Naomi, overcome with self-pity, their greetings were hollow. "Do not call me *pleasant* [Naomi]," she said. "Call me *bitter* [Mara], for the Almighty has dealt very bitterly with me. I went away full, and the LORD has brought me back empty. Why call me Naomi, when the LORD has testified against me and the Almighty has brought calamity upon me?" (Ruth 1:20-21).

Naomi had surveyed her circumstances and concluded that the Lord had no further blessings for her. But *God* was not finished. For standing next to Naomi was the Lord's provision for material and relational blessing—Ruth. And just beyond Ruth, the barley harvest was ripening in the fields of her kinsman-redeemer, Boaz. God's quiet providence was already peeking forth, but Naomi couldn't perceive it. Naomi assumed her future was as barren as she was, but that wasn't true. Even as she uttered her complaint, God was quietly orchestrating the circumstances that would lead not only to the redemption of Naomi's family line and property but also to the ancestry of Jesus Christ.

We must never forget that what we can see of our circumstances is not all that is there.

The second narrative features Martha and Mary, two single women from Bethany. You might think I'm going to refer to Martha's infamous kitchen outburst of, "Lord, do you not care that my sister has left me to serve *alone?*" (Luke 10:40). But there's a more poignant New Testament scene recorded for us in the Gospel of John. Henry Blackaby painted it in *Experiencing God*:

> One morning I was reading the story of the death of Lazarus (John 11:1-45). Let me go through the sequence of what happened as I read. John reported that Jesus loved Lazarus, Mary, and Martha. Having received word that Lazarus was sick unto death, Jesus delayed going until Lazarus died. In other words, Mary and Martha asked Jesus to come help their brother, and there was silence. All the way through the final sickness and death of Lazarus, Jesus did not respond. They received no response from the One who *said* He loved Lazarus. Jesus even said He loved Mary and Martha. Yet, there was still no response.
>
> Lazarus died. They went through the entire funeral process. They fixed his body, put him in the grave, and covered it with a stone. Still they experienced silence from God. Then Jesus said to His disciples, "Let's go."
>
> When Jesus arrived, Lazarus had been dead four days. Martha said to Jesus, "Lord, if you had been here, my brother would not have died" (v. 32).
>
> Then the Spirit of God began to help me understand something. It seemed to me as if Jesus had said to Mary and Martha: "You are exactly right. If I had come, your brother would not have died. You know that I could have healed him, because you have seen me heal many, many times. If I had come when you asked me to, I would have healed him. But, you would have never known any more about Me than you already know. I knew that you were ready for a greater revelation of Me than you have ever known in your life. I wanted you to come to know that I am the resurrection and the life. My refusal and My silence were not rejection. It was an opportunity for Me to disclose to you more of Me than you have ever known."[10]

*We must never forget that God's silences are not his rejections. They are preparation for a greater revelation of him.*

What a tender, compassionate, and personal God we serve! We have

---

[10] Henry T. Blackaby and Claude V. King, *Experiencing God: Knowing and Doing the Will of God* (Nashville: Lifeway, 1990), 94.

to keep that truth about his character foremost in our minds as we wait on him. It's never easy to do. We will be tested and tempted in that wait. We will also grow in trusting God with this hope deferred if we do not succumb to bitterness and unbelief. As we wait, let's take sweet comfort from two precious insights from God's servants in centuries past:

> God has not promised to rescue us according to our time schedule. If it appears that your prayers are unanswered, do not dishonor the Lord with unbelief. Waiting in faith is a high form of worship. In some respects, it excels the adoration of the shining ones above. God delivers His servants in ways that exercise their faith. He would not have them lacking in faith, for faith is the wealth of the heavenly life. He desires that the trial of faith continues until faith grows strong and comes to full assurance. The sycamore fig never ripens into sweetness unless it is bruised; the same is true of faith. Tested believer, God will bring you through, but do not expect Him to bring you through in the way that human reason suggests, for that would not develop your faith. [11]

> Christian, believe this, and think on it: thou shalt be externally embraced in the arms of that love which was from everlasting, and will extend to everlasting—of that love which brought the Son of God's love from heaven to earth, from earth to the cross, from the cross to the grave, from the grave to glory—that love which was weary, hungry, tempted, scorned, scourged, buffeted, spit upon, crucified, pierced—which did fast, pray, teach, heal, weep, sweat, bleed, die; that love will eternally embrace thee.[12]

We're not on hold. Waiting in faith is our high form of worship. And though we may not be married, we are eternally embraced in the arms of everlasting love.

---

[11] Charles H. Spurgeon, *Beside Still Waters* (Nashville: Thomas Nelson, 1999), 148.

[12] Richard Baxter, *The Saints' Everlasting Rest* (Ann Arbor, Mich.: Evangelical Press, 1978), 35.

# CHAPTER 9

# Sex, Romance, and the Glory of God: What Every Christian Wife Needs to Know

CAROLYN MAHANEY[1]

Several years ago at a church leadership conference, I hosted a panel of pastors' wives at a women's session. We fielded questions on a wide variety of topics—from childrearing to counseling women in crisis situations.

A woman from the audience asked the question: "What is one thing you have learned that encourages your husband the most?" As the other women on the panel answered, I pondered my response. *I know what C. J.'s answer would be, but dare I say that here?* Suddenly, it was my turn. "Make love to him," I blurted out. "That's what my husband would say if he were here!"

The room erupted in a wave of nervous, knowing laughter.

It's true! Engaging in this physical expression of marital intimacy and union is one of the most meaningful ways we can encourage our husbands.

## Receiving Sex as a Gift

I sometimes wonder: how many of us would have come up with the idea of sex if we were in charge of designing marriage? This is a question posed by Elisabeth Elliot in her book, *Let Me Be a Woman:*

---

[1] The material in this chapter has been adapted from chapter 5 of my book *Feminine Appeal* (Wheaton, Ill.: Crossway, 2003) and from my chapter titled "A Word to Wives," in C. J. Mahaney, *Sex, Romance, and the Glory of God* (Wheaton, Ill.: Crossway, 2004).

> Who of us, given the chance to arrange the world to our liking, would have had the powers of imagination . . . the courage of the Creator when He conceived the idea of sex? We cannot suppose that He over-looked the potentialities, the pitfalls, the high risks that would accompany it. He saw them all. And He made a woman, suitable, fit in every way, for man.[2]

Do you find yourself amazed when you stop to think about this gift of sex that God has created and given us to enjoy in our marriages? Only God himself could have come up with such an idea! And because it *is* his idea, we glorify God when we cultivate sexual desire for our husbands and welcome their sexual desire for us.

However, if you watch TV, go to the movies, or read magazines today, you can get the impression that the only people having sex (or "good sex") are the ones who aren't married. If marital sex is even portrayed in the popular media, it seems bland or routine. Our culture demeans marital sex and instead celebrates immoral sex.

That's why it is so important that we acquire a *biblical* perspective of sex. God intends for us to experience tremendous joy and satisfaction in our sexual relationship with our husbands. And what greater proof do we need than the fact that God included the Song of Solomon in Holy Scripture—an entire book of the Bible devoted to love, romance, and sexuality in marriage. (If you have not done so recently, I would encourage you to take an hour to read the Song of Solomon and gain a fresh dose of passion for your marriage.) This little book portrays a physical relationship between husband and wife that is *filled* with uninhibited passion and exhilarating delight. This is God's heart and aim for our sexual experience. We are to receive sex as a wonderful gift from him and enjoy it for his glory.

### Sex and Sin

Undoubtedly some of you reading this chapter have had past sexual encounters that yielded much pain and confusion. If you have experienced the negative consequences of sexual sin—either as a willing participant or as a victim—be assured that no situation in your life is beyond the reach of God's grace.

---

[2] Elisabeth Elliot, *Let Me Be a Woman* (Wheaton, Ill.: Tyndale, 1976), 152-153.

Just ask Glenda Revell. Born out of wedlock to a promiscuous mother who hated her all her life, and sexually abused repeatedly by her stepfather, Glenda knew the meaning of suffering. And yet, despite the anguish of her situation, her testimony is of the redeeming power of Christ. In her book *Glenda's Story: Led by Grace,* she explains:

> Sexual defilement of a child is a monstrous sin, and the rape of a child's spirit is on equal footing. The damage from either would appear irreversible. But as Dr. David Jeremiah has said, "Our God has the power to reverse the irreversible." It is true, for I have tasted of His cure from both, and it fills me with a longing for Him that the happiest of childhoods could not have given.[3]

The cure that Glenda refers to is the cross of Christ:

> He showed me Calvary once more. . . . I saw the horror of my sin, nailing the Son of God to that miserable cross, torturing Him, mocking Him, spitting on Him. Yet He had forgiven me freely. No one had committed such atrocities against me. How could I do anything less than forgive?
>
> Forgiveness came. And with it came healing, complete peace and freedom—absolute freedom—to serve my God and to enjoy His love and peace now and forevermore.[4]

Maybe you can relate to Glenda's horrendous childhood, or possibly you carry around guilt from your own past sexual sin. Perhaps it is your husband's past or present sin that looms large in your heart and mind. You may wonder if you will ever be free from the guilt, fear, and despair.

But no matter how distorted your view or traumatic your experience, help is available. I want to urge you to pour out your heart to the Lord of love, to draw near to him so that you may receive mercy and find grace to help in time of need (Heb. 4:16). I would also encourage you and your husband to pursue biblical counseling from your pastor and his wife or another mature couple in your church. Because of the transforming power of Jesus Christ, even the most difficult and painful situation can be turned into a story of grace.

---

[3] Glenda Revell, *Glenda's Story: Led by Grace* (Lincoln, Neb.: Gateway to Joy, 1997), 41.
[4] Ibid., 98.

## Five Principles of "Grade A" Passion

By the grace of God, we can all enjoy the sexual relationship within marriage. So let's consider what a passionate sexual relationship looks like from the wife's perspective. Though the Bible does not give explicit instructions regarding marital sex, it does provide us with principles to guide our behavior. We will focus on five biblical principles for cultivating "Grade A" sexual intimacy—how wives can be attractive, available, anticipatory, aggressive, and adventurous.

### Be Attractive

The husband in Song of Solomon was captivated by his wife's beauty: "Behold, you are beautiful, my love; behold, you are beautiful" (Song 1:15). Again in chapter 7 he exclaimed: "How beautiful and pleasant you are, O loved one, with all your delights!" (v. 6). Beauty is just as important in *our* husbands' eyes as it was for the husband in Song of Solomon. Therefore, as wives, we should aim to be beautiful in our husbands' eyes.

Often women who meticulously attended to their physical appearance before marriage neglect it after the wedding ceremony is over. I once overheard a woman negatively comment about another woman's appearance: "She looks married." Ouch! That shouldn't be! We should give the same careful attention to our physical appearance *after* marriage as we did *before*.

We need to discover what makes us attractive to our husbands. What clothing, hairstyle, or makeup do they find most appealing? (As always, the standard of "modesty and self-control" set forth in 1 Timothy 2:8-10 applies.) And we should strive to care for our appearance—not only when we go out, but also at home where only our husbands see us. As my childhood pastor used to say, "If the barn needs painting, paint it!" Well, what color should that barn be painted? The answer is, whatever is attractive to our husbands!

Now I must also acknowledge the reality that physical beauty is passing away. After ten, twenty, or fifty years of marriage, we will not look as lovely as we did on our wedding day. And some of you may be in my season of life—where everything about my physical appearance is headed in one direction, and that would not be uphill!

However, we discover some wonderful news in 1 Peter 3:3-5. This passage exhorts us:

> Do not let your adorning be external—the braiding of hair, the wearing of gold, or the putting on of clothing—but let your adorning be the hidden person of the heart with the imperishable beauty of a gentle and quiet spirit, which in God's sight is very precious. For this is how the holy women who hoped in God used to adorn themselves, by submitting to their husbands.

We learn from these verses that we can actually adorn ourselves or "make [ourselves] beautiful" (v. 5, NIV) by cultivating a gentle and quiet spirit. Although it doesn't explain how this happens, and it certainly is not referring to physical beauty, this passage asserts that we will become more attractive as we grow in godly character.

I must interject here that a gentle and quiet spirit is not necessarily referring to a woman with a quiet personality. It's possible for a woman to have a quiet personality and *not* have a gentle and quiet spirit. It's just as possible for a woman with an effervescent personality to *have* a gentle and quiet spirit. A gentle and quiet spirit is not a personality type. A simple definition for a gentle and quiet spirit is *a steadfast peace because of a steadfast trust in God*. A woman who possesses this spirit humbly responds to whatever God chooses for her life, regardless of the cost.

Mary, the mother of Jesus, is a great example: "Behold, I am the servant of the Lord; let it be to me according to your word" (Luke 1:38) she said, when the angel informed her she would give birth to the Son of God. Mary humbly accepted God's will despite what it cost her. She displayed a steadfast peace because of her steadfast trust in God—*that's* a gentle and quiet spirit. And the unfading beauty of a gentle and quiet spirit will make us attractive to our husbands, even as our physical beauty fades through the years.

## Be Available

Scripture makes it plain that my body belongs to my husband and his body belongs to me. The husband and wife in the Song of Solomon understood this principle: "I am my beloved's and my beloved is mine" (Song 6:3). And in 1 Corinthians 7:3-5 we read:

> The husband should give to his wife her conjugal rights, and likewise the wife to her husband. For the wife does not have authority over her own body, but the husband does. Likewise the husband does not have authority over his own body, but the wife does. Do not deprive one another, except perhaps by agreement for a limited time, that you may devote yourselves to prayer; but then come together again, so that Satan may not tempt you because of your lack of self-control.

As husband and wife, we belong entirely and unreservedly to each other—my body is his possession, and his body is mine. We are to give ourselves without qualification and not withhold the pleasure of sex. The only exception to this rule is for the activity of prayer and then only by mutual agreement and for a limited time.

We must heed this admonition and offer no excuses. As I once heard a man say, "I've heard many excuses for not having sex—not in the mood, headache, too tired, don't have time. Prayer and fasting has never been one of them."

When we choose to obey God and give our bodies to our husbands—even if we don't feel like it—God will reward us with pleasure. As Elisabeth Elliot encourages us: "The essence of sexual enjoyment for a woman is self-giving. . . . You will find that it is impossible to draw the line between giving pleasure and receiving pleasure. If you put the giving first, the receiving is inevitable."[5]

### Be Anticipatory

It has been said that the sexiest organ of the human body lies between our ears. Our brains have a tremendous effect on our sexual experience. How we think influences our sexual desire.

Most of us will confess that before marriage our sexual desire was strong. It was hard *not* to anticipate the wedding night and that first opportunity to express our passion.

But what about now? When was the last time we spent all day looking forward to physical relations with our husbands? If it has been awhile, if we no longer anticipate lovemaking as we once did, it may be that we have stopped fantasizing about our husbands. When we neglect

---

[5] Elisabeth Elliot, *Let Me Be a Woman*, 169-170.

to think sexual thoughts, we should not be surprised by our lack of sexual desire.

On the other hand, fantasizing about our husbands throughout the day will heighten our sexual longing. In case you are wondering, it is perfectly holy to think these erotic, sensual thoughts. Let's take our cue from the wife in Song of Solomon:

> My beloved is radiant and ruddy,
>> distinguished among ten thousand.
> His head is the finest gold;
>> his locks are wavy,
>> black as a raven.
> His eyes are like doves
>> beside streams of water,
> bathed in milk,
>> sitting beside a full pool.
> His cheeks are like beds of spices,
>> mounds of sweet-smelling herbs.
> His lips are lilies,
>> dripping liquid myrrh.
> His arms are rods of gold,
>> set with jewels.
> His body is polished ivory,
>> bedecked with sapphires.
> His legs are alabaster columns,
>> set on bases of gold.
> His appearance is like Lebanon,
>> choice as the cedars.
> His mouth is most sweet,
>> and he is altogether desirable. (Song 5:10-16)

This wife's sensual musings culminated in the exclamation: "He is altogether desirable." Do you see how her passion was ignited by fantasizing about her husband? God has furnished us with imaginations, and we should use them to "daydream" about our husbands.

Another common reason for a lack of sexual desire is fatigue. Although weariness is a reality in many seasons of our lives, it is probably most pronounced when a woman is caring for small children.

Recently I had a conversation with a young first-time mother.

"Before our baby was born," she explained, "I had plenty of time to romance my husband, clean my home, and cook delicious meals. But now there are days I'm still in my bathrobe at three o'clock in the afternoon, because I've spent all morning caring for our newborn! So how do I keep my husband a priority when my child requires so much time and attention?" she asked.

"Honey," I replied, "fix your husband a peanut butter and jelly sandwich for dinner and give him great sex after dinner, and he will feel prized by you!"

My response was an attempt to encourage her to curtail her efforts in other areas so she could devote herself to what pleased her husband the most. For many husbands, "great sex" would top their list! They would happily do without gourmet meals and immaculate homes if it meant we saved our energy for sex. So let me encourage you to ask your husband what is most meaningful to him.

If we struggle with fatigue, let's evaluate our lifestyles. Do we need to scale back on tasks of lesser importance? Do we need to pare down our schedules? Do we need to take a nap during the day? Do we need to take a shower before lovemaking? Do we need to vary the time of day we make love? Granted, this requires some pretty creative planning, but it's vital that we make these changes if we are to anticipate lovemaking.

By now I hope you realize where all this "anticipation" is headed. Our longings should culminate in what Proverbs 5:19 describes as intoxicating sex! Husbands desire more than merely having their biological needs met by a bored, passive wife. Rather, they delight in our initiation of the lovemaking experience, and they derive great pleasure when we are eager and excited during the act. But don't just take my word for it. Ask your husband today what would most enhance the sexual experience for him.

### Be Aggressive

When you read the Song of Solomon you can't help but be captivated by the extravagant language of love exchanged between the husband and wife. It is important to note that their love language is a mutual exchange. It is not one-sided. The wife is as aggressive in her sensual praise of her husband as he is of her. We should be the same way.

Some years ago I came across one woman's tender challenge to ponder and communicate our affection and desire for our husbands. She writes:

> Are you in love with your husband? Not, Do you love him? I know you do. He has been around a long time, and you're used to him. He is the father of your children. But are you in love with him? How long has it been since your heart really squeezed when you looked at him? . . . Why is it you have forgotten the things that attracted you to him at first? . . . By the grace of God, I want you to start changing your thought pattern. Tomorrow morning, get your eyes off the toaster or the baby bottles long enough to LOOK at him. Don't you see the way his coat fits his shoulders? Look at his hands. Do you remember when just to look at his strong hands made your heart lift? Well LOOK at him and remember. Then loose your tongue and tell him you love him.[6]

We also need to be aggressive in our pursuit of our husbands. We discover in the Song of Solomon that the husband and wife equally initiated the lovemaking experience and were equally aggressive during sex. The responsibility to initiate lovemaking doesn't rest solely with our husbands; as wives, we should initiate as well.

Let me add here that I have occasionally counseled women whose husbands had less desire for sexual relations than they had. This challenging situation can often produce confusion, pain, and even fear. However, it need not hinder you from pursuing a God-glorifying marriage. Again, I would encourage you and your husband to seek godly counsel from your pastor and his wife. And remember to put your trust in God: He is at work in your marriage for your good and his glory (see Rom. 8:28).

### Be Adventurous

Finally, we should cultivate surprise and excitement in our physical relationship. We should be adventurous. As Joe Dillow says: "The woman who would never think of serving her husband the same frozen television dinner every evening sometimes serves him the same frozen sexual response every night. Sex, like supper, loses much of its flavor when it becomes predictable."[7]

---

[6] Shirley Rice, quoted in Ed Wheat, *Love Life for Every Married Couple* (Grand Rapids, Mich.: Zondervan, 1980), 87-88.

[7] Joe C. Dillow, *Solomon on Sex* (Nashville: Thomas Nelson, 1977), 146.

Let's not allow our lovemaking to become predictable. Let's be ready to make love at different times and be willing to try new places. Let's keep our husbands in eager suspense by our creativity in the sexual relationship. As we do, we will reap rich rewards in our marriage!

## The Arena of Love

Having taught this material on numerous occasions, I am aware that not all wives will be thrilled with this message. Perhaps you are one of them. Maybe you are weighed down by a lack of faith. *My sexual desire will never equal my husband's desire!* Maybe you feel immobilized by the amount of deficiency that has been exposed. *I will never be able to make all those changes!* Or possibly, your past or present sexual sin still appears as an insurmountable obstacle in your view. *My situation is beyond all hope!*

May I implore you not to despair? These thoughts and feelings are contrary to the truth of God's Word. Please be persuaded that God is able to renew your sexual desire, empower you to change, and revive you with hope. You can trust the Savior to gradually transform your sexual relationship with your husband. Remember that sex was God's idea in the first place and he is passionately committed to blessing the marriage bed, for our pleasure and his glory.

In conclusion, I cannot think of more fitting, moving words to leave you with than those of Robert Farrar Capon:

> The bed is the heart of the home, the arena of love, the seedbed of life, and the one constant point of meeting. It is the place where, night by night, forgiveness and fair speech return that the sun may not go down on our wrath; where the perfunctory kiss and the entirely ceremonial pat on the backside become unction and grace. It is the oldest, friendliest thing in anybody's marriage, the first used and the last left, and no one can praise it enough.[8]

---

[8] Robert Farrar Capon, quoted in Debra Evans, *The Mystery of Womanhood* (Wheaton, Ill.: Crossway, 1987), 265.

# Part 5: History and Sex

# CHAPTER 10

# Martin Luther's Reform of Marriage

JUSTIN TAYLOR

If we were asked to name the most significant events in Martin Luther's life, we would likely recount his thunderstorm decision to become a monk, his discovery that righteousness is a gift from God, his nailing of the Ninety-five Theses to the Wittenberg Door, or his courageous "Here I Stand" speech. Asked to name his teachings that impacted the church, many of us would point to the doctrine of justification by faith alone, the distinction between the two kingdoms of God, or the doctrine of Christian freedom. But few of us know the story of his marriage, his teachings on the goodness and necessity of marriage, and its significant impact not only on Reformation Germany but also on the entire evangelical world, continuing to this day. William Lazareth rightly comments:

> It is no exaggeration to say that Luther's monastic revolt and subsequent marriage represent for his ethics what his nailing of the *Theses* and his defense at Worms represent for his theology. Rightly understood both are dramatic symbols of the very heart of the biblical message which was recovered by Luther in his reformation of Christian life and thought.[1]

Martin Luther's fascinating biography is fairly well known—or at

---

[1] William H. Lazareth, *Luther on the Christian Home: An Application of the Social Ethics of the Reformation* (Philadelphia: Muhlenberg, 1960), 1.

least it is readily available for those who want to review it[2]—so I will refrain from recounting it in this chapter. Instead, I will sketch Katherine von Bora's life, focusing upon how she met Luther, how they became married, and what their home and marriage looked like. Along the way, we will see Luther's developments with regard to the prospect of his own marriage, as well as his teaching on marriage, the Christian home, sexuality, and love. Finally, I will briefly explore the ways in which Luther transformed the institution of marriage.

## Katherine von Bora and Martin Luther

*Katherine von Bora*

When Martin was a sixteen-year-old high school student, studying in Eisenach, an event happened 120 miles to the east of him that would eventually change his life. Katherine von Bora was born on January 29, 1499, in Hirschfeld, south of Leipzig, to Hans von Bora and Anna von Haugwitz. Katherine had three brothers, and possibly a sister. Her father, Hans von Bora, had once been a wealthy nobleman, but had fallen into financial hardship. When Katherine was only six years old her mother died. That same year Hans was remarried to the widow Margarete von Seidewitz, who had children of her own. Young Katherine was subsequently placed in the Benedictine cloister at Brehna, near Bitterfeld, in order to be educated. The year was 1505—the same year that Martin Luther entered the Augustinian monastery in Erfurt, ninety-five miles away.

At age ten, Katherine's father had her transferred to the less expensive Marienthron Convent, in Nimbschen near Grimma. Her paternal aunt Magdalene von Bora was a nun there, and her maternal aunt Margarete von Haubitz was her superior. On October 8, 1515, at age sixteen, Katherine took her vows and prepared to live the rest of her days as a nun. Providence, however, had different plans.

By the early 1520s, Katherine and the other nuns were beginning to

---

[2] Two helpful biographies are Roland H. Bainton, *Here I Stand: A Life of Martin Luther* (New York: Meridian, 1977); and Heiko A. Oberman, *Luther: Man Between God and the Devil*, trans. Eileen Walliser-Schwarzbart (orig. 1982; New York: Image, 1992). Two shorter, recent additions are Stephen J. Nichols, *Martin Luther: A Guided Tour of His Life and Thought* (Phillipsburg, N.J.: Presbyterian & Reformed, 2003); and Martin Marty, *Martin Luther*, Penguin Lives (New York: Penguin, 2004). For an excellent biography on Katherine von Bora, see Rudolph K. Markwald and Marilynn Morris Markwald, *Katharina von Bora: A Reformation Life* (St. Louis: Concordia, 2002).

catch wind of Luther's teaching on the goodness and necessity of marriage, as well as the inadvisability of monastic vows. In secret they read passages like these from Luther's sermons:

> Priests, monks, and nuns are duty-bound to forsake their vows whenever they find that God's ordinance to produce seed and to multiply is powerful and strong within them. They have no power by any authority, law, command, or vow to hinder this which God has created within them.[3]

> Marriage is not only an honorable but a necessary state. It is earnestly commanded by God that in every condition and station in life men and women, who were created for it, should be found in this estate.[4]

> Renew your natural companionships without delay and get married, for your vow is contrary to God and has no validity, and say, "I have promised that which I do not have and which is not mine."[5]

> It is certain that all convents and monasteries, where supposedly devout people live and where their spiritual estate is to make them devout and blessed, are worse than common brothels, taverns, or dens of thieves. . . . It is obvious that such human commandments, such as forbidding marriages of priests, are nothing but dictates of mere humans and the devil. . . . So, if you have a daughter or a friend who has fallen into such an estate and you are sincere and faithful, you should help her to get out, even if you have to risk your goods, body, and life for it.[6]

But it was not as if a monk or a nun could *voluntarily* leave a monastery or convent. Leaving—or assisting others to leave—was an offense punishable by death. Some of the nuns began to write letters to their families, asking for their assistance in withdrawing from Marienthron. But few families could afford to do so. The nuns therefore decided to send a secret letter to Luther in which they poured out their hearts to him. They solicited Leonhard Koppe (1464–1552)—a fifty-nine-year-old merchant and leading citizen from Torgau who regularly

---

[3] Martin Luther, *Luther's Works*, American Edition [hereafter *LW*], ed. Jaroslav Pelikan and Helmut T. Lehmann, 55 vols. (Philadelphia: Muhlenberg, 1955–1973), 45:19.

[4] Martin Luther, *What Luther Says: An Anthology* [hereafter *WLS*], ed. Ewald M. Plass, 3 vols. in 1 (St. Louis: Concordia, 1959), 2768.

[5] *LW* 45:27.

[6] Cited in Markwald and Markwald, *Katharina von Bora,* 40.

delivered herring to the convent—to deliver the letter to Luther. Luther struggled deeply with what to do, but he finally seized upon a plan. He would enlist the aid of Koppe to help him carry it out. Although aiding and abetting the escape of the nuns was an act punishable by death, Koppe believed in the cause and decided to risk everything—his reputation, his career, even his life—on it.

In the early morning hours of Easter 1523, Koppe's team of horses pulled a covered wagon filled with fish barrels through the gate of the convent. But as his covered wagon pulled away from the convent, no one knew that the apparently empty fish barrels were carrying twelve runaway nuns—among them Katherine von Bora!

Three of the nuns immediately returned to their families. After a long, cold journey through the night, the remaining nine nuns arrived at the Augustinian monastery in Wittenberg—often called "The Black Cloister" due to the black robes worn by the members of the Augustinian order—which was where Luther lived. One student reported to a friend: "A wagon load of vestal virgins has just come to town, all more eager for marriage than for life. God grant them husbands lest worse befall."[7] Luther greeted the nuns and their liberators:

> You have done a new work that will be remembered by the country and the people. Some will scream and consider it a great detriment, but others, who are on God's side, will praise it as being of great benefit. You have liberated these poor souls from the prison of human tyranny at just the right time: Easter, when Christ liberated the prison that held his own.[8]

A few days later George Spalatin, Luther's friend and frequent correspondent,[9] wanted to know what Luther planned to do with these women. Luther responded:

> You ask what I shall do with them? First I shall inform their relatives and ask them to support the girls; if they will not I shall have the girls

---

[7] Cited in Bainton, *Here I Stand,* 223.

[8] Cited in Markwald and Markwald, *Katharina von Bora,* 50.

[9] George Burkhardt (1484–1545)—from Spalt, near Nuremberg, hence the name Spalatin—worked for Frederick the Wise and was a frequent correspondent of Luther's. None of the letters from Spalatin to Luther have survived, but thankfully, over four hundred letters from Luther to Spalatin still exist.

otherwise provided for. Some of the families have already promised me to take them; for some I shall get husbands if I can. . . . Here are they, who serve Christ, in need of true pity. They have escaped from the cloister in miserable condition. I pray you also to do the work of charity and beg some money for me from your rich courtiers, by which I can support the girls a week or two until their kinsmen or other provide for them.[10]

Around the same time Nicholas von Amsdorf was composing a similar request to Spalatin, emphasizing the women's extreme poverty and their patient spirit:

They are fair, fine, all of noble birth, and none of them is fifty years old. . . . If you want to give anything to the poor, give it to them, for they are poor, wretched and deserted by their kinsfolk. I pity the poor things; they have neither shoes nor clothes. I beg of you, my dear brother, to see if you cannot get something for them from the people of the court, so that they may be provided with food and clothing. Please do all you can, for in their great poverty and anxiety they are very patient. Indeed I am astonished that in such great tribulation and poverty they are so patient and happy.[11]

Luther felt responsible to help these sisters, and he went right to work. He arranged for six of them to find a home, a husband, or a job. Three, however, remained—one of whom was Katherine von Bora. Her family didn't want her back. So Luther arranged for her to be housed with the family of Philipp Reichenbach, the city clerk of Wittenberg.

The Reichenbachs were friends with the Baumgärtner family of Nuremberg. In May/June of 1523, their son, Jerome (Hieronymus) Baumgärtner (1498–1565), an alumnus of the University of Wittenberg, made a return visit to the city, where he became acquainted with Katherine. A romance ensued, and talk of marriage quickly followed. He had to return home, but he promised to return before the month was over. In the next few months, Katherine repeatedly wrote to him, but her letters went unanswered. His patrician family was apparently less than

---

[10] *Luther's Correspondence and Other Contemporary Letters* [hereafter *SJ*], trans. and ed. Preserved Smith and Charles M. Jacobs, 2 vols. (Philadelphia: Lutheran Publication Society, 1918), 2:179-180.
[11] *SJ* 2:181-182.

happy at the prospect of their privileged son marrying a runaway nun with no money.

Luther continued to feel responsible for Katherine, and eventually suggested to her that Dr. Kasper Glatz, a pastor in his sixties who lived at nearby Orlamünde, might make a suitable husband. But Katherine rejected the suggestion in no uncertain terms—a response Luther considered prideful and snobbish! Katherine approached von Amsdorf to talk about this. Von Amsdorf asked her if she thought she was too good for Glatz—after all, he was a doctor, a professor, and a pastor. Katherine said that she'd have no objection to marrying either von Amsdorf or Luther—both doctors, professors, and pastors—but that Glatz was out of the question. Shortly after this conversation, Luther dropped by the von Amsdorf estate. Good naturedly, von Amsdorf asked Luther: "What the devil are you doing, trying to coax and force the good Kate to marry that old cheapskate whom she neither desires nor considers with all her heart as husband?" Luther—perhaps half-joking himself—responded: "What devil would want to have her, then? If she does not like him, she may have to wait a good while for another one!"[12] Years later Luther looks back on this season of his life: "Had I desired to marry fourteen years ago, I would have chosen Eva von Schoenfeld,[13] now Basilius's wife. At that time I did not love my Catherine at all. I always suspected her of pride."[14]

Luther then decided to write a note to Baumgärtner to see if he would change his mind about marrying Katherine. On October 12, 1524 Luther wrote:

> If you want your Katie von Bora, you had best act quickly, before she is given away to someone else who wants her.[15] She has not yet conquered her love for you. I would gladly see you married to each other.[16]

But again, there was no reply. In the spring of 1525 Baumgärtner announced his engagement to Sibylle Dichtel von Tutzing—a beautiful

---

[12] Cited in Markwald and Markwald, *Katharina von Bora*, 61.
[13] One of Katherine's friends who escaped the nunnery with her.
[14] *WLS* 887.
[15] Most likely a reference to Glatz.
[16] Martin Luther, *D. Martin Luthers Werke: Briefwechsel* [hereafter *WABr*], 15 vols., J. F. K. Knaake, G. Kawerau, et al., eds. (Weimar: Hermann Böhlaus, 1930–1985), 3:357-358.

fourteen-year-old girl from a wealthy family. Katherine was no doubt devastated. The Reichenbachs never intervened on Katherine's behalf, and perhaps because of this, Katherine soon moved in with the family of Lucas and Barbara Cranach, friends of Luther. The Schoenfeld sisters, who had escaped the nunnery with Katherine, stayed there as well.

## Martin Luther

Luther, who by this time was in his forties, was still a single man. This did not prevent him, however, from powerfully preaching on the virtues and importance of marriage. Some, like the Bavarian noblewoman Regula von Grimace, began to wonder if Luther himself was planning to marry. Luther responded in a letter to Spalatin (November 30, 1524):

> I am grateful for what Regula writes about my wedding plans; I am not surprised about such gossip, since so many other bits of gossip are around concerning me. Nevertheless give her my thanks and tell her I am in God's hand as a creature whose heart God may change and rechange, kill and revive again at any moment. Nevertheless, the way I feel now, and have felt thus far, I will not marry. It is not that I do not feel my flesh or sex, since I am neither wood nor stone, but my mind is far removed from marriage, since I daily expect death and the punishment due to a heretic. Therefore I shall not limit God's work in me, nor shall I rely on my own heart. Yet I hope God does not let me live long.[17]

Luther here acknowledges the presence of sexual desire. Earlier, in connection with a sermon on Isaac's marriage to Rebekah at age forty,[18] Luther—himself around that age—had written: "Nature is so constituted that it feels sexual desires (*fervores carnis*) at about the age of twenty. To bear and to overcome these until the age of forty is truly a grievous and great burden."[19] But at this time, Luther truly believed that his death was imminent and that God had called him to a life of singleness. Hence marriage would be unhelpful and unnecessary, and chastity could be maintained.

A few years earlier, in his *Estate of Marriage* (1522) Luther had spo-

---

[17] *LW* 48:93.
[18] Genesis 25:20.
[19] *WLS* 891 n. 11.

ken of those rare Paul-type individuals who were able to refrain from sex and marriage for the purpose of ministry involvement. By implication including himself in this category, he wrote of those:

> spiritually rich and exalted persons, bridled by the grace of God, who are equipped for marriage by nature and physical capacity and nevertheless voluntarily remain celibate. These put it this way, "I could marry if I wish, I am capable of it. But it does not attract me. I would rather work on the kingdom of heaven, i.e., the gospel, and beget spiritual children." Such persons are rare, not one in a thousand, for they are a special miracle of God. No one should venture on such a life unless he finds God's grace to be so powerful within him that the divine injunction, "Be fruitful and multiply," has no place in him.[20]

Luther's reservations about his own prospects for marriage did not deter him from enthusiastically counseling *others* to marry! Spalatin wanted Luther to encourage Wolfgang Reissenbusch, the preceptor of the Antonia's in Lichtenberg, to get married. So on March 27, 1525, Luther wrote him a letter which was to be later published as a booklet.[21] Luther wrote:

> Your body urges you to marry and needs it; God wills and forces it. What will you do about it? It would also be a fine, noble example if you married, that would help many feeble ones, broaden their paths and give them more scope, so many others might escape the dangers of the flesh and follow you.

On April 10, 1525, Luther offered similar counsel to Spalatin: "Why don't you go on and get married? I urge matrimony on others with so many arguments that *I am myself almost moved to marry*, though our enemies do not cease to condemn that way of life, and our wiseacres laugh at it all the time."[22] This is the first recorded hint that perhaps Luther was opening up to the possibility of being married.

One week later Luther, along with Philipp Melanchthon and John Agricola, left on a trip to Eisleben to discuss the formation of a Christian

---

[20] *LW* 45:21.
[21] *A Christian Writing for W. Reissenbusch, Encouraging Him to Marry*, in *LW* 44:300-301. Reissenbusch married Hanna Hertzog on April 26, 1525—one month after Luther wrote his letter.
[22] *SJ* 2:304, emphasis mine.

school. Apparently marriage was very much on his mind. On April 16, the day of the trip, he paused to pen a letter to Spalatin about his traveling plans. At the end of the note he could not refrain from making a few more jokes about himself and the possibility of marriage:

> Incidentally, regarding what you are writing about my marrying: I do not want you to wonder that a famous lover like me does not marry. It is rather strange that I, who so often write about matrimony and get mixed up with women, have not yet turned into a woman, to say nothing of not having married one. Yet if you want me to set an example, look, here you have the most powerful one, for I have had three wives simultaneously,[23] and loved them so much that I have lost two who are taking other husbands; the third[24] I can hardly keep with my left arm, and she, too, will probably be snatched away from me. But you are a sluggish lover who does not dare to become the husband of even one woman. Watch out that I, who have no thought of marriage at all, do not some day overtake you too eager suitors—just as God usually does things which are least expected. I am saying this seriously to urge you to do what you are intending.[25]

On April 21 Luther left Eisleben for Thuringia to visit his parents, friends, and relatives, and also to advocate for peace with regard to the uprising of the peasants. When he mentioned the idea of marriage to his parents—perhaps again in a joking manner—his father enthusiastically encouraged him to follow through on marriage, expecting that Martin would have a son through whom he would pass along the family name.

The straw that broke the camel's back, however, may have been when Hieronymus Schurrf wrote: "If this monk [Luther] were to take a wife, then all the world and the very devil would laugh, and [Luther] himself would ruin everything that he had created."[26] On May 4, Luther responded in a letter to John Rühel, offering the first definitive statement that he was thinking of marrying Katherine: "If I can arrange it, I will marry Kate in defiance of the devil and all his adversaries."[27] In early June he wrote to Albrecht von Mainz, encouraging him to marry: "If my marrying will strengthen him, I am ready. I believe in marriage."[28]

---

[23] A tongue-in-cheek reference, most likely to Ave (Eva) von Schoenfeld, Ave Alemann, and Katherine.
[24] Probably a reference to Katherine.
[25] *LW* 48:104-105.
[26] Cited in Markwald and Markwald, *Katharina von Bora*, 63.
[27] Cited in ibid.
[28] *WABr* 3:479-482.

He later recounted: "As I considered taking Kate as my wife, I entreated our Lord God earnestly to help me."[29] Though we don't know the details, we do know that Luther proposed to Katherine at the Cranach residence. And that she accepted.

On June 10, in response to Spalatin's question about Luther's view of how long an engagement should be, he wrote: "Don't put off till tomorrow! By delay Hannibal lost Rome. By delay Esau forfeited his birthright. Christ said, 'Ye shall seek me, and ye shall not find.' Thus Scripture, experience, and all creation testify that the gifts of God must be taken on the wing."[30] Just three days later, Luther heeded his own counsel by becoming officially engaged and married on the very same day! Luther later wrote of the danger of putting off marriage: "We should help partners get together with no delay. If I had not married quietly with the knowledge of only a few friends, people would certainly have prevented it."[31]

### The Wedding of Martin and Katie

On the evening of June 13, 1525, which was a Tuesday—the customary day for weddings—the couple became legally engaged in Luther's home, which was the former Augustinian monastery. The witnesses included Justus Jonas (Luther's best friend), Johann Bugenhagen (pastor of the Wittenberg city church), Lucas and Barbara Cranach (whose family Katherine was living with at the time), and Johann Apel (a professor of jurisprudence and an ex-Dean of the Cathedral of Bamberg, who had himself married a nun). Although it was not the customary practice of that time, the couple was immediately married by Bugenhagen after the engagement. After the ceremony, the witnesses escorted the bride and groom to the nuptial bed. Then, in accordance with an ancient German custom, the couple consummated their marriage in the presence of Jonas, who served as a witness.

On the following morning Luther entertained his friends at breakfast. Jonas hired a special messenger to deliver a firsthand account of the marriage to Spalatin:

---

[29] Cited in Markwald and Markwald, *Katharina von Bora*, 70.
[30] Bainton, *Here I Stand*, 225.
[31] Cited in Lazareth, *Luther on the Christian Home*, 23.

This letter will come to you, my dear Spalatin, as the bearer of great news. Our Luther has married Catharine von Bora. I was present and was a witness of the marriage yesterday (and saw the bride lying in the marriage chamber). Seeing that sight I had to give way to my feelings and could not refrain from tears. Now that it has happened and is the will of God, I wish this good and true man and beloved father in the Lord much happiness. God is wonderful in His work and ways.[32]

The Luthers decided to have a public ceremony two weeks later, on June 27, so that out-of-town guests (including his parents) could be notified and join in the celebration. Examining the personal wedding invitations written by Luther himself gives us interesting insight into Luther's mind-set at the time. We see a man obviously excited and enthusiastic—even surprised—about this new stage of his life. These invitations also make it clear that this wedding was more than just an act of love between two people. Luther clearly had one eye cocked to the watching world.

To Spalatin he writes:

I have stopped the mouths of my calumniators with Catharine von Bora. . . . I have made myself so cheap and despised by this marriage that I expect the angels laugh and the devils weep thereat.

The world and its wise men have not yet seen how pious and sacred is marriage, but they consider it impious and devilish in me. It pleases me, however, to have my marriage condemned by those who are ignorant of God.[33]

In some of the invitations Luther stresses what an unexpected turn of events this is—even for him. To Wenzel Link: "Despite the fact that I was otherwise minded, the Lord has suddenly and unexpectedly contracted a marriage for me with Catharine von Bora, the nun."[34] As he would later write: "A good wife is not found accidentally and without divine guidance. On the contrary, she is a gift of God and does not come, as the heathen imagine, in answer to our planning and judging."[35]

And to Leonhard Koppe, without whom Martin and Katie would

---

[32] *SJ* 2:322. The parenthetical clause is from another version of this letter. See n. 3.
[33] *SJ* 2:323-324.
[34] *SJ* 2:328.
[35] *WLS* 906.

not have met, Luther writes: "God has suddenly and unexpectantly caught me in the bond of holy matrimony.[36] I am going to get married. God likes to work miracles and to make a fool of the world."[37]

And to von Amsdorf:

> Indeed, the rumor is true that I was suddenly married to Catherine; [I did this] to silence the evil mouths which are so used to complaining about me. For I still hope to live for a little while. In addition, I also did not want to reject this unique [opportunity to obey] my father's wish for progeny, which he so often expressed. At the same time, I also wanted to confirm what I have taught by practicing it; for I find so many timid people in spite of such great light from the gospel. God has willed and brought about this step. For I feel neither passionate love nor burning for my spouse, but I cherish her.[38]

We should pause here to examine this final line. Does it indicate that Luther didn't truly love Katie? It's difficult to determine the precise intent of Luther's remark, but it is important to remember that at this point the length of their romance had been exceedingly short! It may have been the case that Luther saw in Katie not someone with whom he felt passionate love, but someone with whom he could *foresee* passionate love. William Lazareth comments:

> Modern marriage counselors probably would have questioned the marriage itself. It was an open secret in Wittenberg that Martin and Katie did not get along very well because of their clashing temperaments and personalities. Certainly they were not romantically in love, and there is no evidence that any kind of courtship preceded their marriage. . . . We have no reason to doubt Luther's contention that he married primarily as a testimony of faith.[39]

Luther's comment about cherishing Katherine but not feeling passionate love for her must also be set within the context of the day and the wagging tongues that were going on all around Luther. Even Luther's friend Melanchthon—invited neither to the engagement nor to

[36] *SJ* 2:328.
[37] Cited in Bainton, *Here I Stand*, 226.
[38] *LW* 48:117.
[39] Lazareth, *Luther on the Christian Home*, 22-23.

the later public ceremony—suspected that Luther had been taken in by carnal lust:

> ... at this unfortunate time, when good and excellent men everywhere are in distress, he not only does not sympathize with them, but, as it seems, rather *waxes wanton* and diminishes his reputation, just when Germany has especial need of his judgment and authority.... The man is certainly pliable; and the nuns have used their arts against him most successfully; thus probably society with the nuns has softened or even *inflamed* this noble and high-spirited man.[40]

Erasmus helped spread the slanderous rumor that Katherine had borne Martin's child two weeks before the ceremony. After their marriage, Duke George the Bearded wrote that Martin and Katherine were "now feasting in carnal lust."[41] When Katie became pregnant a year later, it was predicted that the union of this monk and this nun would produce a two-headed baby, or the Antichrist. Set within this contentious context, it is perhaps not surprising that Luther wanted to clarify that though he "cherished" his spouse, he was not marrying because of "passionate love," so as not to add fuel to the fire of this demagoguery.

At 10 A.M. on June 27 the Luthers and their wedding party traveled from the Black Cloister to the parish church, accompanied by the sounds of bells and pipers, to participate in the public ceremony. The recessional took them back to the Black Cloister, where they had a dinner and then a dance in the town hall. Another banquet followed in the evening, followed by the dismissal of the guests by the magistrates at 11 P.M.

A couple of months after the wedding, Luther was still reveling in his marriage—and obviously delighting in the consternation of others toward it:

> I have now testified to the gospel not only by word but also by deed: I have married a nun to spite the triumphant enemies who yell "Hurrah, hurrah!" [I have done this] so that it does not seem that I am yielding.[42]

---

[40] *SJ* 2:324-325, my emphasis.
[41] Cited in Markwald and Markwald, *Katharina von Bora,* 78.
[42] *LW* 48:123.

The guests who had been invited to Luther's wedding had no idea of the significance of the event that they witnessed.

> Little did the sixteenth-century world realize the tremendous significance—both religious and social—of this simple and reverent ceremony in the backwoods of rural Germany. The union of Martin and Katie was not cursed with the birth of the Antichrist. Instead, it was blessed with the birth of the Protestant parsonage and the rebirth of a genuinely Christian ethos in home and community. Luther's marriage remains to this day the central evangelical symbol of the Reformation's liberation and transformation of the Christian daily life.[43]

We now turn to look at their married life together.

### The Marriage and Family of Martin and Katie

*Their Home*

The dilapidated Black Cloister—which had once housed forty monks—was the Luthers' home for the first eight years of their marriage. Prior to marriage, Luther slept there on a smelly straw bed. Wolfgang Seberger, Luther's lazy servant, had neglected to air out the straw in Luther's bed for a year, and Luther was apparently too busy to care! He later remarked: "Before I was married the bed was not made for a whole year and became foul with sweat."[44] Shortly after their wedding Luther wisely ordered a new mattress for him and his new bride![45] Luther—who once famously boasted, "If I break wind in Wittenberg they smell it in Rome"—undoubtedly had to make some adjustments to his bachelor lifestyle. It took some time for him to get used to it:

> A man is likely to wonder a great deal when he first gets married. Sitting at the table, he muses, "Not long ago I was by myself, but now there are two of us." When he is in bed and wakes up, he sees two pigtails next to him—something he did not see there before.[46]

The Black Cloister was quite large—and often quite full. It seems

---

[43] Lazareth, *Luther on the Christian Home,* vii.

[44] Bainton, *Here I Stand,* 226.

[45] *LW* 49:142.

[46] Martin Luther, *D. Martin Luthers Werke: Tischreden* [hereafter *WATr*], 6 vols., J. F. K. Knaake, G. Kawerau, et al., eds. (Weimar: Hermann Böhlaus, 1912–1921), 3:211.

that this was the case from the very beginning of their marriage. On the night of their public wedding, Andreas Karlstadt—a frequent adversary of Luther's—was fleeing from the Peasants' War and seeking shelter. Martin invited him to stay—and Karlstadt stayed for eight more weeks! A few years into their marriage, the Luthers took into their home the six children of Luther's sister.[47] They also raised Katherine's nephew. University students often ate and boarded there, and Luther's letters make reference to a steady stream of guests either coming or going.[48] Their household could, at times, number as high as twenty-five!

For many years Luther didn't charge anyone for room and board. (In fact, there was a waiting list for those who wanted to room and board with the Luthers.) This, combined with his refusal to charge for lecturing, his refusal to accept honoraria for his writing, and his generosity toward the poor, led the Luthers quickly into debt. But as Luther once wrote: "God put fingers on our hand for the money to slide through them so He can give us more. Whatever a person gives away, God will reimburse."[49] Another time Luther said: "Riches are among the most trivial things on earth and the smallest gift God gives to a person."[50]

Their poverty, however, was of no comparison to the richness that Martin found in his bride Katie: "My Katie," he wrote, "is in all things so obliging and pleasing to me that I would not exchange my poverty for the riches of Croesus."[51] Once, when Luther thought he was dying, he wrote: "My dear son and my dear Kate. I have nothing [in worldly goods] to bequest to you, but I have a rich God. Him I leave to you. He will nourish you well."[52]

## Katie

Her biographers describe Katherine as "patient, focused, and stubborn." Lucas Cranach's paintings of her portray her as having an "interesting face: expressive, almond-shaped eyes; high cheekbones; and a mouth

---

[47] Scholars lack information about Luther's sister, but it is probable that she had died.

[48] For example, see Luther's references to household guests in *LW* 49:122; 50:81; 50:126; 50:149; 50:223; 50:292.

[49] Cited in Markwald and Markwald, *Katharina von Bora*, 86.

[50] *WATr* 5:240.

[51] A proverbial saying referring to King Croesus (sixth century B.C.). Cited in Lazareth, *Luther on the Christian Home*, 31.

[52] *WATr* 3:90.

that appears ready to talk."[53] Katie was the sort of person who could take a joke—and Martin was certainly the type who enjoyed dishing it out. In his letters he often teased her about matters such as her frugality, negligence, and worries.[54] Katie also had a sense of humor, along with a way of correcting her husband in just that way that he needed. Once, when Luther was so depressed that no words of counsel seemed capable of penetrating his darkness, Katie decided to don a black dress. Luther asked: "Are you going to a funeral?" "No," she replied, "but since you act as though God is dead, I wanted to join you in the mourning." Luther quickly recovered![55]

Katie performed innumerable tasks for the family. While Martin lectured and wrote and debated and preached and traveled, Katie drove the wagon, took care of the field, bought cattle and put them out to pasture, brewed the beer, prepared food for the graduation banquets, rented the horses, sold linen, served as Martin's publishing agent, and often nursed him back to health during his frequent illnesses.[56] Martin often called her the "morning star of Wittenberg" since she rose at 4 A.M. to begin her many responsibilities—and often worked until 9 in the evening. Luther often had to urge her to relax.

### Their Children

Katie bore six children—three sons and three daughters: Hans (John), Elizabeth, Magdalena, Martin, Paul, and Margaretha. The children brought great joy to their household. Martin often told them stories, taught them songs and games, played melodies on his lute, and instructed them in the faith. Four of the children lived to adulthood; Elizabeth died at the age of 13 months, and Magdalena died at the age of 13 years. Luther's letters tell of the deep pain their deaths caused him and Katherine.

### Their Final Days

Martin Luther died early in the morning on February 18, 1546, in Eisleben at the age of 62. Katie wrote in a rare letter that she was "deeply

---

[53] Markwald and Markwald, *Katharina von Bora*, 197.
[54] *LW* 50:150, 174, 305, et al.
[55] Cited in Markwald and Markwald, *Katharina von Bora*, 140.
[56] *LW* 50:108-109, 81, 94, 167, et al.

grieved and saddened over the loss of such a dear and precious man as my husband has been."[57] Katie was to live for nearly seven more difficult years until her death on December 21, 1552, at the age of 53. Among her final recorded words was that the desire of her heart was to "cling to Christ like a burr to a dress."[58]

## Luther's Teachings on Marriage, Love, and Sex

We now turn from looking at the Luthers marriage itself to offering a cursory review of Martin Luther's teachings on marriage. A comprehensive treatment would make for a very large volume, so we will only scratch the surface of Luther's rich teaching on these issues.

### The Necessity of Marriage

Luther once asked a very simple but provocative question: "Why should one not forestall immorality by means of marriage?"[59] Luther believed in the gift of celibacy—in fact, God granted it to him for many years. Paul had been granted the gift, and commended it in 1 Corinthians 7 as a blessing for the furtherance of the kingdom. But Luther also believed that it was a very *rare* gift. He suggested that many young men and women without the divine gift of celibacy were rejecting the divine gift of marriage. His counsel was that if you are struggling with lust, then your duty is simple: get married!

> Whoever finds himself unsuited to the celibate life should see to it right away that he has something to do and to work at; then let him strike out in God's name and get married. A young man should marry at the age of twenty at the latest, a young woman at fifteen to eighteen; that's when they are still in good health and best suited for marriage.[60]

Obviously the specifics here were not to be written in stone. After all, Katie was 26 and Luther was 41 years old when they were married! Further, this is not meant to be a discouragement for those earnestly desiring to marry. But it is an exhortation to those who are practicing what Albert Mohler has called "extended adolescence." Mohler com-

[57] Cited in ibid., 176.
[58] Cited in ibid., 192.
[59] *LW* 45:45.
[60] *LW* 45:48.

ments on the troubling trend of the "marginalization of marriage" in the church and world today:

> Demographic trends, cultural shifts, and a weakening of the biblical concept of marriage have produced a situation in which marriage is in big trouble, even among many Christians. . . . By any calculation, the statistics indicate that young adults are marrying much later in life than at any time in recent human history. As a matter of fact, demographers have suggested that this new pattern of delay in marriage has established a statistical pattern that in previous generations had been most closely associated with social crises like war and natural disaster.[61]

"From Genesis to Revelation," Mohler writes, "the Bible assumes that marriage is normative for human beings."[62] Marriage is biblically normative. Therefore, it should be both expected and sought. Luther's counsel is both blunt and necessary:

> If you have the gift of abstinence and can live without sex, well and good. Then abstain from sex life. But if you cannot without sin abstain from uniting with a woman, then make use of the remedy God points out to you.[63]

Luther's words could not be any more relevant for the current crisis that Mohler identifies.

### The Essence and Purpose of Marriage
Luther defined marriage in this way:

> Marriage is the God-appointed and legitimate union of man and woman in the hope of having children or at least for the purpose of avoiding fornication and sin and living to the glory of God.[64]

---

[61] Albert Mohler, "Looking Back at the Mystery of Marriage: Part One," http://www.cross walk.com/news/weblogs/mohler/?adate=8/19/2004 (accessed 1/19/05). *Time Magazine* recently ran a cover story (Jan. 16, 2004), entitled "Grow Up? Not So Fast," observing that "This isn't just a trend, a temporary fad or a generational hiccup. This is a much larger phenomenon, of a different kind and a different order. Social scientists are starting to realize that a permanent shift has taken place in the way we live our lives." See http://www.time.com/time/covers/1101050124/story.html (accessed 1-19-05).

[62] Ibid.

[63] *WLS* 898.

[64] Ibid., 884.

And here is how he identified the purpose of marriage:

> The ultimate purpose is to obey God, to find aid and counsel against sin; to call upon God; to seek, love, and educate children for the glory of God; to live with one's wife in the fear of God and to bear the cross; but if there are no children, nevertheless to live with one's wife in contentment; and to avoid all lewdness with others.[65]

We see a number of important elements in this definition. First, its ultimate purpose is the glory of God. Second, we see that children are not just the blessed by-products of marriage; they are part of the very essence of the marital design. I will have more to say on this below. Third, sanctification is at the very heart of marriage. Marriage is a God-appointed means of obeying God, fulfilling our God-given desires, avoiding sin, and instructing children in the faith.

## MARRIAGE IS AN INSTRUMENT OF SANCTIFICATION

One of Luther's early metaphors for marriage was that of a hospital. "The temptation of the flesh has become so strong and consuming that marriage may be likened to a hospital for incurables which prevents inmates from falling into graver sins."[66] Roland Bainton notes that:

> After his own marriage Luther's tone shifted to a stress upon the home as a school for character. It is the area where the Christian virtues find their readiest exemplification, and, whereas in Catholicism monasticism is the sphere for the cultivation of the counsels of perfection, in Protestantism the home is as it were a functional substitute.[67]

Both metaphors—a school and a hospital—signal the important role of marriage as an agent of sanctification and rehabilitation. Our selfishness and pride are exposed. And if we respond in God-honoring humility, marriage can be used by God to cleanse us of our sin. The shift away from the monastic metaphor is also significant, for it signifies that marriage is never a purely private affair. Christian marriage is not to be *of* the world, but it must certainly be *in* the world. This leads to our next point.

---

[65] Ibid.

[66] *LW* 44:9.

[67] Roland H. Bainton, *What Christianity Says About Sex, Love, and Marriage* (New York: Association Press, 1957), 79.

## MARRIAGE IS NOT A SACRAMENT

One of Luther's most significant teachings was that marriage is not a sacrament. The tradition of viewing marriage as a sacrament was due in part to a mistranslation of the Latin Vulgate, which rendered *mysterion* (lit., mystery) as *sacramentum* in Ephesians 5:32.[68] Luther argued instead that marriage was a public, civic matter: "Marriage is a civic matter (*res politica*). It is really not, together with all its circumstances, the business of the church. It is so only when a matter of conscience is involved."[69] As Lazareth summarizes: "Marriage is a wonderful blessing of God but it is not a Christian sacrament. . . . Marriage is still under the law of God but not under the wing of the church."[70] This does not in any way lessen the spiritual significance of marriage. As we saw above, Luther viewed marriage as a school for sanctification. But why relegate it to the civic realm? Because marriage is not designed only for Christians. It is a creation ordinance—a rule of God established for all people. Obviously we desire that all people bow their knees and acknowledge Jesus as their Lord—as all will do one day (Phil. 2:10-11). But that is not a prerequisite for a legitimate marriage. Marriage is not to be "regarded as a holy sacrament in the realm of grace, but honored rather as a divine ordinance in the realm of creation."[71] Marriage, therefore, is designed as an institution to serve the public good and is to thereby be the foundation for a well-ordered society.

## SEX IS GOOD, NECESSARY, AND SHOULD BE CELEBRATED WITHIN MARRIAGE

Against those who downplayed marriage, denigrated sex, and urged life-long continence, Luther taught that unless one has the rare gift of celibacy, marriage and sex are both natural and necessary:

> It is not a matter of free choice or decision but a natural and necessary thing, that whatever is a man must have a woman and whatever is a woman must have a man. . . . It is just as necessary as the fact that I am a man, and more necessary than sleeping and waking, eating and drinking, and emptying the bowels and bladder. . . . And wherever men

---

[68] *LW* 36:93-94.
[69] *WLS* 885.
[70] Lazareth, *Luther on the Christian Home*, 185.
[71] Ibid.

try to resist this, it remains irresistible nonetheless and goes its way through fornication, adultery, and secret sins, for this is a matter of nature and not of choice.[72]

In other words, God designed us as sexual beings, and this should lead the majority of us to seek sexual relations in a covenantal marital relationship comprised of one man and one woman.

Physical union between man and wife, however, is not a sufficient condition for a healthy marriage:

> I have observed many married couples coming together in such great passion that they were ready to devour each other for love, but after a half year the one ran away from the other.[73]

> A bride is taken quickly; to love her for a lifetime is quite a different matter. . . . For merely sleeping together . . . will not do it alone; there must also be unity and harmony of mind, habits, and life. Each must be patient and helpful with the other for things cannot always go smoothly.[74]

Sex by itself can do nothing. There must also be a union of the heart and mind. In fact, sex in marriage can be overdone:

> It is indeed true that sexual intercourse in marriage should be moderate, to extinguish the burning of the flesh. Just as we should observe moderation in eating and drinking, so pious couples should refrain from indulging their flesh too much.[75]

Luther also wrote that "intercourse is never without sin,"[76] which has led some to imagine that he thought the sex act was inherently evil. This conclusion, however, ignores the qualification that Luther immediately adds:

> Intercourse is never without sin; but God excuses it by his grace because the estate of marriage is his work, and he preserves in and through the sin all that good which he implanted and blessed in marriage.[77]

---

[72] *LW* 45:18.
[73] *WLS* 899.
[74] Cited in Lazareth, *Luther on the Christian Home*, 227.
[75] *WLS* 2812.
[76] *LW* 45:49.
[77] *LW* 45:49.

So there *is* sin bound up with the sex act, but marriage is the matrix for the redemption of sex. Allan Carlson comments on this passage: "Through marriage, sex became a moral good, an expression of God's will. This was the heart of Luther's sexual revolution."[78] It is also important to note that Luther extolled the virtues and beauty of pre-Fall sex:

> [T]ruly in all nature there was no activity more excellent and more admirable than procreation. After the proclamation of the name of God it is the most important activity Adam and Eve in the state of innocence could carry on—as free from sin in doing this as they were in praising God.[79]

But the Fall introduced disastrous results:

> If Adam had not fallen, the love of bride and groom would have been the loveliest thing. Now this love is not pure either, for admittedly a married partner desires to have the other, yet each seeks to satisfy his desire with the other, and it is this desire which corrupts this kind of love. Therefore, the married state is now no longer pure and free from sin.[80]

In sum, then, we see that Luther praised the virtues of pre-Fall sex, saw marriage as the matrix of redemption for sexuality, and yet still saw sin lurking in the marital bed. If all we knew was the above, then we might conclude that Luther had a low—or at least a reserved—view of sex and its place in the Christian life. But Luther was also an advocate for *celebrating* the gift of sexual union. When Luther's longtime correspondent Spalatin got married just five months after Martin and Katie, Luther wrote him a note, obviously delighted that his friend would be able to experience the joy of sex with his new bride. Heiko Oberman notes that this "erotic passage" "was stricken from editions of Luther's letters very early on."

> When you sleep with your Catherine and embrace her, you should think: "This child of man, this creature of God has been given to me

---

[78] Allan C. Carlson, "A Revolutionary Theology of Sex: Martin Luther on Sex, Marriage and Family," Witherspoon Lectures (July 2, 2004), http://www.witherspoonfellowship.org/index.cfm?get=item&b=7&item=WT04G01# (accessed 1-14-05).

[79] *LW* 5:117-118.

[80] *LW* 44:9.

by my Christ. May he be praised and glorified." On the evening of the day on which, according to my calculations, you will receive this, I shall make love to my Catherine while you make love to yours, and thus we will be united in love.[81]

Furthermore, in accordance with Scripture (1 Cor. 7:3-5), Luther celebrated the idea of regular sexual intercourse within the bounds of marriage. Whereas the apostle Paul's counsel was only in general, unspecified terms, Luther was more than happy to give specific detail! William Lazareth writes: "As to the recommended frequency of marital coitus, the hale and hearty spirit (if not the actual words) of Luther's sexual counsel is reflected in the humorous couplet traditionally ascribed to him: 'Twice a week, hundred-four a year, should give neither cause to fear.'"[82]

We see then in Luther a healthy, joyful appreciation for the gift of sex in marriage. Lazareth summarizes Luther's view: "Christians who have been transformed by the gospel are not to avoid sex, but to dedicate their sexual gifts—like all others—both joyfully and shamelessly to the glory and service of God."[83] Finally, Lazareth rightly captures Luther's view of marriage, family, and sex with the following description: "Luther's faith was simple enough to trust that after a conscientious day's labor, a Christian father could come home and eat his sausage, drink his beer, play his flute, sing with his children, and make love to his wife—all to the glory of God!"[84]

## CHILDREN ARE THE SWEETEST FRUITS OF MARRIAGE

As mentioned above, Luther believed that the main purposes of marriage were companionship and children.[85] "Children," he said, "are the sweetest fruits of marriage; they tie and strengthen the bonds of love."[86] He described the raising of children as the most noble task God assigns:

> The greatest good in married life, that which makes all suffering and labor worth while, is that God grants offspring and commands that

---

[81] Cited in Oberman, *Luther,* 276.

[82] Lazareth, *Luther on the Christian Home,* 226 n. 82.

[83] Ibid., 226.

[84] Ibid., 145.

[85] *LW* 44:8.

[86] Cited in Markwald and Markwald, *Katharina von Bora,* 93.

they be brought up to worship and serve him. In all the world this is the noblest and most precious work, because to God there can be nothing dearer than the salvation of souls.[87]

The arrangement of marital fellowship and procreation to the glory of God offers a faint echo of paradise:

This living together of husband and wife—that they occupy the same home, that they take care of the household, that together they produce and bring up children—is a kind of faint image and a remnant, as it were, of that blessed living together [in Eden].[88]

Specifically, the task of childrearing is the most valuable work in the kingdom of God:

This at least all married people should know. They can do no better work and do nothing more valuable either for God, for Christendom, for all the world, for themselves, and for their children than to bring up their children well.[89]

It is preaching and teaching like this that leads Steven Ozment to conclude, "Never has the art of parenting been more highly praised and parental authority more wholeheartedly supported than in Reformation Europe."[90] This vision of childrearing yielded a new vision for the Christian home:

With them God makes of your house a hospital, and sets you over them as chief nurse, to wait on them, to give them good words and works as meat and drink, that they may learn to trust, believe, and fear God. . . . O what a blessed marriage and home were that where such parents were to be found! Truly it would be a real church, a chosen cloister, yea, a paradise.[91]

This is really quite stunning when you stop to think of it. Luther is saying that of all the things you can do in the world—of all the ministries

---

[87] LW 45:47.

[88] LW 5:133.

[89] LW 44:12.

[90] Steven Ozment, *When Fathers Ruled: Family Life in Reformation Europe* (Cambridge, Mass.: Harvard University Press, 1983), 132.

[91] Cited in Lazareth, *Luther on the Christian Home*, 145.

you can start and all of the hours you can invest—the most significant and meaningful task takes place right in our homes. This leads to our next point.

## THE ORDINARY MUST BE SANCTIFIED

One of Luther's great contributions to our view of the family involved the sanctification of the ordinary. Many sadly neglect their family and their friends because they are pouring all of their time into "ministry"— neglecting to see that all of life should be ministry and every sphere should be sanctified. We must have eyes to see that the ordinary duties of life contain great spiritual significance. Luther describes the message that the world whispers in our ear:

> Now observe that when that clever harlot, our natural reason . . . , takes a look at married life, she turns up her nose and says, "Alas, must I rock the baby, wash its diapers, make its bed, smell its stench, stay up nights with it, take care of it when it cries, heal its rashes and sores . . . ?"[92]

But into this context Luther breathes fresh gospel air:

> What then does Christian faith say to this? It opens its eyes, looks upon all these insignificant, distasteful, and despised duties in the Spirit, and is aware that they are all adorned with divine approval as with the costliest gold and jewels. It says, O God, because I am certain that thou hast created me as a man and hast from my body begotten this child, I also know for a certainty that it meets with thy perfect pleasure. I confess to thee that I am not worthy to rock the little babe or wash its diapers, or to be entrusted with the care of the child and its mother. How is it that I, without any merit, have come to this distinction of being certain that I am serving thy creature and thy most precious will? O how gladly will I do so, though the duties should be even more insignificant and despised. Neither frost nor heat, neither drudgery nor labor, will distress or dissuade me, for I am certain that it is thus pleasing in thy sight. . . . God, with all his angels and creatures is smiling—not because the father is washing diapers, but because he is doing so in Christian faith.[93]

---

[92] *LW* 45:39.
[93] *LW* 45:39–40.

We must put on the spectacles of faith and see all of life as infused with meaning and significance by our Creator. Set in this context, Luther greatly elevated the place of the family within the church of Christ.

### THE INSTITUTION OF MARRIAGE IS TO BE PRAISED

When studying Luther's teaching on marriage, one of the things that stands out is the freedom and frequency with which Luther sung the praises of marriage. It is not just that he is teaching about how to have a good marriage. It is not just that he is praising a specific marriage—whether his own or another's. But Luther judges it to be of great importance for pastors and preachers—and all of us, really—to exclaim the beauty and the wonder of *marriage itself*. Whereas at one point he seemed to regard marriage mainly as a place to avoid the lusts of the flesh, he soon came to speak of the sweetness of the institution itself:

> Ah, dear God, marriage is not a thing of nature but a gift of God, the sweetest, the dearest, and the purest life above all celibacy and single-ness, when it turns out well, though the very devil if it does not. . . . If then these three remain—fidelity and faith, children and progeny, and the sacrament—it is to be considered to be a wholly divine and blessed estate.[94]

Though he did not shy away from acknowledging the difficulties of marriage, he could write: "I consider marriage to be a paradise, even if it has to endure greatest poverty."[95] "The union of man and woman is a great thing."[96] "One should not regard any estate as better in the sight of God than the estate of marriage."[97] "I say these things in order that we may learn how honorable a thing it is to live in that estate which God has ordained."[98] For Luther, an important element of a joyful marriage was to be found in the belief that the marital institution itself was a good, God-ordained gift. "No one can have real happiness in marriage who does not recognize in firm faith that this estate together with all its works, however insignificant, is pleasing to God and precious in his

---

[94] Cited in Bainton, *What Christianity Says About Sex, Love, and Marriage,* 82-83.
[95] *LW* 48:321.
[96] *WLS* 2773.
[97] *LW* 45:47.
[98] *LW* 45:41.

sight."[99] The church would do well today to emulate Luther's example and to speak often of the *goodness* of the gift of marriage.

## Love in Marriage

Luther also wrote often about the importance of love within marriage. At first blush this might seem rather insignificant. As the old Frank Sinatra song goes: "Love and marriage, love and marriage, go together like a horse and carriage. This I tell you, brother, you can't have one without the other!"[100] It is easy to forget, though, that such was not always the conventional wisdom. Marriage had a terrible reputation in Luther's day, and women were looked upon as a necessary evil. Luther lamented:

> The estate of marriage has universally fallen into such awful disrepute. There are many pagan books which treat of nothing but the depravity of womankind and the unhappiness of the estate of marriage, such that some have thought that even if Wisdom itself were a woman that one should not marry. . . . They concluded that woman is a necessary evil, and that no household can be without such an evil.[101]

Part of Luther's legacy is that he reintroduced love as an essential element of marriage. He wasn't the first to do so, and obviously there were already married couples at that time who loved each other deeply. But Luther was at the forefront of advocating marital love and making it the norm for entering into marriage and thriving within marriage.

An important part of this teaching was the distinction between initial lust and sustaining love: "The first love is drunken. When the intoxication wears off, then comes the real marriage love."[102] He explains:

> It is the highest grace of God, when love continues to flourish in married life. The first love is ardent, is an intoxication love, so that we are blinded and are drawn to marriage. After we have slept off our intox-

---

[99] *LW* 45:42.
[100] "Love and Marriage," words by Sammy Cahn and Jimmy Van Heusen, sung by Frank Sinatra on the album *The Reprise Collection* (Capitol-Reprise, 1955).
[101] *LW* 45:36.
[102] Luther, cited in Bainton, *Here I Stand*, 235.

ication, sincere love remains in the married life of the godly; but the godless are sorry they ever married.[103]

The essence of this biblical, sincere, marital love, Luther argued, was wholehearted devotion and faithfulness to the good of one's spouse:

> Where conjugal chastity is to be maintained, husband and wife must, above all things, live together in love and harmony, so that one cherishes the other wholeheartedly and with complete fidelity. This wholehearted devotion is one of the chief requirements in the creation of a love and desire for chastity. Where it is found, chastity will follow as a matter of course, without any command. Therefore St. Paul (Eph. 5:22-25) so diligently admonishes married people to love and honor each other.[104]

This love is given by God and praised by God as an example of divine love:

> Conjugal love or the desire to marry is a natural affection, implanted and inspired by God. Therefore conjugal love is praised so highly in Scripture and is so frequently adduced as an example of the relations existing between Christ and His Christendom.[105]

If this is true, then forcing or arranging marriages is sinfully unwise. Luther continues:

> Therefore parents are sinning against God and human nature when they force their children to marry or accept a spouse for whom they have no desire. . . . Daily experiences clearly teach and show us what sort of trouble has come from forced marriages. . . . And even though God and human nature did not demand that marriage is to be unforced, *a heart of fatherly and motherly affection toward children should refuse to tolerate anything but love and delight as the basis of marriage.*[106]

"Christian love," Luther believed, "should be a gushing, surging kind of love which overflows from the inner heart like a fresh stream or brook

---

[103] *WLS* 899.
[104] Ibid., 2807.
[105] Ibid., 2792.
[106] *WLS* 2792, emphasis added.

that is always in motion and never dries up."[107] And this should be at the foundation and essence of our marriages.[108]

## Love Your Neighbor as You Love Yourself

When we hear Christ's commands to "love one another" (John 13:34; 15:12) and to "love your neighbor as yourself" (Matt. 22:39), we often think of love for those outside of our family. But Luther believed that the two commands could not be separated. Bainton, in commentating upon Luther's view, summarizes it in this way: "Love indeed there is in Christian marriage, but it is only a heightening of that Christian love which is enjoined toward all. We are told to love our neighbors. The wife is the nearest neighbor. She should therefore be the most beloved."[109] Or as Lazareth puts it: "It is in this all-inclusive, self-giving sense that the Christian is to love his neighbor—the nearest and dearest of whom is his own God-given wife."[110] Love your neighbor as yourself—that is, love your spouse.

## Luther's Example of Love

It would be one thing for Luther to preach the importance of love within marriage. But he also intentionally modeled this love in his own marriage. As we saw above, their marriage did not have the most romantic of beginnings. But a deep and passionate love soon developed. Martin's praise for Katie was often on his lips, and the letters and references that remain are an enduring testimony to his respect and affection for her. "Kate," he wrote, "you have a God-fearing man who loves you. You are an empress; realize it and thank God for it."[111] He often referred to her

---

[107] Cited in Lazareth, *Luther on the Christian Home*, 232.

[108] I hasten to add—lest any reader conclude otherwise from this study—that not all of Luther's teachings on marriage are fully biblical. One of the intentions of this chapter is to highlight the positive, biblical, revolutionary teachings and example of Luther that had such a tremendous impact upon the church. But Luther also had his blind spots. For example, though he advocated love as the foundation for marriage, he failed to insist on the Scriptural teaching that Christ must be the foundation for both marital partners. In conjunction with 1 Corinthians 7:12-13, Luther thought that it was permissible for a Christian to marry a non-Christian. He wrote: "You will find plenty of Christians—indeed the greater part of them—who are worse in their secret unbelief than any Jew, heathen, Turk, or heretic" (*LW* 45:22-30). 1 Corinthians 7:12-13, however, does not sanction a believer and a non-believer to enter into marriage; it only speaks to the issues of divorce once that marriage has occurred. And 1 Corinthians 7:39 contradicts Luther's reasoning by insisting that the only absolute prerequisite for marriage is that a man and the woman be "in the Lord."

[109] Bainton, *What Christianity Says About Sex, Love, and Marriage*, 81.

[110] Lazareth, *Luther on the Christian Home*, 231-232.

[111] *WATr* 1:554, no. 1110.

as "Lord Catherine, doctor and preacher," "Sir Katie," "the empress," "my rib," "my true love," "my sweetheart," "Gracious Lady," "wise woman and doctor," "Your Grace," "holy lady," and "a gift of God."[112] And he referred to himself as "Your obedient servant," "Your loving Martin Luther," or "Your Holiness' willing servant."[113]

When Luther devised the plan to rescue Katherine and the other nuns from their monastic bondage, marriage was one of the furthest things from his mind. At one point he had even exclaimed: "Good Lord! Will our people at Wittenberg give wives even to the monks? They will not push a wife on me!"[114] But as we have seen, the Lord had different plans for Martin Luther. As the following quote indicates, Luther learned to treasure Katie for her virtues and her faithfulness—and saw her as a good and gracious gift from God:

> I would not want to exchange my Kate for France nor for Venice to boot; to begin with (1) because God has given her to me and me to her; (2) because I often find out that there are more shortcomings in other women than in my Kate; and although she, of course, has some too, these are nonetheless offset by far greater virtues; (3) because she keeps faith and honor in our marriage relation.[115]

It is obvious that Katherine von Bora had brought tremendous change into the life of Martin Luther. But their love and commitment and example also brought significant reform to the church and to the world.

## The Impact of Luther on Marriage and the Home

Few marriages have had a greater impact upon the church and upon the culture than that of Martin Luther and Katherine von Bora. Luther himself marveled at the transformation he had witnessed in his lifetime:

> When I was a boy, the wicked and impure practice of celibacy had made marriage so disreputable that I believed that I could not even think about the life of married people without sinning. Everybody was fully persuaded that anyone who intended to lead a holy life acceptable to God could not get married but had to live as a celi-

---

[112] *L W* 49:236, 267, 154; 50:208, 209, 210, 218, 305, et al.
[113] *L W* 49:238; 50:223, 292, 304, 306, et al.
[114] *L W* 48:290.
[115] *WLS* 2774.

bate and take the vow of celibacy. Thus many who had been husbands became either monks or priests after their wives had died.
Therefore it was a work necessary and useful for the church when
men saw to it that through the Word of God marriage again came
to be respected and that it received the praises it deserved. As a
result, by the grace of God now everyone declares that it is something good and holy to live with one's wife in harmony and
peace.[116]

It is not as though distortions of the marital institution disappeared because of the marriage of Martin Luther to Katherine von
Bora. But they helped to lay a theological foundation and an exem-
plary model that would forever impact how we view marriage. Marital
laws were changed[117] and the understanding of the Protestant family
was transformed.

In assessing Luther's cultural impact with respect to marriage,
Bainton writes:

> The Luther who got married in order to testify to his faith actually
> founded a home and did more than any other person to determine the
> tone of German domestic relations for the next four centuries.[118]

Thomas Miller comes to a similar conclusion:

> Luther established marriage as a centerpiece of evangelical social orga-
> nization in a remarkably brief time. The changes he introduced, how-
> ever, altered permanently Western attitudes toward marriage. . . .
> [O]ur civilization has been shaped by the pattern of family life that he
> established.[119]

Luther preached passionately on marriage for years as a single man.
And likely he would have left an impact on the state of marriage even if
he had remained single. But the fact that he did enter into marriage made

---

[116] *LW* 1:135.

[117] For a detailed study of the Lutheran reformers' transformation of the Roman Catholic theology
and law of marriage, see John Witte, Jr., "The Reformation of Marriage Law in Martin Luther's
Germany: Its Significance Then and Now," *The Journal of Law and Religion* 4, no. 2 (1986): 293-
351.

[118] Bainton, *Here I Stand*, 233.

[119] Thomas F. Miller, "Luther: Father of the Christian Home," *Christianity Today*, October 21,
1983, 17.

his teaching and preaching on these issues all the more significant. It enabled Luther not only to teach God's Word on this subject, but to model it as well. We must therefore look to God and thank him for Martin Luther—but also for a young nun who had the grace and courage to follow her convictions, her conscience, and the authoritative Word of Christ.

# CHAPTER 11

# Christian Hedonists or Religious Prudes? The Puritans on Sex

MARK DEVER

## Introduction

### Puritan Stereotypes

What would the Puritans of the seventeenth century think of the new and sensuous Saab 500 coupe? A recent Saab radio commercial considered this matter. "The seventeenth-century New England Puritans," the deep, velvety voice begins, "were people who devoted their entire lives to work and prayer. They would not have approved of the sensual beauty of the new Saab 500 coupe. The Puritans believed that to have fun was a sin. There was no place in their lives for the pleasure and luxury of a new Saab convertible. For the Puritans, the only reason for living was to sacrifice and prepare for an eternity of holy peace. Aren't you glad you're not a Puritan? See your nearest Saab dealer."[1]

If that is what the Puritans thought about the Saab, we can only imagine what they must have thought about sex. The two words "Puritans" and "sex" almost seem shocking in the same sentence, unless of course one is referring to a "puritanical suppression of sex." That

---

[1] Historian David Allyn has written that "the Puritans left an undeniably powerful legacy of sexual repression. After Massachusetts passed the New World's first anti-obscenity law in 1711, so many books, plays, and newspapers were censored that the slogan 'Banned in Boston' acquired a familiar ring and was adopted by promotion men as a tongue-in-cheek advertising ploy" (David Allyn, *Make Love Not War: The Sexual Revolution: An Unfettered History* [New York: Routledge, 2001], 54).

much we can understand, at least if our understanding of the Puritans is anything like the Saab advertiser's.

Two of the most commonly asked questions today about the Puritans are, "What ever happened to them?" and "What did they think about sex?" I don't know if anyone has ever put together their apparent extinction and their reputed prudishness, but the Puritans are certainly viewed as the archetypical religious prudes. Somehow they garnered a reputation for legalism and pleasure-hating that has followed them through the ages. Kenneth Hare wrote that,

> The Puritan through life's sweet garden goes
> 　To pluck the thorn, and cast away the rose;
> And hopes to please, by this peculiar whim,
> 　The God who fashioned it and gave it him.[2]

Nineteenth-century historian Thomas Macaulay wrote in his *History of England* that "The Puritan hated bear-baiting, not because it gave pain to the bear, but because it gave pleasure to the spectators."[3] Early twentieth-century journalist H. L. Mencken said that "Puritanism" was "the haunting fear that someone, somewhere may be happy."[4] And contemporary radio personality Garrison Keillor has continued the tradition by telling us that the Puritans "arrived here in 1648 in the hope of finding greater restrictions than were permissible under English law at that time."[5]

Is there not a reason so many commentators have described the Puritans this way? After all, couldn't you be fined or placed in the stocks if you kissed your wife in public in colonial Massachusetts? Surely the Puritans were puritanical when it came to sex.

## Our Situation Today

We look to the past for wisdom because times change. In God's providence we live in a day that is challenging for Christians. Every era in a

---

[2] Cited in J. I. Packer, *A Quest for Godliness* (Wheaton, Ill.: Crossway, 1990), 259.
[3] Thomas B. Macaulay, *History of England from the Ascension of James II*, 5 vols. (Philadelphia: Lippincott, 1879), vol. 1, chapter 3.
[4] H. L. Mencken, *A Mencken Chrestomathy* (New York: Vintage, 1982), 624.
[5] Garrison Keillor, *Garrison Keillor and the Hopeful Gospel Quartet* (CD) (New York: Epic Records, 1992).

fallen world is challenging, but some eras have respected and reinforced the basic principles of Christian morality more than is the case today. Even in the last fifty years, Christian ideals of sexuality have been eroded by divorce, contraception, abortion, increased levels of cohabitation, higher rates of illegitimacy, and the legitimization of homosexual relationships. The shame, shock, disgrace, and danger once associated with fornication and adultery have declined. Marriage itself is decreasingly associated with sexual activity. Singleness, in fact, is often viewed as the period for sexual activity and the time to "sow one's wild oats." In fact, if we are honest, marriage these days is not viewed as the permanent *introduction to* sex, but as the temporary *limitation of* it!

In the pornographic pop hit song "The Bad Touch," the European group Bloodhound Gang thumps out the refrain, "You and me baby ain't nothin' but mammals, so let's do it like they do on the Discovery Channel." In our society people create desires and associate fulfillment with the product they sell. Today people sell sex, and everything else by it. Perhaps we should sing instead, "You and me baby ain't nothin' but money, for people and comp'nies that want to sell us their honey."

In a time marked by the rapid dissolution of a Christian understanding of sex, what do the Puritans have to teach us?

## The Background of the Reformation

### The Roman Catholic Tradition

The Protestant Reformation began against the backdrop of a Roman Catholic church that valued virginity above marriage. Prudery very much characterized the Roman Catholic disposition toward sex. Many in the Roman church believed you could not have sex without sinning, even with your spouse. So Aquinas wrote, "It would seem that impotence is not an impediment to marriage. For carnal copulation is not essential to marriage, since marriage is more perfect when both parties observe continency by vow."[6] In consequence, Roman Catholic theologians suggested abstinence "on Thursday in memory of Christ's arrest, on Friday in memory of his death, on Saturday in honour of the Virgin Mary, on Sunday in honour of the Resurrection and on Monday in com-

---

[6] Thomas Aquinas, *Summa Theologia,* supplement, question 58, article 1, objection 1.

memoration of the departed."[7] Their message was clear: sex is shameful; virginity is best.

## The Lutheran Revolution

Luther reversed the emphasis. He said that clerical celibacy was a disaster. Apparently, in Luther's day cardinals who limited themselves *to women* were championed as saints. Neither parents nor the pope could forbid marriage, Luther said, any more than they could rightly forbid eating and drinking. He stressed 1 Corinthians 7:2 and marriage's purpose in protecting against immorality, more than its purpose in procreation.

Overall, Luther had a positive outlook on marriage, though he said some things that have cast doubt on his reputation for enjoying life with gusto. He once said, "The reproduction of mankind is a great marvel and mystery. Had God consulted me in the matter, I should have advised him to continue the generation of the species by fashioning them of clay." Luther was also realistic about the challenges of marriage. He wrote, "Good God, what a lot of vexation there is in marriage! Adam has made a muck of our nature. Think of all the rows Adam and Eve must have had in the course of their nine hundred years. Eve would say 'You ate the apple,' and Adam would reply, 'You gave it to me.'"

## The Situation in the World of the Puritans

The sixteenth and seventeenth centuries knew much immorality, as can be seen in everything from court records to Shakespeare's plays, from surviving songs to the lewd books sold on the streets. The Puritan view of sex, in part, was informed by a desire to protect it from such widespread spoil and debauchery. Allen Carden writes, "The Puritans put strict biblical parameters around sex because they valued it, not because they were embarrassed by it or opposed to it."[8] The Puritan minister Richard Baxter warned: "Take heed of ribald filthy talk, and Love Songs, and of such incensing snares."[9] And, "Take heed of a delight

---

[7] Derrick S. Bailey, *Sexual Relation in Christian Thought* (New York: Harper & Brothers, 1959), 133 n.3., cited in Daniel Doriani, "The Puritans, Sex, and Pleasure," *Westminster Theological Journal* 53 (Spring 1991): 142 [125-143].

[8] Allen Carden, *Puritan Christianity in America: Religion and Life in Seventeenth-Century Massachusetts* (Grand Rapids, Mich.: Baker, 1990), 219.

[9] Richard Baxter, *Christian Directory* (London: Robert White, 1673), 272.

in Romances, Play-books, feigned stories, useless news, which corrupt the mind, and waste your time."[10]

## The Puritan Practice of Marriage

Some famous Puritan ministers avoided marriage altogether, like John Knewstub of Cockfield, Suffolk, who maintained that he was content being single. His disciple Richard Sibbes also never married. But most married, and many married again when a spouse died. The Puritans preferred to be married. One Puritan widow remarried within twenty-four hours of her husband's demise.[11] Looking in on a few of the well-known figures from this period can give some idea of what life was like. Probably the Puritans were all aware of the example of Martin Luther. At age forty-two, Luther married for the first time. He married Katherine von Bora, age twenty-six, in 1525. William Chaderton, bishop of Chester, married off his only daughter Joan, age nine, to a boy of eleven. At age thirty-five, John Milton (1608–1674) married for the first time. He married Mary Powell, a young girl of seventeen, who deserted him within a month and returned home. A few years later, Mary rejoined him, bore him three daughters, and died in 1652. Milton's second wife died in childbirth. Four years later Milton married Catherine Woodcock. Catherine also died in childbirth. In 1662 Richard Baxter married Margaret Charlton, who was twenty-one years younger than he. They were married for nineteen years, until Margaret died in 1681. Margaret discovered that Richard had an impatient temper and a sharp tongue (which surprises no one who has read his books). Thomas Goodwin married his second wife when he was fifty years old and she was sixteen. John Owen had eleven children by his first marriage, all of whom died young except one daughter.[12] In short, marriage was a common part of the Puritans' lives.

Puritans were plain people in their lives and in their ceremonies. In 1656, the justice of the peace at Woolwich asked Sir James Halkett if he intended to marry Anne Murray. He answered "yes." The justice then asked Anne Murray if she intended to marry Sir James Halkett.

---

[10] Ibid.

[11] Cited in John Adair, *Founding Fathers: The Puritans in England and America* (1982; reprint Grand Rapids, Mich.: Baker, 1986), 268.

[12] James W. Bruce III, *From Grief to Glory* (Wheaton, Ill.: Crossway, 2002), 86-87.

She also answered "yes." The justice concluded, "I pronounce you man and wife."[13] The plain gold ring was a Puritan-inspired modification from the more elaborate rings that were common before the 1650s. Many Puritans wore none at all. Plainness could adorn even the joys of marriage.

### Finding a Wife or Husband

While the idea of marrying for romantic love was present in the seventeenth century, the Puritans typically did not do so. In our day, we think that if a couple falls in love, they should marry; if they do not fall in love, they should not marry; and if they fall out of love once married, they should divorce. Normally, a Puritan decided first that it was time to marry, even though no potential spouse was firmly fixed in mind. With this goal in mind, a Puritan man would then seek out a partner who met certain, generally biblical criteria. He did not simply wait to be smitten by the first woman who made his stomach flutter and his head dizzy and then decide to act. Once married, he would then bend his purposes toward loving his wife entirely. Edmund Morgan put it this way:

> Puritan love . . . was not so much the cause as it was the product of marriage. It was the chief duty of husband and wife toward each other, but it did not necessarily form a sufficient reason for marriage. . . . The advice was not that couples should not marry unless they *love* each other but that they should not marry unless they *can* love each other.[14]

London Puritan preacher Richard Steele (1629–1692) expressed it pithily: "Do not first love, and then consider; but first consider, and then love."[15]

### Puritan Thoughts on Marriage and Sex

Reading Puritan sermons—from Richard Sibbes to Jonathan Edwards— we find much "affectionate" language of heart, beauty, and love. And they wrote at length about marriage, but without ever explicitly men-

---

[13] Adair, *Founding Fathers,* 225.
[14] Edmund Morgan, *The Puritan Family: Religion and Domestic Relations in Seventeenth-Century New England* (1944; reprint New York: Harper & Row, 1966), 54.
[15] Richard Steele, "What Are the Duties of Husband and Wife Toward Each Other?" in *Puritan Sermons 1659–1689,* 6 vols. (1674; reprint Wheaton, Ill.: Richard Owen Roberts, 1981), 2:200.

tioning its sexual aspects, or if mentioning it, doing so briefly by main-taining that the marriage bed is honorable (see Heb. 13:4) and perhaps by giving a glancing blow to Rome's wrong exaltation of virginity and denigration of marriage. One might expect to find such remarks in their sermons on the Song of Solomon, which was a favorite Puritan book. But they uniformly interpreted the book as pertaining to Christ and the church. They preached it often, but only as allegory.

When Puritans do mention marriage, their comments are warm, even sweet. Thomas Gataker (1574–1654) wrote, "There is no society more near, more entire, more needful, more kindly, more delightful, more comfortable, more constant, more continual, than the society of a man and wife, the main root, source, and original of all other soci-eties."[16] Over against the traditional Roman Catholic vilification of women as snares, John Cotton (1584–1652) wrote, "Women are crea-tures without which there is no comfortable living for man. . . . They [referring to the Roman Catholics] are a sort of blasphemers then who despise and decry them, and call them a necessary evil, for they are a nec-essary good."[17] Oliver Cromwell (1599–1658) wrote to his daughter Bridget: "Dear heart, let not thy love for thy spouse in any way cool thy desire for Christ. That which is most lovable in thy spouse is the image of Christ in him. Look to this and love it most and everything else for this."[18] Cotton Mather (1663–1728) called his second wife "a most lovely creature and such a gift of Heaven to me and mine that the sense thereof . . . dissolves me into tears of joy."[19] Jonathan Edwards's (1703–1758) last words were of his wife Sarah: "Give my kindest love to my dear wife, and tell her that the uncommon union which has so long subsisted between us has been of such a nature as I trust is spiritual and therefore will continue forever."[20] These are typical Puritan attitudes toward sex and marriage.

---

[16] Cited by Leland Ryken, *Worldly Saints: The Puritans as They Really Were* (Grand Rapids, Mich.: Zondervan, 1986), 42.

[17] Cited in ibid., 52.

[18] Cited by Roland Bainton, *Sex, Love, and Marriage: A Christian Survey* (London: Fontana, 1957), 99.

[19] Cited in Ryken, *Worldly Saints,* 39.

[20] Sereno E. Dwight, "Memoirs of Jonathan Edwards," in *The Works of Jonathan Edwards,* ed. Edward Hickman, 2 vols. (1834; reprint, Edinburgh: Banner of Truth, 1974), 1:clxxviii.

## Romance Among the Puritans in the Seventeenth Century

At Colworth Church in Bedfordshire, there is a monument erected in 1641 to Sir William Dyer and his wife Katherine. He died first, and carved upon his monument are several lines of verse written by his widow Katherine to him:

> My dearest dust, could not thy hasty day
> Afford thy drowszy patience leave to stay
> One hower longer: so that we might either
> Sate up, or gone to bedd together?
> But since thy finisht labour hath possest
> Thy weary limbs with early rest,
> Enjoy it sweetly: and thy widdowe bride
> Shall soone repose her by thy slumbring side.
> Whose business, now, is only to prepare
> My nightly dress, and call to prayer:
> Mine eyes wax heavy and ye day growes cold.
> Draw, draw ye closed curtaynes: and make roome:
> My dear, my dearest dust; I come, I come.[21]

Tenacity and tenderness clearly went together in Puritan views not only of divine love but of marital love as well.

### Sexual Sin

*The Sexual Sin of Wrongful Indulgence*

For all of their affirmation of marriage and the sexual nature, much of what the Puritans said about sex was negative. "Toward sexual intercourse outside marriage the Puritans were as frankly hostile as they were favorable to it in marriage."[22] There was a lot to declare sinful in the seventeenth century. Edmund Morgan, after extensively researching seventeenth-century New England court records, concluded, "Illicit sexual intercourse was fairly common."[23] And it vexed and mystified Puritan ministers in old and New England why sexual sin should be so prevalent. John Flavel (1630–1691) marveled, "It is

---

[21] Cited in Adair, *Founding Fathers*, 259.
[22] Edmund S. Morgan, "The Puritans and Sex," *The New England Quarterly* (December 1942): 594.
[23] Ibid., 596.

a matter of just admiration, how the sin of uncleanness should grow so epidemical and common as it doth. . . . And yet for all this, to the amazement of all serious observers, never was any age more infamous for this sin, than the present age is; and that under the clear shining light of the gospel."[24] Flavel assumed his age was particularly "unclean" for four reasons: first, the bad examples of great men; second, the near inevitability which comes when individuals are neither able to contain themselves nor marry[25] (much like our own day, and the too-frequent delay of marriage); third, the absence of lawful remedies and the presence of temptations, as with soldiers and seamen; and fourth, decreasing levels of shame surrounding sexual sin due to its commonness.[26] With regard to the second point above, it is possible that indentured servitude and artisan apprenticeships, central aspects of the social structure in seventeenth-century old and New England, virtually forbade marriage to young men of all but the most wealthy families.

Jonathan Edwards also believed society was experiencing a moral decline:

> The land is vastly corrupted as to this sin within this few years. Young people take more and more of a licentious liberty in their keeping company. . . . And there is not that discountenance of such things as there formerly used to be. It is not now such a discredit; 'tis not accounted such a blot and disgrace to a person. . . . I believe there is not a country in the Christian world, however debauched and vicious, where parents indulge their children in such liberties in company-keeping as they do in this country. . . .[27]

---

[24] John Flavel, *The Reasonableness of Personal Reformation and the Necessity of Conversion,* in *The Works of John Flavel,* 6 vols. (1820; reprint London: Banner of Truth, 1968), 6:515.

[25] "They are not yet arrived at an estate sufficient to maintain a family with reputation: But when they have gotten enough by trade, or by the fall of their paternal estates, to live in equal reputation with their neighbors; then they design to alter their course of life, and abandon these follies" (ibid., 516). Preventatives for the complaint of uncontrollable lust were, according to Flavel, "temperance, and more abstemiousness in meats and drinks; avoiding lascivious books, play-houses, and filthy company; laborious diligence in your lawful callings, and fervent prayer, for mortifying and preventing grace: And if temptations shall stir amidst all these preventives; then casting yourselves upon the directions and supply of providence, in the honourable estate of marriage" (ibid., 517).

[26] Flavel, *The Reasonableness of Personal Reformation,* 515-519.

[27] Jonathan Edwards, "Sin and Wickedness Bring Calamity and Misery on a People," in *The Works of Jonathan Edwards,* vol. 14, *Sermons and Discourses 1723–1729,* ed. Kenneth P. Minkema (New Haven, Conn.: Yale University Press, 1997), 502. On 503, Edwards reflects that parents say their parents were too strict, so they are now being too lenient.

## The Sexual Sin of Wrongful Abstinence

On the other hand, one of the most famous facts about the Puritans is that they worked to encourage, and even enforce, sexual relations between spouses. So, "If a husband deserted his wife and remained within the jurisdiction of a Puritan government, he was promptly sent back to her."[28] Over sixty years ago, Edmund Morgan's research unearthed a case in the First Church of Boston where James Mattock was excommunicated because "he denyed Coniugall fellowship unto his wife for the space of 2 years together upon pretense of taking Revenge upon himself for his abusing of her before marriage."[29] Either for engaging in sex with the wrong person, or for engaging too little with the right person, sex was regarded as a matter easily beset by sin.

## Their Theology of Sexual Sin

The Puritans were not naïve. They knew that not all pleasures are good. They had read Jesus' interpretation of the parable of the sower and the seed, where he mentions that "the desires for other things" or "life's pleasures" could choke out true life.[30] As Richard Sibbes (1577–1635) said, "Take heed of worldly-mindedness, which will glue thy affections to the earth, and will not suffer them to be lifted up to Christ. Take heed of the pleasures of the world, lest they drown thy soul, as they do the souls of many that profess themselves to be Christians."[31] They perceived Bunyan's city of Vanity Fair not only on the pages of *Pilgrim's Progress*, but in their world around them, as well as in their own hearts. They were not stoics, but they were suspicious of pleasure. Citing Eve in the Garden, Benjamin Needler (1620–1682) cautioned his hearers, "Learn to suspect things that are delightful."[32]

In order to gain a Christian view of pleasure, I have been helped by meditating on two Puritan ministers who preached and wrote in the second half of the seventeenth century in England: John Flavel (1630–1691)

---

[28] Morgan, "Puritans and Sex," 604.
[29] Cited by Morgan, "Puritans and Sex," 593.
[30] Mark 4:19; Luke 8:14.
[31] Richard Sibbes, "The Spouse, Her Earnest Desire After Christ," in *Works of Richard Sibbes,* vol. 2, ed. Alexander B. Grosart (1862–1864 edition; reprint Edinburgh: Banner of Truth, 1983), 205-206.
[32] Benjamin Needler, "How May Beloved Lusts Be Discovered and Mortified," in *Puritan Sermons 1659–1689,* 1:65.

and Richard Baxter (1615–1691). John Flavel said that "Most of those souls that are now in hell, are there upon the account of their indulgence to the flesh; they could not deny the flesh, and now are denied by God."[33] In his book *A Caution to Seamen: A Dissuasive Against Several Horrid and Detestable Sins,* Flavel provides a terrifyingly direct, sustained attack on sexual immorality, making argument after argument against it.[34]

Sex outside of marriage cannot please God because it is contrary to God's purpose and command. And yet, as part of our depravity, Flavel said, we live believing that there is "no fruit so sweet to corrupt nature, as forbidden fruit."[35] Such self-knowledge must make us be careful. Baxter warned:

> When you are looking on the cup, or gazing on alluring beauty, or wantonly dallying and pleasing your senses with things unsafe, you little know how far beyond your intentions you may be drawn, and how deep the wound may prove, how great the smart, or how long and difficult the cure.[36]

And Baxter was one of the most insightful reflectors and writers on what he calls "flesh-pleasing." He continues:

> Flesh-pleasing is the Grand Idolatry of the world: and the Flesh the greatest Idol that ever was set up against God. . . . That is a man's God which he taketh for his chief Good, and loveth best, and trusteth in most and is most desirous to please: And this is the flesh to every sensualist.[37]

> It [flesh-pleasing] is the sin of sins; the end of all sin, and therefore the very sum and Life of all. All the evil wicked men commit, is ultimately to please the flesh: The love of flesh-pleasing is the cause of all. Pride and Covetousness, and Whoredom, and wantonness, and gluttony and drunkenness, and all the rest are but either the immediate works of sensuality and Flesh-pleasing, or the distant service of it, by laying in provision for it. . . . Cure this sin and you have taken off the poise, and

---

[33] John Flavel, *A Treatise of the Soul of Man,* in *The Works of John Flavel,* 2:607.
[34] John Flavel, *A Caution to Seamen: A Dissuasive Against Several Horrid and Detestable Sins,* in *The Works of John Flavel,* 5:315-324.
[35] Flavel, *The Reasonableness of Personal Reformation,* 513.
[36] Baxter, *Christian Directory,* 58.
[37] Ibid., 268.

cured all the positive sins of the soul; Though the privative sins would be still uncured, if there were no more done; Because that which makes the clock stand still, is not enough to make it go right: But indeed nothing, but the Love of Pleasing God, can truly cure the Love of flesh-pleasing: and such a cure is the cure of every sin, both positive and privative, active and defective.[38]

Even more graphically, he warns:

When the skull is cast up with the spade, to make room for a successor, you may see the hole where all the meat and drink went in, and the hideous seat of the face which sometime was the discovery of wantonness, pride and scorn: but you'll see no signs of mirth or pleasure. . . . Go to the Grave, and see there the end of fleshly pleasure, and what is all that it will do for you at the last.[39]

Baxter continues with this careful advice:

Seek not the ease and pleasure of a little walking breathing clay, when you should be seeking and fore-tasting the everlasting pleasure. Here lyeth your danger and your work: Strive more against your own flesh, than against all your Enemies in Earth and Hell: If you be saved from this, you are saved from them all. Christ suffered in the flesh, to tell you that it is not pampering, but suffering that your flesh must expect, if you will reign with him.[40]

Baxter was typical among the Puritans in perceiving that sexual sins were particularly devastating sins. Matthew Henry wrote, "no sin doth more deface the image of God's holiness upon the soul, than uncleanness doth, nor render it more odious in the eyes of the pure and holy God."[41] Some may think that all of these warnings are too ascetic or even stoic, but after reading and meditating on hundreds of pages like this in my own research, I would disagree. Their warnings are simply based upon meditating on the apostle Paul's caution in 1 Corinthians 6:18: "Flee from sexual immorality. Every other sin a

---

[38] Ibid., 267-268.
[39] Ibid., 272.
[40] Ibid., 273.
[41] Matthew Henry, *Four Discourses Against Vice and Profaneness*, in *The Complete Works of the Rev. Matthew Henry*, 2 vols. (1705; reprint Grand Rapids, Mich.: Baker, 1979), 1:105 [83-152].

person commits is outside the body, but the sexually immoral person sins against his own body."

## All Pleasures Subordinate to Pleasure in God

So what is the positive Puritan message about sexual pleasure? *All pleasures must be subordinate to pleasure in God.* Baxter again:

> Every pleasing of the flesh, which is capable of being referred to a higher end, and is not so referred, and used, is a sin. . . . That which is not desired as a Means to some Higher end, is desired as our ultimate end itself (in that act). But *God only is man's lawful ultimate end.*[42]

Baxter says that,

> Pleasure is so much the End of man, which his Nature leadeth him to desire, that the chief thing in the world to make a man Good and Happy is to engage his heart to those Pleasures which are Good, and make men Happy: And the chief thing to make him Bad and Miserable, is to engage him in the pleasures which make men Bad and end in Misery.[43]

Sexual pleasure is naturally suspect because it can be found so quickly apart from God:

> Suspect all that Love which selfishness and fleshly-interest have a hand in. Is it some bodily pleasure that you love so much? . . . We are so much apter to exceed and sin in carnal fleshly mindedness, than in Loving what is good for our souls, that there we should be much more suspicious. . . .[44]

Baxter brings truths down to the practical level:

> In sum, All pleasing of the flesh which is lawful must have these qualifications. 1. God's Glory must be the ultimate end. 2. The matter must be lawful, and not forbidden. 3. Therefore it must not be to the hinderance of duty. 4. Nor to the drawing of us to sin. 5. Nor to the hurt of our health. 6. Nor too highly valued, or too dearly bought. 7. The

---

[42] Baxter, *Christian Directory,* 266; emphasis mine (cf. 1 Cor. 10:31).
[43] Ibid., 396.
[44] Ibid., 329.

measure must be moderate: where any of these are wanting it is sin: And where flesh-pleasing is Habitually in the bent of Heart and Life preferred before the Pleasing of God it proves the soul in captivity to the flesh and in a damnable condition.[45]

John Adair sums up well the balance Puritans struck by enjoying God-given pleasure for *his* sake, not for their own:

The Puritan could enjoy a good bed because he knew that the end of all sleep and rest was refreshment for activity. To love sleep and ease for their own sake was to mistake their end. Meat and drink existed not for the purpose of pleasure, but so that we might serve God better. If a man's mind delights in eating and drinking for their own sake, he has succumbed to the lust of the flesh. In enjoying good things the Puritan kept in mind why they had been ordained.[46]

The Puritans were not ascetics, but neither were they sensualists. Sensual pleasure was not life's uppermost goal, but neither did they deny it entirely. Rather, it was always to be subjected to the glory of God.

Baxter again:

Remember still that God would give you more pleasure, and not less, and that he will give you as much of the Delights of sense, as is truly good for you, so you will take them in their place, in subordination to your heavenly delights. And is not this to encrease and multiply your pleasure? Is not health, and friends, and food, and convenient habitation much sweeter as the fruit of the love of God, and the fore-tastes of everlasting mercies and as our helps to Heaven, and as the means to spiritual comfort, than of themselves alone? All your mercies are from God: He would take none from you, but sanctifie them, and give you more.[47]

## Summary of the Achievement of Puritanism

### The Purposes for Marriage

Marriage, for the Puritans, was a theater for godly pleasure. The Puritan understanding of the purpose of marriage is well summarized in the

45 Ibid., 267.
46 Adair, *Founding Fathers*, 253.
47 Baxter, *Christian Directory*, 272.

Westminster Confession (1648): XXIV:ii: "Marriage was ordained for the mutual help of husband and wife, for the increase of mankind with a legitimate issue, and of the church with a holy seed, and for preventing of uncleanness." The Puritans all enunciated this threefold purpose for marriage.[48]

We might summarize their views this way. If the Roman Catholics tended to emphasize Genesis 1:28 ("Be fruitful and multiply") and the Lutherans emphasized 1 Corinthians 7:9 ("It is better to marry than to be aflame with passion"), the Puritans tended to go to Genesis 2:18— "It is not good that the man should be alone." In other words, the Roman church emphasized procreation, the Lutherans pointed to protection, and the Puritans, while agreeing with both of these, stressed companionship in life and partnership in the service of God.

It was this emphasis that has been taken to be the lasting historical achievement of Puritanism in regard to sex.

## Lessons for Today

In conclusion, here are eight lessons for us today—eight marks, you might say, of healthy sex.

1. *Sex is supposed to be limited.* God created sex, but he has also placed certain boundaries around it. The fact that we have sexual appetites is from God, but those appetites are also fallen.[49] Our culture has a romantic, rosy understanding of human sexuality that is false, and dangerously so. Our depravity affects our sexuality.

We must keep in mind that sex is temporary. It is not an ultimate, life-fulfilling reality. Baxter warns even the newly married that their time in this state will be short. They will soon go to a world in which there is no marriage.[50] Do not make a god of sex.

2. *Sex in marriage is made by God.* It should not be avoided. Matthew 19:10-11 and 1 Corinthians 7:7 clearly teach that not all people either can or should be celibate. The Puritans were not the first ones

---

[48] E.g., William Ames, *The Marrow of Theology,* John De. Eusden, trans. from Latin ed. 1629 (Durham, N.C.: Labyrinth, 1983), 319-320; and William Gouge's "Ends of marriage. . . . They are especially three: That the world might be increased. . . . That men might avoid fornication. . . . That man and wife might be a mutual help to one another. . . ." (William Gouge, *Of Domesticall Duties: Eight Treatises* [London: John Haviland, 1622], 209-210). Cf. Henry Bullinger in *The Decades of Henry Bullinger* (Cambridge: Cambridge University Press, 1849), 396.

[49] Baxter, *Christian Directory,* 264.

[50] Ibid., 486.

to see this idea in the Bible, though they did champion it. Thomas Vincent preached that:

> There is no uncleanness or unholiness in marriage itself, or in any use thereof; which is evident, because marriage was instituted in Paradise, in the state of man's innocency; and marriage, being God's ordinance, must needs be holy, because all God's ordinances are so. . . . Adultery and fornication, indeed, do both wound and stain the spirit, as well as pollute the body; but there is a real innocency, holiness, and chastity in marriage, and the use of it according unto God's ordinance.[51]

Sex outside of marriage is a temptation to be avoided.

3. *Sexual sin can be repented of and forgiven through Christ.* In the process of repenting, or turning away, from sexual sin, we must get practical. Richard Baxter offers a list to combat inward lust: 1. Eat less. 2. Don't be idle. 3. Avoid the tempting object. He went on to give sixteen specific directions to cure inward lust.[52] Ultimately, he said one can fight fornication by avoiding the temptation, by "reverencing your own conscience," and by remembering that God sees and will judge. Beyond that, he says, "If thou be unmarried marry, if easier remedies will not serve. . . . It is God's Ordinance partly for this end."

We must also *get humility.* Baxter recommends accountability partners. "If less means prevail not open thy case to some able faithful friend, and engage them to watch over thee; and tell them when thou art most endangered by temptation." If a friend does not work, he suggests telling the pastor, and even asking openly for the prayers of the whole congregation!

> Begin thus to crave the fruit of Church Discipline thy self; so far shouldst thou be from flying from it, and spurning against it as the desperate hardened sinners do. . . . If the shame of all the Town be upon thee, and the Boys should hoot after thee in the Streets, if it would drive thee from thy sin, how easie were thy suffering in comparison of what it is like to be? Concealment is Satan's great advantage. It would be hard for thee to sin thus if it were but opened.[53]

---

[51] Thomas Vincent, "That Doctrine in the Church of Rome Which Forbids to Marry, Is a Wicked Doctrine," in *Puritan Sermons 1659–1689,* 6:354.
[52] Baxter, *Christian Directory,* 400-401.
[53] Ibid., 398-400.

The repentant ones who trust in Christ can be assured that God forgives. Beware thinking that moral reformation is all Christianity has to offer: "A Thief doth not become a true man when the Prison or Stocks do hinder him from stealing, but when a changed heart doth hinder him."[54]

Christ offers us a new life! God made us in his image to know him, but we have sinned, sexually and otherwise, and separated ourselves from him. We are now the objects of our good God's righteous wrath. And it is only because of Christ—God come in the flesh, fully God and fully man—that we have hope. He lived a perfect life and died on the cross, taking the punishment that we deserve. He was then raised from the dead as a sign of God's acceptance of his sacrifice. Christ calls us all to come and know his forgiveness now by repenting of our sins and trusting in him. Then his righteousness, even his sexual righteousness, becomes ours!

4. *Sex is not mainly for ourselves.* And,

5. *Sex is for ourselves, but only with our spouses.* William Gouge (1575–1653) wrote:

> One of the best remedies that can be prescribed to married persons (next to an awfull feare of God, and a continuall setting of him before them, wheresoever they are) is, that husband and wife mutually delight each in other, and maintaine a pure and fervent love betwixt themselves, yielding that due benevolence one to another which is warranted and sanctified by God's word, and ordained of God for this particular end. This due benevolence (as the Apostle stileth it) is one of the most proper and essentiall acts of marriage: and necessary for the maine and principall ends thereof: as for preservation of chastity in such as have not the gift of continency, for increasing the world with a legitimate brood, and for linking the affections of the married couple more firmly together. These ends of marriage, at least the two former, are made void without this duty be performed. As it is called benevolence because it must be performed with good will and delight, willingly, readily and cheerefully; so it is said to be due because it is a debt which the wife oweth to her husband, and he to her (1 Cor. 7:4).[55]

## Puritan Richard Steele taught that,

---

[54] Ibid., 271.

[55] Gouge, *Of Domesticall Duties*, 215-216; cf. 234-235. This is why desertion is a potential ground of divorce. Baxter criticized husbands and wives who choose to live apart (Baxter, *Christian Directory*, 521).

1 Cor. 7:3-5 . . . plainly shows that even the sober use of the marriage-bed is such a mutual debt, that it may not be intermitted long without necessity and consent. . . . Neither desire of gain, nor fear of trouble, nor occasional distastes, nor pretence of religion, should separate those from conjugal converse and cohabitation, (unless with consent, and that but for a time,) whom God hath joined together.[56]

He said that they "should be . . . sober, seasonable, and regular in the use of the marriage-bed."[57]

6. *Sex should be passionately enjoyed within marriage.* The Puritans offered cautions to excess. Too much of anything is a sin. "Put a restraint upon thine appetite: feed not to excess," Flavel said.[58] And so their writings frequently encourage self-denial. Matthew Henry, for instance, suggested that Christians must "Pamper not the body with varieties and dainties, lest it grow wanton, but use yourselves to deny yourselves, so shall it become easy to you."[59]

But there is also the clear biblical theme of delighting in your spouse. In Ezekiel 24:16, the LORD calls Ezekiel's wife "the delight of your eyes." And in Psalm 37:4, we are commanded to "Delight yourself in the LORD, and he will give you the desires of your heart." John Howe preached a long series on this verse called "A Treatise of Delighting in God."[60] Certainly the Puritans thought pleasure was a good thing.

Even though we assume the human is totally depraved, we do not assume that everything that constitutes human nature, such as sexual desire, is opposed to virtue, especially those aspects of our nature which were created before the Fall and which have legitimate ways for being fulfilled, such as sex within marriage.

Again, the Puritans had a balanced understanding of pleasure and its rightful place. So Richard Sibbes could say, "The more sense we have of the love of Christ, the less we shall regard the pleasures or riches of the world."[61] His good friend William Gouge, though, could also say:

[56] Steele, "Duties of Husband and Wife," 275.
[57] Ibid., 279.
[58] Flavel, *Caution to Seamen*, 323.
[59] Henry, *Four Discourses*, 117.
[60] In *The Works of the Rev. John Howe, M.A.*, 3 vols. (New York: John P. Haven, 1835), 1:349-411.
[61] Sibbes, "Spouse," 207.

The doatage of Stoicks who would have all naturall affection rooted
out of man, is contrary to this patterne, and unworthy to finde any
entertainment among Christians: for what doe they aime at, but to root
that out of man, which God hath planted in him, and to take away the
meanes which God hath used for the better preservation of man? That
wise man who they frame to themselves is worse then a brute beast: he
is a very stocke and blocke. Not only the best and wisest men that ever
were in the world, but also Christ himselfe had those passions and
affections in him, which they account unbeseeming a wise man. Their
doatage hath long since been hissed out of the schooles of Philosophers,
should it then finde place in Christ's Church? Let us labour to cherish
this naturall affection in us, and to turne it to the best things, even to
such as are not only apparently, but indeed good: and among good
things to such as are most excellent, and the most necessary: such as
concerne our soules, and eternall life. For this end we must pray to have
our understandings inlightened . . . and to have our wills and affections
sanctified, that we embrace, pursue, and delight in that which we know
to be the best. Thus shall our naturall affection be turned into a spiritual affection.[62]

And Baxter concludes the point: "Passions are not sinful in themselves;
for God hath given them to us for his service."[63] Therefore:

Turn all your passions into the right chanel, and make them all Holy,
using them for God upon the greatest things. This is the true cure:
The bare restraint of them is but a palliate cure; like the easing of pain
by a dose of opium. Cure the fear of man, by the fear of God, and
the Love of the creature, by the Love of God, and the cares for the
body, by caring for the soul, and earthly fleshly desires and delights,
by spiritual desires and delights, and worldly sorrow, by profitable
godly sorrow.[64]

Christ is passionate for his people, and therefore a husband should
be passionate for his wife. This has been intended ever since creation.
Flavel remarks, "It is not the having, but the *delighting* in a lawful wife,
as God requires you to do, that thou must be a fence against this sin. So
Solomon, Prov. 5:19: 'Let her be as the loving hind, and pleasant roe; let

---

[62] Gouge, *Of Domesticall Duties*, 83-84.
[63] Baxter, *Christian Directory*, 327.
[64] Ibid., 329.

her breasts satisfy thee at all times, and be thou ravished always with her love.'"[65] Commenting on the same verse, Matthew Henry writes, "Desire no better diversion from severe study and business than the innocent and pleasant conversation of thy own wife; let her lie in thy bosom . . . and do thou repose thy head in hers, and let that satisfy thee at all times; and seek not for pleasure in any other."[66]

7. *Sex is ultimately for the glory of God.* Sex is a merciless master and a super servant! We need to re-couple sex and the glory of God as part of our evangelism. When we use another person for money or for a one-night stand, when we use pornography, we de-couple sex from its intended purpose. Whenever we use other people to achieve our own gratification and ends, we idolize ourselves and our appetites. However, God set up good sex as part of evangelism. That does not mean we practice evangelistic dating, let alone evangelistic mating. It means that the sexual intimacy of marriage helps our spouse to love God, it helps us understand how Christ loves the church, and it builds a marriage that is distinct from unfaithful and non-Christian marriages. Baxter writes, "When Husband and Wife take pleasure in each other, it uniteth them in duty, it helpeth them with ease to do their work, and bear their burdens; and is not the least part of the comfort of the married state."[67] In short, sex within marriage helps display the Christian gospel by teaching us how to love and how we are loved by One who is different than ourselves—by God himself.

8. *Sex is a preview of everlasting love.* Baxter sensibly admits, "The intending of God's Glory or our spiritual good, cannot be distinctly and sensibly re-acted in every particular pleasure we take, or bit we eat, or thing we use: But a sincere Habitual Intention well laid at first in the Heart, will serve to the right use of many particular Means."[68] How can you form such "a sincere Habitual Intention"? Grow as a Christian, and join a healthy local church. Believe it or not, this will help your sex life. As Baxter says:

> Dwell in the delightful Love of God, and in the sweet contemplation of his Love in Christ, and rowl over his tender mercies in your

---

[65] Flavel, *Caution to Seamen*, 324.
[66] Matthew Henry, *Commentary on the Whole Bible* (1710).
[67] Baxter, *Christian Directory*, 522.
[68] Ibid., 266.

thoughts, and let your conversation be with the Holy Ones in Heaven, and your work be Thanksgiving and Praise to God: And this will habituate your souls to such a sweetness, and mellowness, and stability, as will resist sinful passion even as heat resisteth cold.[69] The greatest of all means to cast out all sinful Love, is to keep the soul in the Love of God.[70]

Heaven is what Jonathan Edwards once called "A World of Love," while Richard Sibbes observed love's tendency to always increase and desire more: "The nature of true love . . . is never satisfied. . . . there is a continual desire to have a further taste and assurance of his love."[71] Perhaps this gives us some indication of what Heaven will be like.

In this body, what comes through our eyes goes directly into the soul. So Adam's banishment from the vision of God in the Garden constituted the center of his punishment. And thus Moses was unable to see God, as has been the case with all of Adam's progeny. But there is hope. In Isaiah 33:17 we read the prophecy, "Your eyes will behold the king in his beauty." God promises his people that he will restore their sight of him. This restoration began in the Incarnation, and now the body of Christ, the church, is called to present a reflection of that glory in this world. So Jesus taught his disciples, "You are the light of the world. A city set on a hill cannot be hidden. . . . Let your light shine before others, so that they may see your good works and give glory to your Father who is in heaven" (Matt. 5:14, 16). The climax of the Bible is found in Revelation 22:4, where we read the promise, "They will see his face." If you are a Christian, do you not look forward to that day when we are done with hearing and faith, and can return to the unmediated seeing of God that we were made for?

And what about feeling? In heaven, there will be no marrying or giving in marriage (Matt. 22:30). But what senses will our resurrected bodies know? We can only imagine what our good God has in store. And to do this kind of meditation and heart-setting, few can help us like the Puritans. Certainly not our local Saab dealer.

---

[69] Ibid., 328.
[70] Ibid.
[71] Sibbes, "Spouse," 204.

**Recommendations for Further Reading**

Four books that you might read, if you want to pursue this conversation further:

1. J. I. Packer, *A Quest for Godliness* (Crossway, 1990)
2. J. I. Packer, *A Grief Sanctified* (Richard Baxter's Memoir of His Wife) (Crossway, 2002)
3. Elisabeth Dodds, *Marriage to a Difficult Man: Jonathan and Sarah Edwards* (Westminster, 1971)
4. Doreen Moore, *Good Christians, Good Husbands? Leaving a Legacy in Marriage and Ministry* (on the marriages of Wesley, Whitefield, and Edwards) (Christian Focus, 2004)

**Appendix: Academics on the Achievement of Puritanism**

After the Puritans, the Restoration comedies of John Dryden and others from the 1660s on were based on "all the old hackneyed truths or half-truths—familiarity breeds boredom, the same person cannot excite someone year after year, one cannot be excited when sexual relations are a marital duty. . . ."[72] God's plan for love was submerged in a romantic revolt, and the Puritan understanding of marriage and sexual love was among the chief casualties. Today, centuries later, we still labor with the disinformation that has been circulated on the Puritan view of sex. Literary figures from William Shakespeare to Nathaniel Hawthorne have contributed to these misunderstandings.

How did the Puritans change society's attitudes about sex? Did they in fact succeed in spreading the seeds of sexual repression in all of us? The middle of the twentieth century saw important new research on the Puritans on this important topic. Edmund Morgan's important 1942 article, "The Puritans and Sex," was a crucial call for a reevaluation of the Puritans based on Morgan's own careful work in some New England primary sources.[73] Morgan concluded that they

---

[72] Edmund Leites, *The Puritan Conscience and Modern Sexuality* (New Haven, Conn.: Yale University Press, 1986), 14.

[73] Morgan, "Puritans and Sex," 591-607; reprinted in Edmund Morgan, "The Puritans and Sex," in *The American Family in Social-Historical Perspective*, ed. Michael Gordon (New York: St. Martin's, 1978).

concentrated their efforts on prevention more than on punishment. The result was not a society in which most of us would care to live, for the methods of prevention often caused serious interference with personal liberty. It must nevertheless be admitted that in matters of sex the Puritans showed none of the blind zeal or narrow-minded bigotry which is too often supposed to have been characteristic of them. The more one learns about these people, the less do they appear to have resembled the sad and sour portraits which their modern critics have drawn of them.[74]

Elsewhere, Morgan writes:

> In short, the Puritans were neither prudes nor ascetics. They knew how to laugh, and they knew how to love. But it is equally clear that they did not spend their best hours in either love or laughter. They had fixed their eyes on a heavenly goal, which directed and informed their lives. When earthly delights dimmed their vision, it was time to break off. Yet even this side of the goal there was room for joy.[75]

Probably the best book on the Puritan view of marriage is by James Turner Johnson, professor of religion at Rutgers University in New Jersey, called *A Society Ordained by God: English Puritan Marriage Doctrine in the First Half of the Seventeenth Century.*[76] He describes the Puritan idea of marriage as a covenant that is ratified, or signed, by the couple's sexual union.[77]

Leland Ryken, professor of English literature at Wheaton College, helped rehabilitate the Puritans' reputation more popularly in his book *Worldly Saints.*[78] He quoted earlier scholars—such as C. S. Lewis—who wrote in a more balanced fashion than the Puritans'

---

[74] Morgan, "Puritans and Sex," 607.

[75] Morgan, *Puritan Family*, 64.

[76] James Turner Johnson, *A Society Ordained by God: English Puritan Marriage Doctrine in the First Half of the Seventeenth Century* (Nashville: Abingdon, 1970).

[77] "The argument advanced in this chapter and throughout this book, that Puritan marriage doctrine reverses the traditional listing of the marriage ends to put companionship first and procreation last, supports what here can only be stated. Another formulation of the same point is this: Thomas discusses friendship between husband and wife in the context of a marital relationship founded on companionship and aimed at producing the greatest mutual love between the spouses. The two positions are quite opposite, and it would therefore be erroneous to make any argument for similarity rest on the coincidence in language noted above" (Johnson, *Society Ordained by God*, 92 n. 5). "Sexual desire is not to be smothered or denied, for that is both impossible (the desire is too strong) and wrong (it is rebellion against God's will in nature). The proper means of using sexual desire is to channel it into relations with a loving spouse" (Johnson, *Society Ordained by God*, 102).

[78] Leland Ryken, *Worldly Saints* (Grand Rapids, Mich.: Zondervan, 1986).

many detractors.[79] And J. I. Packer worked to repay his own intellectual and spiritual debt to the Puritans by pulling together a number of earlier articles, and writing some new ones in his book *Quest for Godliness,* cited earlier in this chapter. His chapter on the Puritans and marriage is particularly helpful.

In *Worldly Saints,* Ryken points out that "The Puritans rejected asceticism because of their firm grip on the doctrine of creation. In their view, it was God who had created people as sexual beings."[80] Sexuality was not a consequence of the Fall, as some Roman Catholic writers suggested. He writes, "The Puritan doctrine of sex was a watershed in the cultural history of the West. The Puritans devalued celibacy, glorified companionate marriage, affirmed married sex as both necessary and pure, established the ideal of wedded romantic love, and exalted the role of the wife."[81] Ryken notes that while procreation and protection from sin were considered legitimate and important ends of sexual union in marriage, companionship became the leading end. As Edmund Leites summarizes the Puritan understanding of marriage: "In marital love, with its sexuality, we find a true friend and companion, a second self: we are redeemed from our loneliness."[82]

So, most fundamentally, the Puritans believed marriage is a positive gift of God. And most fundamentally, they believed sex in marriage is a positive gift of God, to be used and enjoyed in moderation with the glory of God as the ultimate end. They clearly disagreed with the medieval Roman Catholic preference for virginity above marriage, and they particularly disliked the Roman Catholic prohibition against priests marrying.

A couple of significant qualifications have been added to this rehabilitated understanding of the Puritan view of marriage and sex. First, Margo Todd has offered a *historical qualification,* by asking whether the move away from the medieval Catholic view should be attributed to the Puritans. She argues that a larger movement toward Christian humanism was the source of changed attitudes toward sex, with Puritanism

---

[79] C. S. Lewis writes, "The conversion of courtly love into romantic monogamous love was . . . largely the work of English, and even of Puritan, poets" (cited in Ryken, *Worldly Saints,* 51). Levin Schucking has called the Puritan marriage ideal "Puritanism's greatest and most admirable cultural achievement" (cited in ibid., 40).

[80] Ryken, *Worldly Saints,* 44.

[81] Ibid., 53.

[82] Leites, *Puritan Conscience and Modern Sexuality,* 89.

blossoming as one expression of this new fascination with the ancient texts including the Protestant recovery of the primacy of Scripture.[83]

A second significant qualification has been made by Daniel Doriani.[84] Doriani points out that Puritans do not deserve to be entirely exonerated from their cautious tone toward all pleasures, not least of which was sexual pleasure. The Puritans warned against excess in the marriage bed.[85] And so they placed several restrictions on the sexual relations between marriage partners: sex should not occur during menstruation, and it should not occur too frequently.[86] Doriani also argues that Puritans sometimes required prayer before intercourse, and would even recommend special seasons of prayer for some days before.[87] "The Puritans never attacked sexual activity in itself, but they rarely praised its intrinsic value. Further, they so restricted sexual activity that, if the man in the pew believed the preachers, then spontaneous, passionate, physical love would be almost impossible."[88]

Doriani concludes that the typical Puritan cautions about sex inside marriage sound more like Aristotelian moderation, and less like the Bible. Also, the Bible does not give the prominence to sexual sin the Puritans did, for example, by characterizing it as the worst of sins. Aristotelian "moderation" can be described as biblical insofar as it pertains to self-control, yet it is unbiblical insofar as it entails an avoidance of zeal and passion. "The question is, assuming a couple marries for companionship, partnership, and progeny, can they go on to enjoy 'immoderate,' passionate, sensual love?"[89] Clearly, Doriani assumes there is a place for healthy passion in marriage. Still, he agrees that "Puritan preachers successfully attacked the worst errors from the Middle Ages and began to restore biblical thinking about sexuality to Reformation and post-Reformation England."[90]

Doriani is undoubtedly correct in some of his concerns. Yet Todd's work of placing the Puritans within the larger historical context of a

---

[83] Margo Todd, *Christian Humanism and the Puritan Social Order* (New York: Cambridge University Press, 1987). For Luther's influence, see Justin Taylor's chapter in this volume.

[84] Doriani, "Puritans, Sex, and Pleasure," 125-143. Doriani here deals only with the years 1542–1642.

[85] Ibid., 133-134.

[86] Ibid., 134.

[87] Ibid., 135.

[88] Ibid., 136.

[89] Ibid., 141.

[90] Ibid., 143.

Christian humanist recovery of ancient teaching is applicable here as well. It was typical throughout Christian Europe to call for moderation. Luther wrote, "It is indeed true that sexual intercourse in marriage should be moderate, to extinguish the burning of the flesh. Just as we should observe moderation in eating and drinking, so pious couples should refrain from indulging their flesh too much."[91] Calvin taught, "Let not married persons think that all things are permitted to them, but let each man have his own wife soberly, and each wife her own husband. So doing, let them not admit anything at all that is unworthy of the honorableness and temperance of marriage."[92] And yet Calvin, too, saw a place for pleasure: "Did he [God] not, in short, render many things attractive to us, apart from their necessary use?"[93] Further, if Doriani's research had gone beyond 1642, he would have found more positive words about passion, as some of the quotations in this chapter evidence.

---

[91] *WLS* 2812.
[92] John Calvin, *The Institutes of the Christian Religion,* ed. John T. McNeill, trans. Ford Lewis Battles, in *The Library of Christian Classics* (Philadelphia: Westminster, 1977, 8th printing), 2.8.44.
[93] Ibid., 3.10.2.

# Recommended Resources for Further Reading

Black, Jeffrey S. *Sexual Sin: Combating the Drifting and Cheating.* Resources for Changing Lives. Phillipsburg, N.J.: Presbyterian & Reformed, 2003.

Harris, Joshua. *Boy Meets Girl: Say Hello to Courtship.* Sisters, Ore.: Multnomah, 2000.

_____, *Not Even a Hint: Guarding Your Heart Against Lust.* Sisters, Ore.: Multnomah, 2003.

Heimbach, Daniel R. *True Sexual Morality: Recovering Biblical Standards for a Culture in Crisis.* Wheaton, Ill.: Crossway, 2004.

Köstenberger, Andreas J. with David W. Jones. *God, Marriage, and Family: Rebuilding the Biblical Foundation.* Wheaton, Ill.: Crossway, 2004.

Mahaney, C. J. *Sex, Romance, and the Glory of God: What Every Christian Husband Needs to Know.* Wheaton, Ill.: Crossway, 2004.

Mahaney, Carolyn *Feminine Appeal: Seven Virtues of a Godly Wife and Mother.* Wheaton, Ill.: Crossway, 2004.

McCulley, Carolyn *Did I Kiss Marriage Goodbye? Trusting God with a Hope Deferred.* Wheaton, Ill.: Crossway, 2004.

Ortlund, Raymond C., Jr. *Whoredom: God's Unfaithful Wife in Biblical Theology,* New Studies in Biblical Theology. Downers Grove, Ill.: InterVarsity Press, 2003.

Powlison, David *Pornography: Slaying the Dragon,* Resources for Changing Lives. Phillipsburg, N.J.: Presbyterian & Reformed, 1999.

Powlison, David, and John Yenchko. *Pre-Engagement: Five Questions to Ask Yourself,* Resources for Changing Lives. Phillipsburg, N.J.: Presbyterian & Reformed, 2000.

Tripp, Paul David. *Teens and Sex: What Should We Teach Them?* Resources for Changing Lives. Phillipsburg, N.J.: Presbyterian & Reformed, 2000.

Welch, Edward T. *Addictions, a Banquet in the Grave: Finding Hope in the Power of the Gospel,* Resources for Changing Lives. Phillipsburg, N.J.: Presbyterian & Reformed, 2001.

_____, *Homosexuality: Speaking the Truth in Love,* Resources for Changing Lives. Phillipsburg, N.J.: Presbyterian & Reformed, 2000.

# Scripture Index

# Person Index

# Subject Index

# ✳ desiringGod

Desiring God is a ministry that exists to spread a passion for the supremacy of God in all things for the joy of all peoples through Jesus Christ. We love to spread the truth that God is most glorified in us when we are most satisfied in him. John Piper receives no royalties from the books he writes—they are all reinvested into the ministry of Desiring God. It's all designed as part of our vision to spread this passion to others.

With that in mind, we invite you to visit the Desiring God website at desiringGod.org. You'll find twenty years' worth of free sermons by John Piper in manuscript, and hundreds in downloadable audio formats. In addition there are free articles and information about our upcoming conferences. An online store allows you to purchase audio albums, God-centered children's curriculum, books and resources by Noël Piper, and over 25 books by John Piper. You can also find information about our radio ministry at desiringGodradio.org.

DG also has a whatever-you-can-afford policy, designed for individuals without discretionary funds. If you'd like more information about this policy, please contact us at the address or phone number below.

We exist to help you treasure Jesus Christ above all things. If we can serve you in any way, please let us know!

---

**Desiring God**
2601 East Franklin Avenue
Minneapolis, MN 55406-1103

Telephone: 1.888.346.4700
Fax: 612.338.4372
Email: mail@desiringGod.org
Web: www.desiringGod.org

This book is available in DVD format at:
www.gnpcb.org/sites/supremacy/